A Guide to Great
FIELD TRIPS

KATHLEEN CARROLL

Zephyr Press

Chicago

Library of Congress Cataloging-in-Publication Data
Carroll, Kathleen.
A guide to great field trips / Kathleen Carroll.
    p. cm.
Includes bibliographical references and index.
ISBN-13: 978-1-56976-209-7
ISBN-10: 1-56976-209-0
1. School field trips—United States. I. Title.
LB1047.C37 2007
371.3'84—dc22

                                  2006016576

Cover and interior design: Rattray Design

© 2007 by Kathleen Carroll
All rights reserved
Published by Zephyr Press
An imprint of Chicago Review Press, Incorporated
814 North Franklin Street
Chicago, Illinois 60610
ISBN-13: 978-1-56976-209-7
ISBN-10: 1-56976-209-0
Printed in the United States of America

In gratitude to all the children and adults who
have taught me about field trips—and life

"Learning is experience. Everything else is just information."

—Albert Einstein

Contents

5 *Handling Logistics: A Field Trip Essential* 215

1

Why Take Field Trips?

"We are now at a point where we must educate our children for what no one knew yesterday and prepare our schools for what no one knows yet."
—MARGARET MEAD

Think back to your elementary school days. What do you remember most vividly? If you are like most of us, at least some of those memories are of field trips. These were special days, different from the ordinary routine. As you and your classmates stepped out of the classroom and into the world, your senses were heightened, and your perceptions were indelibly imprinted in your memory.

In this age of standards and accountability, some think that field trips are unnecessary frills. Some say that field trips take away from instruction time, time needed to master standards. But, what does mastering standards mean, anyway? Is mastering standards covering facts and skills for students to bubble in the right answer on a test and then move on to the next set of facts and skills? Or does mastering standards mean leading children beyond a purely two-dimensional world of television, computers, Gameboys, and books, and out into the fresh air? Does mastering standards mean delving into a three-dimensional world of seeing, hearing, smelling, and touching soil, rocks, trees, animals, buildings, beaches, and oceans, working with real issues and learning from real human beings? Does mastering standards mean understanding and remembering concepts, skills, and ways of thinking and relating that will serve students now and as adults? Does mastering standards mean learning how to transfer learning to new situations and use that learning to solve real problems and make meaningful products? If so, then field trips are not frills; they are basics of education. What better way is there for students to master the standards than in conjunction with well-planned field trips?

A Guide to Great Field Trips is designed for teachers, after school and summer program coordinators, faith-based groups, museum educators, home-schoolers, and other families who desire to help children learn with joy in a real-world context and foster the skills to help them thrive in a world of increasing change.

This chapter gives you a rationale to demonstrate to the powers-that-be why field trips are an important aspect of every child's education. Chapter 1 discusses the many advantages of taking field trips from the perspective of each succeeding section of the book. In addition, an overview of each chapter describes practical guidance on how to make the world the classroom. Use that information to plan safe, successful, and rewarding learning experiences for children.

Field Trips Are Real!

The question is not, "Why take field trips?" but "Why don't you take field trips?" Field trips bring the world into the classroom. They enable the learners to see things from their own perspective, but also from the perspectives of their peers—thus, broadening and deepening learning.

Field trips are real, not virtual. They enable students to visit places they might never have seen, to see precious artifacts, to hear magnificent music played by symphony orchestras, to sail on the ocean and bring up creatures that reside on the ocean floor, to go from the theoretical to the practical, to have an indelible experience in the learners' future careers. When a field trip is wisely planned, it can take the travelers back in time (Plimoth Plantation), or up in space (planetarium), or to the ballet, a play, a special event, or to a historic moment.

The field trip can serve as a culminating experience at the end of a course of study, as a catalyst to provoke interest in a new topic, or in the middle of the term for children to test out their ideas and concepts with expert advice from the people they meet at the site.

—Miriam Kronish, principal, Needham, Massachusetts

A Rationale for Chapter 2: The World as the Classroom: Where to Go and What to Do

Chapter 2 provides hundreds of field trip options inside and beyond the local community, in the neighborhood, the schoolyard, the school building, and even in the classroom itself. These field trips connect children to life outside the classroom walls. They broaden the child's perspectives, informing the child of community resources that are available. In addition, these varied field trips may enrich the child with lifelong interests and new possibilities for future careers.

Connect Children to Life

Ellen Bauman, a 25-year veteran first grade teacher in Rockville, Maryland, was the one who told me that the little children she teaches now are living in a two-dimensional world.

> When you read a book to a child and you say, "Remember when you went to the zoo?" they have no idea what you are talking about. They don't even know about wild animals, except as pictures from books; they have no sense of the size. Many of these children don't experience anything except through TV and pictures. They don't see expanses such as a real live beach. I try to help them understand by telling them that the beach is like a huge sandbox with no edges. It's amazing how little knowledge kids have of the world. The parents often work two jobs and the children stay inside. When I ask, "What did you do on this beautiful weekend we just had?" their answer is "I watched TV." There is no immersion in the world.

There is just watching, no feeling for the world around them. Everything is two-dimensional; life is two-dimensional. As a result, they have lost the ability to ask questions. If the rare child does come up with a question, it is often discouraged because that question doesn't matter. It isn't on the test.

Author and CEO Randy White of Kansas City, Missouri, quotes research that backs up Ellen Bauman's observations. In an article about the relationship between children and nature (2005), he speaks of "children's extinction of experience." Research that Randy White has compiled shows that:

> Children today have few opportunities for free play and regular contact with the natural world. Their physical boundaries have shrunk (Devereaux 1991, Kyttä 2004) due to a number of factors. A "culture of fear" has parents afraid for their children's safety. Due to "stranger danger," many children are no longer free to roam their neighborhoods or even their own yards unless accompanied by adults (Pyle 2002, Herrington and Studtmann 1998, Moore and Wong 1997). Many working families can't supervise their children after school, giving rise to latchkey children who stay indoors or attend supervised after-school activities. Furthermore, children's lives have become structured and scheduled by adults, who hold the mistaken belief that this sport or that lesson will make their children more successful as adults (Moore and Wong 1997, White and Stoecklin 1998). The culture of childhood that played outside is gone and children's everyday life has shifted to the indoors (Hart 1999, Moore 2004). One researcher has gone so far as to refer to this sudden shift in children's lives and their loss of free play in the outdoors as a "childhood of imprisonment" (Devereaux 1991).

Randy White states further that, "With children's access to the natural world becoming increasingly limited, schools, where children spend 40 to 50 hours per week, may be mankind's last opportunity to reconnect children with the natural world and create a future generation that values and preserves nature" (Herrington and Studtmann 1998, Malone and Tranter 2003).

Randy White's focus is to have students go outside and learn in their own schoolyard. Chapter 2 of this book provides many suggestions for using the schoolyard for learning. But White's research is relevant to any field trips to natural settings. His article also quotes research indicating the following:

- Children with symptoms of Attention Deficit Hyperactivity Disorder (ADHD) are better able to concentrate after contact with nature (Taylor 2001).
- Children with views of and contact with nature score higher on tests of concentration and self-discipline. The more exposure to nature, the better the scores (Wells 2000, Taylor 2002).

- Children who play regularly in natural environments show more advanced motor fitness, including coordination, balance, and agility, and they are sick less often (Grahn et al. 1997, Fjortoft 2001).

- When children play in natural environments, their play is more diverse with imaginative and creative play that fosters language and collaborative skills (Moore and Wong 1997, Taylor et al. 1998, Fjortoft and Sageie 2000).

- Exposure to natural environments improves children's cognitive development by improving their awareness, reasoning, and observational skills (Pyle 2002).

- Nature buffers the impact of life stress on children and helps them deal with adversity. The greater the amount of nature exposure, the greater the benefits (Wells 2003).

- Play in a diverse natural environment reduces or eliminates bullying (Malone and Tranter 2003).

- Nature helps children develop powers of observation and creativity and instills a sense of peace and being at one with the world (Crain 2001).

- Children who play in nature have more positive feelings about one another (Moore 1996).

- Natural environments stimulate social interaction among children (Moore 1986, Bixler, Floyd, and Hammutt 2002).

- Outdoor environments are important to children's development of independence and autonomy (Bartlett 1996).

This research is not presented as an argument against the world of technology. Chapter 2 also has a section on virtual field trips and teleconferencing and covers how to use the Internet to take children to the Louvre in Paris to see da Vinci's *Mona Lisa*. It describes how students were able to follow a young American's solo trip to the North Pole and speak with him directly when he arrived there, using the Internet and other technologies. But children also need to get out into the world and have some firsthand experiences using their own senses; they need to encounter some three-dimensional space!

There are very exciting learning experiences that combine real-world field trips with technology described in chapter 4. For instance, students might use the Internet to prepare for the field trip. They record their experiences with tools such as digital cameras and videos. Then they employ a variety of innovative technologies, such as podcasts, classroom blogs, and photo-sharing sites, to communicate their learning to family, friends, and other schools around the world. On the other hand, there are museums that combine real artifacts along with their teleconferences. North Carolina's Museum of Natural Sciences program, for instance, encourages students to learn through their senses by mailing schools boxes of artifacts, such as spices from the rainforest or shells from the coast, in line with the teleconferences they present.

Technology is a powerful tool to enhance student learning. The mistake is when technology becomes a total substitute for real-world experience.

Broaden Perspectives

Like Ellen Bauman, other educators I've spoken with have also attested to how limited their students' real-world experiences are. Jaime Piscator, a teacher in Virginia Beach, Virginia, tells of her students who live 20 minutes away from the beach but have never seen the ocean. Principal Miriam Kronish tells of fifth graders living in Staten Island, one of the five boroughs of New York City, who had never been off the island. I have taught children who live 10 minutes from Washington DC's downtown Mall with the Capitol, the Washington Monument, and a slew of free galleries and museums but have never visited any of them. Field trips through schools and summer programs may be the only ways to open doors to the rest of the world for these children.

Texas author and teacher Jo Ann Lohl Spears makes this clear when she says "Where do children learn more: seeing a picture of a milk cow or petting one in a dairy? Talking about a hospital or walking through one? Hearing you talk about fire safety, or hearing a uniformed firefighter talk about it? Field trips can enrich the entire curriculum," she says. "They give children an opportunity to learn in the way they learn best—firsthand experience. They open children's eyes to their community and widen their horizons" (www.parentinginformation.org/fieldtripplanning.htm).

Sometimes broadening one's perspective can be scary, though. Ellen Bauman described a summer program that she participated in in New York City in which she took children on field trips every day. When the program first started, a very tough girl in the group made life difficult for the coordinators. She would yell at the top of her lungs, "I'm not doing this. I'm not getting off the bus! This is a stupid field trip!"

Ellen figured out what might be underneath the defiance. "Stay with me; we'll have fun," Ellen said. And the girl asked diffidently, "I'm not going to get lost, right?" For the rest of the summer, this girl was one of the most cooperative students. Once she felt safe enough, she enjoyed the adventure. Ellen said that they used public transportation so that when the children were older, they would know how to get out and use the resources of their city and its environs.

Teri Brown is a homeschooler mother and author of *Day Tripping: Your Guide to Educational Family Adventure*. She, like many home schooling parents, makes field trips an integral part of her children's education. She says, "When a child first approaches me with a new interest my mind automatically asks, 'What field trip can we go on?' Even more than, 'What book can we get?' I want to know, 'Where can we go?' Her insights are relevant to all families and to teachers and other program leaders. When children get to describe the trips they take with their parents, they become the experts, and everyone in the class benefits.

Learning Through Family Field Trips

"Dad! Stop! What's that one?"

The brakes slammed yet again. Binoculars rose and heads swiveled. The people driving behind us, instead of being annoyed, followed my son's pointing finger, their own binoculars already in place. My daughter grabbed the *National Audubon Field Guide* and started leafing through the pages.

This scene was played out a dozen times over the weekend of the Spring Bird Festival. It was one of the best field trips we've ever taken, bound to become a yearly tradition.

Field trips are the stuff that education is made of. Sometimes a field trip taken for the sheer pleasure of it will turn out to be the most educational of all. With family day trips . . . you just never know. Field trips aren't just icing on the cake. For our family they are elementary.

Let's look at some of the positive ways regular family day trips can influence your family.

- **Family Bonding:** Families are fracturing in this fast-paced modern world where time is the most precious resource a family has. Day trips are one way a family can slow down and spend some time together as a unit. The experience, whether it's a trip to a museum, wildlife viewing area, or farm, becomes a part of the family's collective memory, something to share and recollect for years to come.
- **Historical Perspective:** History is filled with real people doing real things. I care more about my children having a historical perspective than I do about them knowing dates and places. I want them to know that children have always made mud pies; they just wore different clothes while doing it. Before they can care about the important events in history, children must first realize that these events involved real people. Historical day trips to interactive museums or reenactments do more to foster this perspective than any textbook could.
- **Love and Knowledge of, and Empathy for, the Natural World:** As humanity's abuses of the environment mount, it becomes even more important that our children have a working knowledge of the natural world. Ignorance can ruin fragile ecosystems and doom animals to extinction; this in turn has affected our

own health and well-being. By taking day trips to wildlife viewing areas, hatcheries, and reserves, I am nurturing a relationship between my children and the natural world that will last a lifetime.

Day trips have led my family to some extraordinary places and given us unforgettable experiences. Our love for field trips led us to the incredible Spring Bird Festival where we viewed sandhill cranes, great egrets, loons, and the most breathtaking sight of all, a flock of tundra swans feeding in a meadow. Field trips have given my children more hands-on knowledge than they could have received at any school.

—Teri Brown, author and homeschooler parent, Portland, Oregon

Peter Chausse, a walking-tour guide who is also based in Portland, Oregon, takes students and their teachers on tours of their city on foot, looking at art, architecture, bridges, urban parks, and fountains. Along the way, he tells anecdotes that help bring the city's history to life. He has pointed out to me a mindset some children have that the only place you learn is in school. Peter Chausse is committed to helping children find out that "learning is a lifelong endeavor, and that it can take place anywhere and at any time." He told me, "field trips, if organized correctly, can teach kids that there is so much to learn, even when they aren't in school." That understanding is the basis for lifelong learning.

Develop Lifelong Interests

Field trips open students up to new worlds they may not have known existed and can spark interests that may sustain them for the rest of their lives. Peter Kline, author of *The Everyday Genius*, shared these memories of his childhood field trips with me:

When I was young, probably in the second grade, our class made a field trip to the FBI. The thing I remember best from that was something that looked like a fountain pen, but was really a lethal weapon. I can trace my interest in solving mysteries, looking for aspects of things that don't meet the eye, and so on, to that field trip, and that interest is a big part of my life, especially now.

Another event that changed my life was a presentation made in my first grade class by a couple of parents who visited one day. I remember nothing about my first grade teacher or the class apart from that, but I remember that presentation as if it were happening now. The parents told us about the stars and the planets, and inspired in me an interest in astronomy that was so strong that I actually went down to the Library of Congress to look up books on astronomy when I was too young to be admitted. Because I cried, they let me in anyway, and I got a chance to see some of the old books firsthand. It wasn't until the eighth grade that we studied astronomy in school, and that was very sketchy and superficial. However, I have been an avid reader of books on astronomy and cosmology ever since, and it plays a big part in my life.

Ron Fairchild, executive director of the Center for Summer Learning at Johns Hopkins University in Baltimore, Maryland, recognizes the opportunities inherent in field trips for an individual student's development. "We often think of field trips as stand-alone, one-shot deals." He notes, however, "Some kids take a field trip and discover a subject that they absolutely love, something they really get into. Our job as adults is to figure out how to help kids go back to that special museum, how to help them find activities or a school club that will take them further. We need to encourage children to develop the individual talents or interests they have."

Field trips also take kids outside of the box of the culture in which they were born and its unexamined assumptions. This doesn't mean they give up their convictions, but the world becomes more accessible to them. Learning about faraway people and places helps young people become more accepting of those who are different from them. And it may spark a lifelong interest in other cultures.

For example, a former student of mine who is now an adult remembers many details of a study we did of the Japanese culture when she was in first grade. She told me that she remembers fashioning her raku tea cup out of clay, then watching it fire in a barrel full of leaves, of taking part in the tea ceremony with a Japanese visitor to the class, of planting her own bonsai tree, acting out a Japanese fairy tale, *The Tale of the Shining Princess*, and sitting on the floor eating a Japanese meal in a Japanese restaurant. She shared that when she joined the Army and was stationed in Kuwait, the experiences she had enjoyed as a young child helped her. While some of her coworkers preferred to stick with the familiar American culture on base, she was open and eager to learn about the ways of life of the Kuwaitis. That kind openness and interest gives people of other countries a positive impression of Americans. Tim Rider, president of Adventure Student Travel in Kirksville, Missouri (www.adventurestudenttravel.com), adds to this view when he states, "Because of all the travels I've done, wherever I go and whoever I meet, there is something I can talk about that relates to them. Travel tears down walls."

Expose Children to Career Options

Ray Bledsoe, a newly retired principal in Washington, DC, recalls taking a class on a field trip to the Department of Commerce some years ago. The presenter there was describing to the students how he went up in airplanes and took photographs for the government. One of the students in the class, a kid who was good at art but not reading, raised his hand and asked, "How do you get a job like this?" Ray said, "There are so many jobs we don't know about unless we get out and network. I was learning like the students were."

Ron Fairchild agrees. He encourages us to think about field trips as not just for education but also for career development. Any of the field trips suggested in chapter 2 can introduce children to people who might provide models for careers in the future. Ron Fairchild notes that some kids either expect to do what their parents do or else they want to be teachers, doctors, or football stars. They don't know what else is out there. Field trips start them thinking about their future and what they might want to do when they grow up.

Ron Fairchild suggests that on the field trips, we encourage children to ask people questions about their careers. At the gallery students can talk to the artists, curators, and security guards. At the baseball game students can see that in addition to the athletes, there are coaches, trainers, contract negotiators, broadcasters, salespersons, advertisers, and other careers.

Ray Bledsoe adds to this line of thinking. "Consider all the possible careers with newspapers, for instance," he says. "There are reporters, editors, artists, printers. If you can't be a doctor, there are a lot of people who support the doctor to be successful; those are careers worth looking into. Kids need to learn how to network, how to talk with people to find out about jobs, how to get in on the ground floor and work their way up. Somebody has to pull you up," he says. "Someone out there might recognize a student's talent, take them under their wing, and see that they get the breaks needed to succeed. How many students have equal talent but don't get the break?"

Chapter 2 suggests many ways to use field trips to connect children to life and broaden their perspective. This allows children to gain the background experiences that give them more hooks to hang knowledge on. As a result, children may develop interests in hobbies or careers they never would have been exposed to without the trip. Children often pass on their new knowledge to their friends and parents. The whole community becomes richer for it.

A Rationale for Chapter 3: Caring and Curiosity: The Foundations of Field Trips

Chapter 3 is about two attributes, caring and curiosity, the foundations of successful field trips and successful education. Many Americans believe that caring is the most necessary quality in adult life (Elias et al. 1997). Chapter 3 addresses caring by showing ways to encourage students to develop responsibility through service projects, become stewards of the earth, help develop ground rules for behavior on field trips, care about one another, and express sincere thanks to people who have helped them.

Albert Einstein was one of the great models of an inquiring mind. Einstein said, "The important thing is not to stop questioning. Curiosity has its own reason for existing. One cannot help being in awe when contemplating the mysteries of eternity, of life, and of the marvelous structure of reality." Curiosity is a prime motivator for learning and remembering what is learned. Chapter 3 provides a number of approaches to spark children's curiosity about field trips. A graphic organizer encourages students to ask and plan ways to find answers to their own questions. There are plans to help students develop Essential Questions, and a Taxonomy for Discovery provides step-by-step instructions for true inquiry learning. There are strategies that create a dissonance or a cognitive incongruity through information or experiences that run counter to expectations. Piaget called that creating "disequilibrium," which compels the learner to try to understand the unexpected phenomena such as discrepant events and weird facts. ThinkTrix, a thinking skills and questioning strategy, helps students build their mental muscles for seven fundamental types of thinking. The Six Thinking Hats strategy expands curiosity by expanding perspectives, which helps children and adults make better decisions and reflect more fully on evaluations of field trips, as well as historical events and other subjects studied.

Develop Citizenship

Chapter 3 is built around Daniel Goleman's theory of emotional intelligence (EQ). This chapter advocates using field trips as opportunities for students to be of service. Daniel Goleman made the connection when he said, "There is an old-fashioned word for the body of skills that emotional intelligence represents: *character*" (1995, 285). Citizenship is character in action.

Spencer Kagan, the renowned expert on cooperative learning, asserts that there is more to true education than test scores. In an article entitled, "Kagan Structures: Research and Rationale," Kagan states that, ultimately, educational practices must pass tougher tests than boosting student test scores. If the practice raises test scores, but does little to cultivate understanding or develop the whole student, in the long run it too will fade. To endure, an educational practice must help students function successfully and with dignity across the range of (often unpredictable) situations in their lives. In deciding on the worth of any educational innovation, Spencer Kagan says, "We must look beyond initial excitement and narrow achievement data; we must ask if the innovation aligns with fundamental principles of learning, and if it is likely to make an enduring difference for teachers and students along the various dimensions we most value, including thinking skills, social relations, and character virtues. We must ask, 'Does the innovation help us become who we most want to be?'" Fostering citizenship through service is one way to become who we want to be.

Author and professor (at State University in New York) Thomas Lickona, in a lecture entitled "Educating for Character, The School's Highest Calling" (1997), referred back to Aristotle's insight that virtues are not mere thoughts; they are habits we develop by performing virtuous acts. Practice is key in this view. Thomas Lickona spoke of a study performed by psychologist Paul Vitz, who like Aristotle concluded that character development is a performing art. According to Vitz, when the young are repeatedly led to perform virtuous actions, they will come to think of themselves as good people.

Encourage Environmental Stewardship

Author and CEO Randy White of Kansas City, Missouri, has brought together research about the necessity of giving children experiences in nature for them to become stewards of the environment. Research indicates that it is not enough to have children read books or hear lectures about environmental issues to care about the environment. Children need frequent firsthand experiences with nature so that they learn to love and cherish the natural world (Bunting 1985; Chawla 1988; Wilson 1993; Pyle 1993; Chipeniuk 1994; Sobel 1996, 2002, and 2004; Hart 1997; Moore and Wong 1997; Kals, Schumacher, and Montada 1999; Moore and Cosco 2000; Lianne 2001; Kellert 2002; Bixler, Floyd, and Hammutt 2002; Kals and Ittner 2003; Schultz et al. 2004). As Randy White points out, we need to allow children to develop their love for the Earth before we ask them to save it. Rather than books and lectures, nature itself is children's best teacher (Coffey 2001). He notes that the more personal children's experience with nature, the more environmentally concerned and active children are likely to become (Bunting and Cousins 1985, Harvey 1989). Many authorities believe the window of opportunity for the formation of bonding with and positive attitudes toward the natural environment develops sometime during early and middle childhood and requires regular interaction with nearby nature (Cohen and Horm-Wingerg 1993; Wilson 1993; Sobel 1990, 1996, and 2004; Kellert 2002).

Frequent contact with and stewardship of nature extends a sense of care into students' academics and relationships with other people and with the school building and grounds. A study of 40 schools in California that used the natural environment as "an integrated context of learning" with hands-on, project-based learning found that student performance improved in standardized test scores, grade point average, willingness to stay on task, adaptability of different learning styles, and problem solving (Leiberman and

Hoody 1998). Studies also show a reduction in antisocial behavior such as violence, bullying, vandalism, and littering, as well as a drop in absenteeism (Coffey 2001, Moore and Cosco 2000). Learning expert Dr. Larry Martel says that when students plant trees, they are making a difference in a situation; they return and see what the difference is. Perhaps as children discover that they can make a difference, and they get into the habit of doing so, their stewardship expands into other areas of their lives.

Build Community in the Class

Students are more disposed to learning in classrooms where they feel cared about. When the classroom is a community of learners, everyone is accepted and respected. Well-designed field trips help build community.

A Student's View

Field trips are awesome! They are so much fun and you get to do stuff with your class that you don't get to do in the classroom. I remember when my class went to Quebec and Montreal. We played football in the parking lot. It was short but so much fun. I feel much closer and more confident around my classmates now that we've spent some quality time together. All kids should be allowed to take some time off, go someplace with their friends, have fun, and do stuff that they normally wouldn't be able to do.

—Vest Davis, student, Blue Hill, Maine

Maine teacher Catherine Razi notes that on field trips there is a chance for the kids to interact with each other in ways that are not set. Kids who don't talk to each other, talk to each other. On a trip, the students experience themselves in a different way. Field trips engender a cohesiveness that promotes group solidarity. Over the years Razi has seen new friendships form and previous relationships deepen through field trips. "Conversations happen that would never take place otherwise," she recalls. As one of her graduating students noted in looking back over his favorite memories of school, "It was the songs on the bus!" he said. His greatest joy was in the spirit of friendship and unity that shone forth as everyone sang together.

The book *Promoting Social and Emotional Learning: Guidelines for Educators* points out that employers want employees with group effectiveness, including interpersonal skills, negotiation, and teamwork (Elias 1997). Spencer Kagan adds,

No one person can build a modern computer; it takes teams working on components, coordinating efforts with other teams. Thus teamwork skills and communication skills become survival skills for the workplace of the future. Further, because of our increased ability to communicate and trade at a distance and our changing demographics, increasingly we must learn to work well with others different from ourselves—diversity skills are at a premium. . . . Because diversity will be the hallmark of the workplace of the future, we will do well to place a premium on teaching methods that foster diversity skills.

Well-designed field trips give students opportunities to get to know and accept others who are different from them. The projects that emerge from the field trip experience make students with diverse skills valued. The artist with poor reading skills or computer geek with undeveloped social skills becomes a prized member of the team. Beyond that, as classrooms become caring communities, all are valued, not just for what they do, but for who they are.

A Student's View

I love taking field trips. Every single thing about them gives me a need to travel even more. When I grow up, I really want a job with a lot of traveling because I love the feeling of when you cross the line between countries. I want to, when I am older, hold my grandchildren on my lap and tell them all my adventures around the world.

My all-time favorite memory is when my friends and I walked with our arms around each other's shoulders in the pouring rain down the streets of Quebec City.

Something I've learned is that there are so many different kinds of people out there with different languages, religions, skin colors, and beliefs, but they still fit in out there and it doesn't matter what they look like. Everyone, if you look closely, has his or her own kind of beauty.

—Marill Hawkins, student, Blue Hill, Maine

Bring Caring into the Curriculum

Emotions are the gateway to learning. Learning will only last if a person has some feelings about it, an emotional connection to it. As we said above, children need to love nature before they want to save it. In the same way, they need emotional hooks in order to retain learning. Renate Caine and her associates state that "all students can learn more effectively when appropriate emotions are elicited by their experiences" (2005, 85). They note that the greatest gift of the neurosciences to education is the recognition that learning cannot be separated from emotions.

Dr. Frank Lyman of the University of Maryland applies this concept to field trips. "Field trips," he says, "need some emotional charge. Students have to be feeling the experience or they won't bother to learn. They need to know why it is important. For instance, in going to a battlefield such as Gettysburg, there needs to be emotion. Students need to learn in advance about that battle and its effects, about the war and what war is. Otherwise all they see is a green field and a gift shop."

Inspire Students to Wonder and Question; Motivate Students to Think, Problem Solve, and Reflect

Learning through curiosity is natural. That is why babies and toddlers are the best learners around. Curiosity and wonder are emotions that feed learning. Unfortunately there has long been a current in education in the opposite direction of this natural inclination. Brain and learning experts Renate and Geoffrey Caine describe this current when they state at the New Horizons Web site (www.newhorizons.org) that our unexamined beliefs have given rise to an educational system based on the following precepts:

1. Only experts create knowledge.
2. Teachers deliver knowledge in the form of information.
3. Children are graded on how much of the information they have stored.

The trouble is not only that those precepts don't fit with the ways students learn best, they also don't fit with the world our students will inherit. Think back to Margaret Mead's observation, "We are now at a point where we must educate our children for what no one knew yesterday and prepare our schools for what no one knows yet." The experts for the world our students will live in don't exist yet. Today's students need to develop the skills required to deal successfully with a world of accelerating change. Perhaps the experts of the future will be those who, like little children, find the world fascinating and learn by following their curiosity. As life and work keep changing, the experts of the future may be those who can deal most readily with constantly shifting targets.

The Caines have offered another set of precepts, more in keeping with society's needs and more in keeping with learning through curiosity:

1. Dynamic knowledge (the sort of knowledge that is naturally and spontaneously invoked in authentic interactions in the real world) requires individual meaning making based upon multiple sources of information

2. The role of educators is to facilitate the making of dynamic knowledge
3. Dynamic knowledge is revealed through real-world performance

What better way is there to evoke dynamic knowledge than through the real-world experiences of field trips?

Field trips, and all learning for that matter, become meaningful when students exercise the EQ trait of self-motivation, when they get emotionally involved, are able to follow their own curiosity, and strive to make meaning from their own questions rather than regurgitate information given them.

Students' motivation to learn when they are curious and lack of motivation when they are not is evident even in field trips. When do students dislike field trips? When they are forced to move through the exhibit in a lockstep fashion, to listen to a speaker drone on, and are prohibited from exploring the interesting places. When do students like field trips? When they can satisfy their curiosity.

Well-planned field trips spark questioning, the key to a life of learning. For example, Tim Rider, president of Adventure Student Travel in Kirksville, Missouri, remembers seeing ice caves in New Mexico as a child. It was July, the temperature was 110 degrees. The ice caves were 30 feet under the ground. This experience put questions in his mind, which he later researched. He learned that the ice caves were in the middle of an ancient lava flow in the middle of the desert. Tim Rider says that you can learn about glaciers, but when you see how the glaciers carved out Yosemite Valley, you can understand glaciers in a different way. You can talk about the force of rivers, but when you see how a river washed away enough land to make the Grand Canyon, the power of rivers takes on new meaning.

Whether a field trip is to the Grand Canyon or outside the school door to a plot of dandelions, well-designed field trips engender awe and curiosity. Author Randy White's compilation of research agrees. It shows that early experiences with the natural world have been positively linked with the development of imagination and sense of wonder (Cobb 1977, Louv 1991). Wonder is an important motivator for lifelong learning (Wilson 1997).

In the typical traditional classroom, the vast majority of questions come from the teacher and are at the most basic thinking level, the recall of facts. So much more is possible from the Essential Questions, along with the ThinkTrix strategies, described in chapter 3. These strategies facilitate dynamic knowledge and the constructing of personal meaning that make field trips and education in general worthwhile. Chapter 3 shows how teachers ignite children's curiosity by helping students formulate their own quality questions and develop the skills to ask and respond to questions on seven different levels.

As the ancient Chinese philosopher Confucius said, "Learning without thought is labor lost." The work of Arthur Wells Foshay, Professor Emeritus, Teacher's College, Columbia University, supported that statement. Foshay dedicated his career to demonstrating that the ultimate purpose of education is teaching for meaning and understanding (1998). "There are people who know the Three Rs who remain unable to think," he said. "Let us not confuse the necessary with the sufficient. The Three Rs do not offer an adequate base for living life." Foshay said that persistence is the goal of education. What do students do after they are away from you? Do they persist in learning, in pursuing answers to their questions and discovering new questions to pursue? Are they learning how to learn for life? For Foshay the highest level of awareness was a sense of awe. Curiosity and awe lead to persistence.

Dr. Luis Machado, a South American education policy maker, told me a story about his encounter with famed cellist Pablo Casals, who was 90 years old at the time of their meeting. Early one morning during his visit, in great excitement, Casals woke up his wife, led her down to the courtyard of their hotel and over to see the source of his elation, a dew-covered rose shimmering in the morning sun. "Genius," Louis Machado told me, "is the ability to maintain a childlike sense of awe coupled with persistence. Pablo Casals, who practiced his cello for five hours a day for over 80 years, was a paragon of awe and persistence. A few years before he died, his response, when asked why he still practiced the cello for hours every day: 'I'm trying to learn my instrument!'"

For children and adults, part of persistence is being curious, finding the pieces, and putting them together to build understanding. Frank Lyman gives an example, "You experience a building and begin to build a concept of architecture from the building. You are curious about when the building was built, why the building was built that way, and the connection of that building with other buildings and with other art forms, such as painting and music from that time. As you do this, you are building a tapestry of understanding in the sense that understanding means concrete and abstract placed together. You are not only curious about a specific event or object; you are curious about how it relates to a wider experience."

Adults can help children create an appetite for learning, for "weaving tapestries of understanding" by presenting emotionally engaging or unusual phenomena about a field trip that inspires thinking and reflection. A teacher might introduce children to a weird fact about an artist's life so that the children will be curious to see how his or her paintings used light to convey a sense of the supernatural. The teacher would show multiple examples of that use of light in the classroom. Then children will look for examples of this use of light at the art gallery. They might begin to see how that use of light relates to other aspects of the artist's work or how other artists use light for a similar effect.

While the children are at the gallery, they might also find weird facts, along with the directions for inquiry those facts inspire, and take them back to make a classroom treasury. This represents the "idea to example" mode of thinking (see pages 122–125) presented in Frank Lyman's ThinkTrix strategy.

Suppose students learn the weird fact that the streets of Boston were laid down to follow the city's original cow paths or that circles were placed in the Washington, DC, street plan to slow down invading armies from reaching the Capitol. Then when students tour the city, they can view the effects of those weird facts. Their observations in relation to that fact might lead to new questions such as the history of a particular traffic circle or square, the person or event it was named for, and why it was named that way. These are also examples of the ThinkTrix, "idea to example" modes of thinking.

On the other hand, children might start on a field trip and systematically observe until they bring forth their own modes of understanding. For instance, they might find a certain kind of nut on the forest floor and discover that the nuts come from this tree and not that one, or hear a strange animal call and then discover that it is coming from a drab little bird on the branch above them. The Taxonomy for Discovery (see page 112) might serve as the structure for this form of inquiry. It represents an "example to idea" mode in the ThinkTrix strategy. With this approach, it is especially important that students are trained to use their senses to observe carefully.

Frank Lyman points out that ThinkTrix operates effectively on any fact or phenomenon. If you or your students research and collect weird facts before a trip or gather them during the trip, it is natural to employ the ThinkTrix modes of thinking: what caused this, how is it similar to or different from something else, what is its essence, and how might you evaluate it?

Chapter 3 also presents ways to spark students' curiosity in relation to field trips through project-based learning and problem-based learning. Further, chapter 3 encourages reflection about what is learned. These learning strategies draw on the "executive functions" of the brain. The executive functions represent a complex system of cognitive behaviors that include the ability to use reason, assess risk, plan for the future, set goals, moderate emotions, think critically and creatively, reflect, and self-evaluate. Would you agree that these behaviors are keys to a fulfilling family life, a successful career, a thriving community, and a democratic system of government?

The executive functions begin to develop in early childhood and continue to evolve through adolescence and early adulthood as the prefrontal lobes of the brain expand. Renate Caine spoke at the Learning and the Brain Conference in Cambridge, Massachussets, in 2005 on "What's Being Left Behind in 'No Child Left Behind'—The Role of the Executive Functions in Teaching and Learning" (www.edupr.com/brain13.htm). According to Caine,

"Learning that expands and utilizes the brain's executive functions must engage actor-centered decision making. This type of teaching requires that educators make fundamental changes in three areas:

1. Create the optimum social/emotional climate for learning
2. Create the optimum teaching approach that emphasizes student decision making
3. Develop questioning and feedback skills that engage and enhance the executive functions of the brain"

Sitting in a classroom memorizing facts for a standardized test doesn't achieve these ends. Taking field trips where students learn to relate with one another, work with Essential Questions, and help solve real-world problems, does. At the same time, field trips can exercise the skills and fix indelibly in students' minds the concepts needed to pass the tests.

As Frank Lyman says, "When it's all over, you want them to learn something, you want them to learn how to learn, and you want them to want to learn, to become persistent."

A Rationale for Chapter 4: Field Trips Are for Learning!

The purpose of chapter 4 is to maximize learning on field trips. This chapter is built around three questions:

Question 1: "What do the students need to learn?"
Question 2: "How will we and they know they learned it?"
Question 3: "How will the students learn it?"

Recognize That Alignment Is Crucial

Alignment of your answers to these questions is the linchpin. The focus of chapter 4 is to design learning experiences where the learning goals, the assessment of those goals, and the activities and tasks for mastering those goals are aligned. Alignment maximizes the learning potential of field trips. When teachers can demonstrate that their field trips and the pretrip plans, posttrip plans, and assessments are aligned with the required standards, the field trips are more likely to be approved by school and district administrators.

The Domain Matrix is a graphic organizer that helps you analyze your plans to ensure that they are in alignment with your learning goals. The Domain Matrix helps make your teaching and assessment valid so that you are teaching and assessing your stated goals and not something else.

Help Students Achieve the Standards

In districts across the nation, curricula are typically overloaded. If we tried to teach all the standards designated in many state K–12 curricula well, students would need to stay in school for 25 years! Since that isn't possible, some teachers muddle along by making their teaching a mile wide and an inch deep. They try to "cover" as many standards as possible, often as discrete facts. These teachers are likely to claim, "How can we take field trips when there are so many standards to cover?"

Assessment gurus Grant Wiggins and Jay McTighe speak of "coverage" as superficial teaching and testing without concern for students' true understanding. (In fact, one definition of "cover" is to obscure.) "Uncoverage," on the other hand, means to go into depth and achieve the mindfulness that comes from analysis, creation, and reflection on what matters most (2005). Chapter 4 revisits Essential Questions to extract the essence, the core understanding, from the standards and curricula and present it in ways that are meaningful to students. Well-designed field trips provide students with opportunities to develop the depth of understanding of the standards that the term "uncoverage" implies.

The need to address standards is as important for summer programs as it is for classrooms during the school year. In a conversation with Ron Fairchild, executive director of the Center for Summer Learning at Johns Hopkins University, he advised:

> It is incumbent on educators to make the case for why field trips are important and how they help students meet challenging academic standards. Rather than relying exclusively on test preparation, outstanding teachers use field trips and other types of hands-on, experiential learning to teach and reinforce the knowledge and skills that children and youth need to be successful. Similarly, after school and summer program staff use field trips not simply for entertainment, but as valuable opportunities for learning. In the current climate of high-stakes testing and accountability, it's increasingly important that we clearly justify field trips in terms of the value they add to the academic and social development of young people. The Domain Matrix can serve as an excellent tool to ensure that community programs reinforce the required standards.

Chapter 4 also addresses another aspect of Question 1: "What do they need to learn?" This aspect is diagnostic assessment, which asks, "What do the students already know?" and "What do they need to know in order to grasp this new knowledge?" Chapter 4 suggests a variety of preassessments and other formative assessments, which can take place throughout the unit, to guide teachers to teach in ways that are most appropriate for the particular students in their classrooms.

Well-planned field trips are a powerful means for achieving lasting student learning and achievement. Martin Storksdieck, PhD, has spent his academic career studying field trips and their effects. His book, *Field Trips in Environmental Education* (2006), and an article he coauthored, "School Field Trip Visits: Understanding the Teacher's World Through the Lens of Three International Studies" (Anderson 2006), summarize research about the effects of field trips.

His compilation of data shows that "field trips, under the right circumstances, lead to improved learning, particularly if learning is properly defined, and that field trips provide a host of other benefits, that go beyond the narrow confines of classroom-based content, including general learning standards, increased motivation, and introduction to lifelong learning and community resources." According to Martin Storksdieck, a range of studies also show clear cognitive gain of students on field trips compared with students who did not attend. His research indicates that a field trip can also be an effective teaching tool for emotional or affective learning since students who visited museums expressed more positive attitudes and motivation toward learning about the topic of study. Investigations on the long-term effect of field trip experiences on elementary school students found strong memories even after many years had passed. He suggests that the positive memories might entice these former elementary students to return to the field trip setting, if only as parents who accompany their own children. The studies also demonstrated the limitations of narrowly defined learning outcomes as the only benchmarks for success or failure.

Field Trips Make Lasting Memories

(The trip described below, a study of the prairie in South Dakota at Oak Lake Field Station, took place in September and the interview was in April. This trip won first place in a NASA Student Involvement Program. Isaac, a second grader, described his trip to me as I transcribed his memories.)

There were different groups: land, air, life, ground, water, and plants. I was in the land group. We did different experiments when we were in school studying to get ready for Oak Lake. We wrote what we were doing and how we did it so we could send it to NASA.

In the first experiment we did, we took three different cups and we put a bunch of sand, soil, and pebbles in them. They all had holes in the bottom. We saw how long it took the water to get through the holes to some cups below. We were trying to find out which was best for plants. We found that the soil was best for holding water.

Another way we got ready for the trip was we made a web of life. Everything went back to the sun. We had string and somebody became a fox, somebody became a grasshopper, and somebody became a plant. Everything will connect in some way with each other.

We learned that fires are good for the prairie. It burns the tops off the prairie grass. It gets rid of the weeds, but the roots of the prairie grass stay and the grass grows back but the weeds can't.

After that we took some soil in the shape of a mountain and we poured water on it and it became flat. I saw how the prairie was made.

At Oak Lake, we went to the prairie and did experiments to see how the animals would hide. We hid in the prairie grass and the grownups tried to find us. If we had on a bright colored shirt, we were found easier.

After that we went to a big pile of dirt. It was actually a thatch ant nest. They were the rulers of the prairie ants. They were like army ants and they made other ants slaves. They made them get the food for them.

After that we went on a trail to the lake. There was a marshy place by the lake with a dock. We found a bunch of nuts and frogs in the grasses near the marsh. They were super small.

Then we went to the forest and saw a bunch of deer prints. We found a lot of grasshoppers and a katydid. After that we went back to the base where there was a lab. We looked over what we learned. We drew pictures and gave them to our teacher.

Three months later during school we looked at the pictures and fixed anything we wanted to make better and then we sent them into NASA. It was looking at the pictures then (about three months ago) that helped me to remember the trip now. I can remember because we looked at the pictures and we did the real thing.

—Isaac Schaal, student, Brookings, South Dakota

Educational consultant Susan Fort has also collected research on the academic benefits of field trips (2004). She has found that benefits include the opportunity for students to gain knowledge and develop as citizens (Jakubowski 2003; Knapp 2000), an increase in cognitive knowledge of the subject presented, as well as an increased confidence and interest or positive attitude toward the subjects covered on the field trip (Knapp 2000; Sprague 2003). Active and experiential field trips also tend to increase absorption and retention of the information presented because the focus is not just on learning about the concepts or skills, but actually putting the concepts into practice and developing the skills personally (Knapp 2000; Lempert 1996; Mierson and Parikh 2000).

Dr. Lynn Tran's doctoral dissertation from North Carolina State University, "Teaching Science in Museums," compiles educational studies relevant to field trips (www.lib.ncsu.edu/thesis/). Her research also indicates that students who take field trips learn and remember more about a subject than students who don't. She notes, further, that there are effects from field trips that go beyond a narrow conceptual change such as inciting curiosity, developing motivation, piquing an interest in the subject, and increasing the likelihood that students will return to the museum in the future.

Assess Learning

Question 2: "How will we and they know the students have learned?" brings backward planning and assessment to the fore. One of the habits that author Stephen Covey speaks of in his bestselling book, *The Seven Habits of Highly Effective People* (1989), is "Begin with the end in mind." This means more than having a purpose. It means that you have fully visualized what you intend to achieve and planned how to accomplish it. You have a clear vision of what your students will understand and what they will be able to do as a result of the field trip and how you will know they have achieved the goals.

Many teachers build their curriculum around the means rather than the end. The means may be the lessons they use each year, a favorite activity, suggestions in the textbook, or the activities provided by the field trip site coordinators, even if the textbook or activities from the site don't match the standards very well.

With backward planning, we follow Covey's advice. First, we visualize our intended results in line with the required standards and other worthy goals. Then we plan how to determine whether the results have been achieved (the summative assessments). It is only after we are clear on how we will assess our students that we systematically begin to plan tasks to lead our students successfully to achieve the ends we have in mind. In this way we can gauge the appropriateness of the field trip site or textbook activities for our learning goals. If needed, we can change the activities or design new ones more likely to achieve the goals.

Grant Wiggins and Jay McTighe have popularized the term *backward design* in their book *Understanding by Design* (2005). These authors have also recommended that students demonstrate their understanding through Performance Tasks at the end of a unit. A Performance Task is a loosely structured challenge that requires students to put together all the concepts and skills they have learned. A well-designed Performance Task is meaningful to students, provides for further learning, and demonstrates that the student is able to transfer the learning to new situations. Examples of Performance Tasks might range from writing a book for younger children to making a multimedia project about the new learning.

Rubrics give students ample time to self-assess—before, during, and after the Performance Task. As education expert Arthur Costa has said, "The purpose of evaluation is for students to learn self-evaluation." The ability to accurately assess one's own performance is necessary for lifelong learning.

Lynn Tran's doctoral thesis, "Teaching Science in Museums," also asserts that field trips need to be well planned and that learning needs to be assessed. According to Tran, "Over 40 studies have shown the benefits of strengthening classroom assessment. Strengthened assessment provides significant and substantial learning gains for all students; however, the gains are even greater for low achieving students. Increased focus on assessment reduces the learning gap, while raising overall achievement" (2004). The bottom line is, whenever we plan field trips, we also need to plan ways to assess student learning.

Plan Activities in Line with the Goals

Question 3: "How will the students learn it?" is the last question to address in backward planning. We save this question until we are clear about the summative assessment, the assessment at the end of the unit of study. Only then do we plan those activities and tasks that will lead students to achieve the summative assessment successfully.

The Domain Matrix helps assure that the planned activities will be in line with the standards and other stated goals. Now the truth is, that with an experience as broad and rich as a field trip, students are going to come to new understandings and develop skills other than the ones you plan for. But this focus on alignment will increase the likelihood that students will achieve the stated goals.

Where do field trips fit in terms of helping to meet the learning goals and when is the best time to have them? Ron Fairchild states:

> Running summer programs for 13 years, we have focused on field trips at the beginning of the program to serve as an anchor, in the middle to reinforce, and at the end as a culmination. Field trips can serve as motivators at the beginning. We might start with a trip to an aquarium to find the most interesting creature. By finding the children's interests at the beginning, we can build instruction around those interests. On the other hand, that same trip to the aquarium might serve as a culmination. If students have just completed a marine life unit, a trip to an aquarium provides an ideal opportunity for them to review key concepts and information they've just learned.

Rockville, Maryland, teacher Ellen Bauman's ideal is to take students to the same trip twice, at the beginning to motivate them and again at the end after they have delved into a subject, "Expose, then teach, then return with new eyes—that's perfection!" she says.

The Domain Matrix is set up to plan for activities before, during, and after the field trip. Chapter 4 has a section on fostering students' abilities to observe carefully using all their senses (see pages 183–187), as well as a section on preparing students to use technology, such as digital cameras and video cameras, during the trip (see pages 197–206). There is a section on ways to make the travel time part of the learning (see pages 192–194), and some exciting technological innovations, such as classroom blogs and podcasts, whereby students can synthesize their learning and report it to a wider audience. Summative activities like these are in line with Lynn Tran's research, which indicates that postvisit activities are crucial for students to develop their understanding and ability to incorporate the field trip into their experience. Teachers need to review the field trip experience with students for them to get the full benefit. Good preparations and follow-up extend a field trip's value a thousandfold.

Help Diverse Learners Succeed

All the activities, whether before, during, or after the field trip, need to be geared toward achieving the stated learning goals. However, providing for student choice about how to reach those goals affords a means of differentiation, a way to appeal to everyone's abilities and interests. One way chapter 4 suggests meeting diverse students' learning needs is through strategies based on Howard Gardner's theory of the Multiple Intelligences (1993). Multiple intelligences or MI theory, as it is often called, proposes that intelligence is not a single entity. Instead, intelligence is reflected in at least eight separate domains: verbal/linguistic, logical/mathematical, visual/spatial, bodily/kinesthetic, musical/rhythmic, interpersonal, intrapersonal, and naturalistic.

Rather than considering the classroom a hierarchy with those with the highest IQ at the top and those with the lowest at the bottom, this perspective honors many ways of being smart. Children who were considered ordinary or low level in the hierarchical model have their own ways to shine when seen through the lens of MI theory—even children who were at the top of the hierarchy benefit. All children are able to find learning more engaging and develop more of their potential in an MI classroom.

In his article, "Research and Rationale," Spencer Kagan points out that much of the research on the effectiveness of using multiple intelligences in the classroom has been conducted through case studies (2004). He refers to the book *Multiple Intelligences and Student Achievement: Success Stories from Six Schools* by Linda Campbell and Bruce Campbell (1999), which summarizes their analyses of the results. In these case studies, the desire to educate the whole student was the primary reason schools adopted MI. The dramatic achievement gains that resulted were not the primary goal, but a by-product of the shift in philosophy. Kagan uses this data to affirm that "Teaching to the test is self-defeating; it does not produce meaningful gains and alienates students. Gains, as the MI schools demonstrate, are obtained not by teaching to the test, but by broadening the curriculum and making it more meaningful." By making the learning more meaningful to diverse learners, the test scores doubled in some cases. Minority and low-income students as well as their middle-income counterparts outshone their peers at state and national levels.

Like Martin Storksdieck and Lynn Tran, Spencer Kagan affirms that defining success only in terms of academic achievement tests is too narrow. The schools adopting MI produced a host of achievements beyond the test scores, including

- raised expectations among teachers and students.
- increased respect of teachers toward students and students toward each other.
- increased staff collaboration, peer review, self-determination, and professionalism.
- greater student engagement and liking for school and learning.
- improved self-esteem, confidence, and positive risk-taking among students.
- increased self-knowledge among students.
- increased understanding of and respect for diversity.
- increased involvement in global issues.
- improved peer relations.
- increased sense of belonging by students and staff.
- improved student attendance.
- increased community involvement: community projects and volunteer work.
- development of musical, poetic, and a range of other artistic skills among all students within regular classes.
- increased range of enrichment classes.
- increased physical fitness.
- increased choice, responsibility, and self-direction among students.
- increased personalization of the curriculum.
- increased involvement in running and improving classrooms and the school.
- responsibility for running businesses such as "The Poet's Cafe."
- student-developed character education handbooks.
- student-run friendship clubs.
- increased engagement of parents.

- ● increased engagement of community experts and mentors.
- ● increased range of ways to demonstrate learning (e.g., audio tapes, videos, rubrics, exhibitions, portfolios, narratives, projects, presentations, role-playing, performances, interviews, tests, checklists, self-evaluations). (Kagan Online Magazine, spring 2001)

As you read through *A Guide to Great Field Trips*, you will see how these results correspond to the potential benefits of a well-planned field trip.

Field trips also help diverse learners succeed by giving them the background knowledge that our educational system assumes is already present. Jennifer Pavol, a teacher in Loudoun County, Virginia, addresses this when she says, "Children from other countries often don't have a clue about aspects of our history and culture we take for granted. They don't necessarily know who George Washington is or what Thanksgiving is about." A lack of expected knowledge isn't confined to immigrant children, as Matthew Wheelock, founder of a nonprofit program to increase field trips for children in Washington, DC, illustrates below.

Field trips help diverse learners develop the background experience, the "hooks" to hang new knowledge on. At the same time, if multiple intelligences options are provided, field trips honor diverse learners in the ways they learn and demonstrate their learning. Field trips that include MI recognize diversity in both what is learned and in how it is learned. As Jennifer Pavol puts it, "Field trips help you see your students in a different light." We may discover new and wonderful qualities in them that we had never noticed before. And they may discover new abilities and a love for learning that might have remained dormant otherwise.

The Need for Experiential Learning

Case Study: Washington, DC, public school teacher, Matthew Wheelock, left the classroom to launch Live It Learn It, a nonprofit designed to create experiential learning opportunities for DC public school students. Field trips include river ecology excursions, early American architecture study, and visits to the home of former slave and abolitionist Frederick Douglass, a history museum, art galleries, and a sculpture garden.

The Need for Experiential Learning

Teaching at a DC public elementary school with a history of low student achievement made stark a simple truth: many students' academic performance is undermined by their lack of background knowledge, which provides the context necessary to absorb and comprehend new information. Such knowledge is best accumulated through firsthand experience, not just textbooks. Unfortunately, many DC public school students seldom have the opportunity to acquire such crucial background knowledge. Weekends and holidays for these students do not feature visits to the Capitol, Air and Space Museum, National Gallery of Art, or boat trips on local waterways. Even at school, they rarely have the chance to participate in these types of meaningful excursions.

This lack of substantive exposure and experience undermines students' ability to master their academic curriculum and envision rich futures. Live It Learn It was formed to address this educational deficit by introducing students directly to area resources through high-value "Experiential Excursions" during the school day. Such excursions are designed expressly to supplement classroom instruction and help teachers utilize available resources. The experiences motivate students, enhance mastery of the curriculum, and introduce potential professional paths.

The Idea in Action: The Live It Learn It Approach

Live It Learn It utilizes existing resources to meet a compelling need. Specifically, Live It Learn It works closely with two sets of educators—those in the public schools system and those at local museums and nonprofits. This approach builds off existing capacity for experiential education while tailoring opportunities to public school students.

- **Collaboration with teachers**: By working closely with teachers, Live It Learn It is able to integrate field trips with ongoing classroom instruction and the district's curriculum. Teachers identify specific field trips they would like to take, and Live It Learn It does the rest. Most importantly, Live It Learn It provides pretrip and posttrip classroom instruction to maximize the academic benefit of each trip. Necessary arrangements, transportation, and admission costs are also handled by Live It Learn It.
- **Collaboration with educators at local resources**: To ensure that each field trip best utilizes available opportunities, Live It Learn It works with educators at local resources to identify the most effective academic approach for each institution's exhibits and materials.

Results

Live It Learn It's approach has yielded impressive results. To date, students working with Live It Learn It master, on average, 87 percent of the academic objectives covered. When asked to assess Live It Learn It's programs on a scale of 1 to 10, students, on average, ranked them a 9.6. Ninety-eight percent of participating students indicated that they would recommend the experience to family and friends.

Teacher comments were similarly enthusiastic. As one teacher put it, "In a four-day lesson the students really gained a lot of solid scientific information. The fact that the lesson is reinforced by a trip so that students can see the application of the theories they learned was optimal learning at work."

—Matthew Wheelock, director of Live It Learn It, Washington, DC

Reflect Elements of Meaningful Learning

Renate and Geoffrey Caine and their associates are on the cutting edge of applying brain/mind research to learning. In *12 Brain/Mind Learning Principles in Action*, the Caines and their coauthors cite research that indicates "meaningful learning occurs when three elements are intertwined: a state of mind in learners that we call relaxed alertness, the orchestrated immersion of the learner in experiences in which the standards are embedded, and the active processing of that experience" (Caine et al. 2005, xiii). All these elements are present in a well-planned field trip.

The Caines have defined "relaxed alertness" as a state of low threat and high challenge where a learner feels competent, confident, and intrinsically motivated. They state that relaxed alertness is present in learning environments in which emotional and social competence are the goals (Caine et al. 2005).

They state further that the human brain is designed to learn through experience. Information comes to the brain through the senses: seeing, hearing, touching, smelling, and moving. So learning begins with interaction with the physical world. Field trips provide that basis for learning—the orchestrated immersion. As students describe, sketch, and make models of their physical experiences, they begin to take steps toward mastery.

Students step beyond description when they begin to connect these new experiences to knowledge that their brains have already stored, when they relate the new information to what they already know and care about. The Caines and their colleagues show that students acquire the what, why, when, and how of academic knowledge when they grapple with puzzles or dilemmas they come across. This grappling is a search that leads to deeper understanding and is another aspect of the orchestrated immersion. This grappling is also the purpose of the strategies to spark curiosity described in chapter 3 of this book.

While there is active processing when students describe, sketch, and find connections with their previous knowledge, the ultimate in active processing happens when students solve a problem or make a product or performance with the new knowledge. The students are demonstrating that they can transfer the learning to a different situation. Well-designed field trips provide the relaxed alertness, the immersion in experiences in which the standards are imbedded, and the active processing that correlate with meaningful learning. Good field trips help students score well on the standardized tests, but they do so much more. They educate the whole child and they help that child retain that learning for life.

A Rationale for Chapter 5: Handling Logistics: A Field Trip Essential

No one can doubt the importance of handling the logistical practicalities required for making a field trip happen. Chapter 5 includes strategies for choosing the right trip, paying for it, getting permission, and arranging for transportation. It also looks at the practical aspects of preparing students for the trip and getting and sharing useful evaluations of the trip from everyone concerned.

While chapter 5 is geared mainly toward helping the teacher or field trip organizer plan for a successful trip, students can also learn while preparing for the trip. Many of these practical matters can serve as motivating learning experiences. The logistical aspects of a trip can become real-world opportunities to foster understandings and skills that will serve students well for life. Even young children can help with some of the preparations for a field trip. In some cases, student help may lessen your load in planning for the trip.

Learn to Use Data for Decision Making

Navajo teacher Gerry King teaches on the Navajo reservation in New Mexico. The students in her class are currently working together with her to choose an ongoing service project. They are attending community meetings to gather information about community needs. At the time of this writing, the students are inclined to gear the service project toward the elderly in their community. Possibilities range from chopping wood to help keep the elders warm through the winter to oral histories to honor and preserve the elders' memories. Service projects can happen in any community. The scale can be made appropriate for the students' age and the time available. Students benefit not only from the giving, but also from helping to choose and plan the project.

According to the National Council of Teachers of Mathematics (NCTM), involving students in planning field trips addresses specific national standards of math proficiency (1995). Whether the trip is a service project or a field trip with a purely academic focus, students build mathematical skills first, as they collect and manipulate data and construct tables to compare the data. NCTM suggests that students help identify the variables that must be considered in planning a class field trip such as distance, time required, and cost. In chapter 5 there are sample data tables for comparing several field trip possibilities.

NCTM also suggests having students look at online maps from links, such as the state and local tourist offices, and calculate the distance and time required for the field trip. A Web site the students can use to explore the attractions in their state is provided by the Library of Congress (www.loc.gov).

Students can also use their mathematical skills in planning a schedule for the trip. On the trip itself, NCTM suggests that students track the actual time and distance, as well as meals and lodging costs. Experiences such as these provide occasions for students to practice methods and tools for computation, estimation, problem posing and solving, interpretation of graphical representations, measuring with standard units, and responding to investigations that require the comparison of data sets.

Robert Moses, a 1960s civil rights proponent and recipient of the MacArthur Fellows Program "genius" grant, currently works for equal rights for poor minorities through his nationally renowned Algebra Project. The Algebra Project, for students from kindergarten through grade 12, uses field trips and other engaging means to help poor children learn mathematical concepts. In talking about mathematicization of field trips, David Dennis, director of the Southern Initiative of the Algebra Project outside of Charleston, South Carolina, gave me this example. "We take children on a field trip to learn about their community," he said. "The trip is used as a basis for teaching mathematical concepts and skills. We may have eight to ten stops that introduce children to their community's history, political structure, economics, and culture. The trip includes landmarks such as the city hall, the library, and a historical church. Along the way children take odometer readings from spot 'A' to spot 'B.' They begin to understand negative numbers when they return to a previous landmark."

Dennis described how when the children return to the classroom, they move from the concrete experience of the field trip toward a mathematical abstraction using a five-step process. They make pictures or murals of the landmarks, discuss what they learned, and develop a model for adding and subtracting. Gradually they move from the concrete to the abstract: the trip line becomes a number line. Dennis pointed out that a foundation for understanding math is for children to get a sense of place. Textbooks can't do that. Field trips can (http://algebra.org/).

Learn About Finance

The previous suggestions from NCTM introduce children to financial issues as they consider the cost of the trip. Costs might include transportation, museum fees, food, lodging, and incidentals.

Opportunities for real-world mathematics are also present when students help with fund-raising. Students can compare projected funds raised with actual funds raised. They can learn how to keep tabs of money pledged and money that comes in. At the same time, they may learn other useful skills such as cooking, cleaning, or making handicrafts. Fund-raisers might foster values such as a responsibility toward the environment. Chapter 5 presents a number of earth-friendly options for fund-raisers. It also describes fund-raisers that improve academic skills, such as a schoolwide spelling challenge, where friends and family make pledges for each word the child spells correctly. All of these benefits are multiplied when children get to exercise their math skills by helping keep tabs on the financial aspects of the field trip. A teacher can provide these opportunities while being careful to honor privacy issues such as who pledged money and which families contributed how much. Field trips can provide a wealth of opportunities to solve real math problems and experience the practical value of learning mathematics.

Dot the i's and Cross the t's

Learning how to take care of the particulars required of an endeavor is a major life skill. Handling the details can mean the difference between a project that actually happens and one that remains an unfulfilled dream. This is as true with field trips as with any other endeavor. If the trip requires fund-raising and the fund-raising comes through a grant, students might follow the grant proposal's checklist and help fulfill the requirements. When the proposal is funded, students can contribute to the documentation of the field trip with drawings, photographs, and writing that spells out what the students have learned, how they have benefited, and why they are grateful for the support they have received.

Field trips require stepping through some hoops. Permissions are required from school administration, field trip site managers, parents, and possibly district administrators. NCTM suggests that an authentic writing project be used for students to write their parents to request permission for the trip and solicit chaperones (http://illuminations.nctm.org/index_d.aspx?id=366). Students might also write to provide parents with information such as the purpose of the trip, whether or not there is a cost, whether a packed lunch is needed, and the type of clothing required. Perhaps students can form an assembly line to make name tags.

When the trip has been approved, students may help develop and use a checklist for items for the class to bring along such as making sure each child has a name tag and that there is a first aid kit, food supplies, art supplies, cameras, journals, and whatever else is needed for the trip.

Become Partners in Safety

The teacher or field trip leader is ultimately responsible for student safety. That job becomes easier when the students are on your team and are committed to their own safety and the safety of their classmates. The National Science Teachers Association (NSTA) speaks of making your students your "partners-in-safety" (www.nsta.org/pressroom&news_story_ID=48320). Children are more likely to become your partners-in-safety if they understand the reasons for safety guidelines and help make the safety guidelines. Chapter 5 discusses students' safety on the bus, when walking through a city, and in small groups with chaperones (see pages 240–245).

Chapter 2 also addresses safety with a scientific study some San Diego students undertook about the difficulty speeding cars have in coming to a sudden stop and the implications for the dangers of jaywalking (see page 62). This study opened these students' eyes to the dangers inherent in their former practice of casually walking across the middle of the street in front of school. It also encouraged students to publicize those dangers to drivers.

With the right preparation, children are likely to internalize a commitment to safety for themselves and others through experiences with field trips. When the commitment is their own and not just imposed by authorities, children are more likely to bring a value for safety wherever they are—in school or out, alone or with others.

Develop Evaluation Skills

It is wise to evaluate the field trip and its value, including what worked, what didn't work, whether the trip is worth repeating, and suggestions to make it better in the future. Chapter 5 has recommendations for evaluating your field trips. While the insights of participating teachers and chaperones are important, who better to ask than the children themselves?

Children feel respected and their self-esteem is enhanced when their observations and judgments are requested. Dr. W. Edwards Deming, a world expert on quality control, had insights that can relate to your field trip (Aguayo 1991). In his system called Total Quality Management (TQM) Dr. Deming recommended keeping data on processes to see how to improve on them. He also recommended asking the workers, the people closest to production, to suggest improvements on the process. The intention is to bring about continual improvement. In like manner, teachers can ask the students what were the greatest moments, what problems arose, and how this trip compared with others. The children's responses can help make for constant improvement in your field trips.

Chapter 5 provides a blueprint to address the many details that must be handled to enjoy successful field trips. When students have the opportunity to help with the details, another level of learning can take place. In helping with logistics, students apply their reading, writing, math, and other academic skills to real-world needs. They also develop practical skills that will serve them well for life.

This chapter presented a rationale both for field trips in general and for the particular information presented in each succeeding chapter. This rationale might be useful in justifying your field trip to decision makers. You may find it helpful to mark ideas on the following checklist that are relevant to your field trip and, perhaps, refer to the particular chapter to review those ideas.

Checklist: Why Take Field Trips?

Rationale for Chapter 2: The World As the Classroom: Where to Go and What to Do

Well-planned field trips
- ☐ connect children to life.
- ☐ broaden perspectives.
- ☐ develop lifelong interests.
- ☐ expose children to career options.

Rationale for Chapter 3: Caring and Curiosity: The Foundations of Field Trips

Well-planned field trips
- ☐ develop citizenship.
- ☐ encourage environmental stewardship.
- ☐ build community in the class.
- ☐ bring caring into the curriculum.
- ☐ inspire students to wonder and question.
- ☐ motivate children to think, problem solve, and reflect.

Rationale for Chapter 4: Field Trips Are for Learning!

Well-planned field trips
- ☐ recognize that alignment is crucial.
- ☐ achieve the standards.
- ☐ assess learning.
- ☐ plan activities in line with the goals.
- ☐ reach diverse learners.
- ☐ reflect elements of meaningful learning.

Rationale for Chapter 5: Handling Logistics: A Field Trip Essential

When students help to handle the planning, they
- ☐ learn to use decision making tools.
- ☐ learn about finance.
- ☐ dot the i's and cross the t's.
- ☐ become partners in safety.
- ☐ develop evaluation skills.

References

Aguayo, R. 1991. *Dr. Deming: The American Who Taught the Japanese About Quality.* NY: Fireside.

Anderson, D., J. Kisiel, and M. Storksdieck. 2006. School Field Trip Visits: Understanding the Teacher's World Through the Lens of Three International Studies. *Curator—The Museum Journal.*

Bartlett, S. 1996. Access to Outdoor Play and Its Implications for Healthy Attachments. Unpublished article.

Bixler, R., M. Floyd, and W. Hammutt. 2002. Environmental Socialization: Qualitative Tests of the Childhood Play Hypothesis. *Environment and Behavior* 34:795–818.

Brown, T. 2003. *Day Tripping: Your Guide to Educational Family Adventures.* Belgium, WI: Champion Press.

Bunting, T. E., and L. R. Cousins. 1985. Environmental Dispositions Among School-Age Children. *Environment and Behavior* 17:6.

Caine, R., and G. Caine, et al. 2005. *12 Brain/Mind Learning Principles in Action: The Fieldbook for Making Connections, Teaching, and the Human Brain.* Thousand Oaks, CA: Corwin Publishing.

Campbell, L., and B. Campbell. 1999. Multiple Intelligences and Student Achievement: Success Stories from Six Schools. Alexandria, VA: Association for Supervision and Curriculum Development.

Chawla, L. 1988. Children's Concern for the Natural Environment. *Children's Environments* 5:3.

Chawla, L. 1994. Editors' Note. *Children's Environments* 11:3.

Chipeniuk, R. 1994. Naturalness in Landscape: An Inquiry from a Planning Perspective. PhD diss., University of Waterloo, Ontario.

Cobb, E. 1977. *The Ecology of Imagination in Childhood.* NY: Columbia University Press.

Coffey, A. 2001. "Transforming School Grounds." In *Greening School Grounds: Creating Habitats for Learning.* ed. Grant, T. and G. Littlejohn. Toronto: Green Teacher and Gabriola Island, BC: New Society Publishers.

Cohen, S., and D. Horm-Wingerg. 1993. Children and the Environment: Ecological Awareness Among Preschool Children. *Environment and Behavior* 25:103–120.

Covey, S. 1989. *The Seven Habits of Highly Effective People.* NY: Simon and Schuster.

Crain, W. 2001. How Nature Helps Children Develop. *Montessori Life* Summer 2001.

Elias, M. et al. 1997. *Promoting Social and Emotional Learning: Guidelines for Educators.* Alexandria, VA: Association for Supervision and Curriculum Development (ASCD).

Fjortoft, I., and J. Sageie. 2000. The Natural Environment as a Playground for Children: Landscape Description and Analysis of a Natural Landscape. *Landscape and Urban Planning* 48:83–97.

Fjortoft, I. 2001. The Natural Environment as a Playground for Children: The Impact of Outdoor Play Activities in Pre-Primary School Children. *Early Childhood Education Journal* 29:111–117.

Fort, S. 2004. Guide to Planning Field Experiences and Trips for Middle and High School Students, Cambridge College.

Devereaux, K. 1991. "Children of Nature." *U. C. Davis Magazine* 9:2.

Goleman, D. 1995. *Emotional Intelligence.* NY: Bantam Books.

Grahn, P., F. Martensson, B. Llindblad, P. Nilsson, and A. Ekman. 1997. UTE pa DAGIS, Stad & Land nr. 93/1991 Sveriges lantbruksuniversitet, Alnarp.

Hart, R. 1997. *Children's Participation: The Theory and Practice of Involving Young Citizens in Community Development and Environmental Care.* UK: Earthscan Publications Limited.

Harvey, M. 1989. The Relationship Between Children's Experiences with Vegetation on Schoolgrounds. *Journal of Environmental Education* 21:9–18.

Herrington, S., and K. Studtmann. 1998. Landscape Interventions: New Directions for the Design of Children's Outdoor Play Environments. *Landscape and Urban Planning* 42:191–205.

Inside TC Volume III, No. 11. 1998. "Arthur Wells Foshay, Who Taught the Quest for Meaning, Dead at 86": Teachers College, Columbia University. www.tc.columbia.edu/news/article.htm?id=2119&tid=48 (accessed October 14, 2005).

Jakubowski, L. M. 2003. Beyond book learning: Cultivating the pedagogy of experience through field trips. *Journal of Experiential Education* 26:24–33.

Kagan, S. 2001. "Kagan Structures: Research and Rationale": Kagan Club. www.kaganonline.com/KaganClub/FreeArticles/ResearchRationale.html (accessed June 3, 2005).

Kals, E., D. Schumacher, and L. Montada. 1999. Emotional Affinity Towards Nature as a Motivational Basis to Protect Nature. *Environment and Behavior* 31:178–202.

Kals, E., and H. Ittner. 2003. "Children's Environmental Identity, Indicators and Behavioral Impacts." In *Identity and the Natural Environment—The Psychological Significance of Nature.* ed. Clayton, S. and S. Opotow. Cambridge, MA: MIT Press.

Kellert, S. 2002. "Experiencing Nature: Affective, Cognitive, and Evaluative Development." In *Children and Nature: Psychological, Sociocultural, and Evolutionary Investigations*. Kahn, P. H. and S. R. Kellert, eds. Cambridge, MA: MIT Press.

Kline, P. 1988. *The Everyday Genius*. Arlington, VA: Great Ocean Publishers Binding.

Knapp, D. 2000. Memorable experiences of a science field trip. *School Science and Mathematics* 100:65–72.

Kyttä, M. 2004. The Extent of Children's Independent Mobility and the Number of Actualized Affordances as Criteria for Child-Friendly Environments. *Journal of Environmental Psychology* 24:179–198.

Leiberman, G., and L. Hoody. 1998. Closing the Achievement Gap: Using the Environment as an Integrated Context for Learning. Paper presented at the State Education and Environmental Roundtable, San Diego, CA.

Lempert, D. H. 1996. *Escape from the Ivory Tower: Student Adventures in Democratic Experiential Education*. San Francisco: Jossey-Bass Publishers.

Lickona, T. 1997. Educating for Character: The School's Highest Calling. Lecture presented at the Georgia Humanities Council, Atlanta, GA. www.georgiahumanities.org/downloads/governors_awards/lickona.pdf (accessed May 13, 2005).

Louv, R. 1991. *Childhood's Future*. NY: Doubleday.

Malone, K., and P. Tranter. 2003. "Children's Environmental Learning and the Use, Design, and Management of Schoolgrounds." *Children, Youth and Environments*. http://www.colorado.edu/journals/cye/13_2/Malone_Tranter/ChildrensEnvLearning.htm (accessed June 9, 2004).

McKendrick, J., M. Bradford, and A. Fielde. 2000. Kid Customer? Commercialization of Playspace and the Commodification of Childhood. *Childhood* 7:295–314.

Mierson, S., and A. Parikh. 2000. Stories from the field: Problem-based learning from a teacher's and a student's perspective. *Change* 32:21–27.

Moore, R., and H. Wong. 1997. *Natural Learning: Rediscovering Nature's Way of Teaching*. Berkeley, CA: MIG Communications.

Moore, R. 2004. "Countering Children's Sedentary Lifestyles by Design": Natural Learning Initiative (North Carolina State University). www.naturalearning.org (accessed June 12, 2004).

Moore, R., and N. Cosco. 2000. Developing an Earth-Bound Culture Through Design of Childhood Habitats, Natural Learning Initiative. Paper presented at the Conference on People, Land, and Sustainability: A Global View of Community Gardening, University of Nottingham, UK. www.naturalearning.org/earthboundpaper.html (accessed June 12, 2004).

Moore, R. 1996. Compact Nature: The Role of Playing and Learning Gardens on Children's Lives. *Journal of Therapeutic Horticulture* 8:72–82.

Moore, R. 1986. The Power of Nature Orientations of Girls and Boys Toward Biotic and Abiotic Play Settings on a Reconstructed Schoolyard. *Children's Environments Quarterly* 3:3.

NCTM. 1995. *Curriculum and Evaluation Standards for School Mathematics.* Reston, VA: National Council of Teachers of Mathematics, Inc.

Piaget, J. 1962. *Play, Dreams, and Imagination in Children.* NY: Norton.

Pyle, R. 1993. *The Thunder Trees: Lessons from an Urban Wildland.* Boston: Houghton Mifflin.

Pyle, R. 2002. "Eden in a Vacant Lot: Special Places, Species and Kids in Community of Life." In *Children and Nature: Psychological, Sociocultural and Evolutionary Investigations.* ed. Kahn, P. H. S. R. Kellert. Cambridge, MA: MIT Press.

Schultz, P., C. Shrive, J. Tabanico, and A. Khazian. 2004. Implicit Connections with Nature. *Journal of Environmental Psychology* 24:31–42.

Sobel, D. 1990. A Place in the World: Adults' Memories of Childhood's Special Places. *Children's Environments Quarterly* 7:4.

Sobel, D. 2002. *Children's Special Places: Exploring the Role of Forts, Dens, and Bush Houses in Middle Childhood.* Detroit, MI: Wayne State University Press.

Sobel, D. 2004. *Place-Based Education: Connecting Classrooms & Communities.* Great Barrington, MA: The Orion Society.

Sobel, D. 1996. *Beyond Ecophobia: Reclaiming the Heart of Nature Education.* Great Barrington, MA: The Orion Society.

Sprague, M. 2003. An academy for Ophelia? *The Clearing House* 76:178–184.

Storksdieck, M. 2006. *Field Trips in Environmental Education.* Berlin, Germany: Berliner Wissenschafts-Verlag.

Taylor, A. F., F. E. Kuo, and W. C. Sullivan. 2001. Coping with ADD: The Surprising Connection to Green Play Settings. *Environment and Behavior* 33:54–77.

Taylor, A. F., F. E. Kuo, and W. C. Sullivan. 2002. Views of Nature and Self-Discipline: Evidence from Inner City Children. *Journal of Environmental Psychology* 22:49–63.

Taylor, A. F., A. Wiley, F. E. Kuo, and W. C. Sullivan. 1998. Growing Up in the Inner City: Green Spaces as Places to Grow. *Environment and Behavior* 30:3–27.

Tran, L. 2004. Teaching Science in Museums. PhD diss., North Carolina State University.

Wells, N., and G. Evans. 2003. Nearby Nature: A Buffer of Life Stress Among Rural Children. *Environment and Behavior* 35:311–330.

Wells, N. 2000. At Home with Nature, Effects of "Greenness" on Children's Cognitive Functioning. *Environment and Behavior* 32:775–795.

White, R., and V. Stoecklin. 1998. "Children's Outdoor Play & Learning Environments: Returning to Nature": White Hutchinson Leisure & Learning Group. www.whitehutchinson.com/children/articles/outdoor.shtml (accessed June 11, 2004).

White, R. 2005. "Interaction with Nature during the Middle Years: Its Importance in Children's Development & Nature's Future": White Hutchinson Leisure & Learning Group. www.whitehutchinson.com/children/articles/nature.shtml (accessed November 18, 2005).

Wiggins, G., and J. McTighe. 2005. *Understanding by Design* (2nd ed.). Alexandria, VA: ASCD.

Wilson, R. 1993. *Fostering a Sense of Wonder During the Early Childhood Years.* Columbus, OH: Greyden.

Wilson, R. 1997. The Wonders of Nature—Honoring Children's Ways of Knowing. *Early Childhood News* 6:19.

2

The World as the Classroom

Where to Go and What to Do

"Learning is a lifelong endeavor, and it can take place anywhere and at anytime."

—PETER CHAUSSE

A field trip gives students a real-world experience, something out of the ordinary from the day-to-day routines in the classroom. Field trips help students understand why it is useful to learn reading, writing, math, history, geography, art, or science. Field trips bring subjects to life! They connect children with the world they live in. They help students broaden their perspectives and help them learn about resources in their own community and beyond. They also expose children to career and networking possibilities. There are many ways to provide students with these real-world experiences. Encourage students to focus their senses during field trips. (See page 183 in chapter 4 for building observational skills.) Use every trip to help students build their vocabulary.

In this section we will consider many traditional and nontraditional field trips that your class could take in your community. These range from galleries and museums to farmers' markets and uniform shops. We will touch on taking trips to faraway places.

We will also consider field trips outside of the classroom that don't require buses and extensive logistics. These include walks in the neighborhood to study birds or perform service and trips to the schoolyard to study shadows or write poetry about a tree. These also include field trips within the school building such as trips with the custodian to the boiler room to learn about energy use, behind-the-scenes trips to the cafeteria, or trips to other classrooms to read stories to younger children or learn what it is like to be in the next higher grade.

Finally we will consider ways to bring field trips into your classroom by hosting experts, teleconferencing with museums and other institutions in your state, picking from the huge number of virtual field trips available online, and inviting students to travel back in time or to exotic places in their own imaginations.

Field Trips in Your Community

The following is a list of field trips—some traditional and some nontraditional—that will help your students learn about their community and the variety of careers open to them as they make real-world connections with their academic subjects.

1. **Airports.** Small, private airports are best. Ask to see the wind sock, the runway, the airplanes, and hangars. Go close to a plane and, if possible, into the cockpit or passenger section. Observe a plane landing or taking off.

2. **Alarm or Security Companies.** Find out what sets off alarms. What are some interesting alarms the company has dealt with? What are the various kinds of alarms and security people have? Why do people feel they need alarms?

3. **American Red Cross.** Find out how they got started. What do they do? What are some recent ways that they have helped in your community, your country, and countries around the world?

4. **Amusement Parks and Theme Parks.** Study the physics of amusement park rides. Have students design their own theme parks based on the history of their state, dinosaurs, or some other subject in their curriculum.

5. **Aquariums.** In addition to viewing the tanks of fish, ask for a guided tour behind the scenes.

6. **Arts and Crafts Festivals.** Interview the artists. Different groups of students could focus on different crafts and report back to the class.

7. **Art Galleries.** If possible, speak with or e-mail the docent in advance to make sure the tour is most relevant to your standards. You might give each student a particular painting to study and report on. Some teachers go to the art gallery in advance to pick out exactly which paintings would address the class objectives. These teachers free up the docent and become the docent themselves. The docent becomes a resource and facilitator rather than a presenter.

8. **Bakeries.** Bread and pastry bakeries can provide behind-the-counter tours through the kitchen. Look at equipment and flour storage areas, compare sizes of pans, see a cake decorating demonstration, and sample some goodies.

9. **Banks.** Discover the purpose of a bank. Learn about the services that banks offer. See the security system. Look inside the big vault. Are there cameras? What should the teller do if held up? What do the students' parents do at banks? What do the banks do with our money?

10. **Beaches.** Comb a nearby beach for shells and sea debris. Catch samples of marine life in nets, and use books to identify what you find. Make a field guide with drawings or photos and include descriptions. For a more in-depth experience, take along an expert such as a marine biologist.

11. **Beauty Shops.** Learn what changes the color of hair. Interview beauticians. Learn what they consider their easiest and hardest work. How do beauticians learn about cutting and styling hair, and how do they keep up with the latest fashions?

12. **Bicycle Shops.** Learn about simple machines and how to fix one's own bicycle when a chain goes off or gears don't work. Learn how to change tires. Compare the pros and cons for owning the simplest to most the elaborate bicycles. Compare the different kinds of bikes such as mountain, racing, or hybrids. Find out about the various gadgets used with bicycles.

13. **Bird Watching Areas.** Look for birds in parks, wildlife preserves, and botanical gardens. Call the local Audubon Society or another environmental organization to find an expert to act as a guide.

14. **Boat Rides or Day Cruises.** Learn the science behind the propulsion the boat uses. Is it wind? a motor? Where do the motors come from? Study the sky; use the Beaufort Wind scale. What is the wind doing to the water? What is the shape of the boat? How easily does it move through the water? Note the wake. The more wake, the harder it is to push through the water. Do tides make any difference? Are there birds, fish, or other life-forms around the boat? Watch the people service the boat. Note the occupations connected with boats.

15. **Book Stores.** Before going in, guess the categories the books are listed in, and then see where they actually are. Where are the most people congregating? What makes the children's section different from other sections? Some stores have tables for coffee. Why? Interview people and find out why they choose to work there.

16. **Botanical and Community Gardens.** These are best in spring, late summer, and early fall when you can observe planting or harvesting. What are they doing to prepare for the next season? What grows at different times? What does it take to grow the plants? Learn from the gardeners what is involved in the planting, care, and harvesting of vegetables. Help to till the soil or weed. Taste some fresh-picked vegetables. Take some back to school and cook and eat a dish. As gardener Hanna Rion says, "The greatest gift of the garden is the restoration of the five senses."

17. **Bus and Train Stations.** These are best scheduled when the station is not too busy. Begin at the ticket area and proceed through the waiting and boarding areas. Observe different types of trains or buses. Interview passengers and employees.

18. **Bus Tours.** Get on a bus and travel around your community. Observe people, land and water forms, architectural styles, bridges, community services, or other aspects of your community.

19. **Cemeteries.** Do grave rubbings on old tombstones (if allowed). Look for family groups. Note the length of life. Do people live longer now on average?

20. **Chambers of Commerce.** Learn about your community. Learn the purpose of a Chamber of Commerce, what it does, and why people belong to one.

21. **Circuses.** Find out if the circus offers tours. Traveling circuses often stage parades when they arrive in town. Some give away free tickets. Students might write reviews for the school newspaper or Web site.

22. **City Halls.** Tour the government offices. See where the council members meet. What other services does your city hall offer? Is there information for tourists?

23. **Clock Shops.** Visit a local clock shop to see different kinds of timepieces and listen to their sounds. Find out how they work. Now most clocks are digital. The old kinds with pendulums teach a piece of history.

24. **Concerts.** Interview the musicians. See how many instruments students can identify. Are there string, wind, brass, and percussion instruments? What is the conductor doing with his or her hands, body, and head? Which musical selections do students find most enjoyable and why?

25. **Courthouses.** Learn how our judicial system works. Experience a trial. What else takes place at a courthouse? Marriage? Adoptions? Records of births and deaths? Records of land deeds?

26. **Dairies.** Schedule a trip early in the morning to see milking machines, barns, and equipment. Ask for a milking demonstration if you must go later.

27. **Daycare Centers.** Learn about the care of babies and young children. Read to and play games with the younger children.

28. **Dentist Offices.** Find a dentist who will give a tour, describe the instruments, and give a demonstration on proper oral hygiene.

29. **Dive Shops.** Learn about underwater breathing equipment and wetsuits and what we need to do to enter a fish's environment. Find out what people see when they dive. Look at films about diving in advance.

30. **Ecology: Rivers, Lakes, Bays, and Streams.** Learn about food chains, the interdependence of different elements, the effects of pollution, and how to restore the waterways. For instance in a Washington, DC, area elementary school, students raised shad from eggs and then released the tiny fry into the Potomac River in an effort to restore a species that had been native to the river. Hundreds of students have participated, both by raising shad fry in the classroom and on the river. Through the students' efforts an estimated 143,000 fry have been released (www.potomacriver.org/living_ resources/shad.htm).

31. **Ethnic Stores.** Visit a Mexican tamale store, Chinese import shop, or whatever is available in your area.

32. **Excavations.** Take advantage of excavations and building in your community. Find out what is under the streets and how buildings are constructed over time.

33. **Exercise Classes.** Learn why people go to an exercise class. Learn about how to build endurance, flexibility, balance, and strength. Find out what is happening to the body and brain as people stretch and flex. What does it do for their emotional health and attitude, as well as their physical health? Take part in an exercise class.

34. **Fabric Stores.** Learn about kinds of fabrics and where and how they are made. Note how they feel. Develop measurement and spatial skills using sewing patterns. Buy a piece of fabric and use patterns to make stuffed animals, pillowcases, or curtains for the classroom.

35. **Family Field Trips, on Their Own.** Let the whole class learn from a family's trip. The family takes videos and digital photos; the child from the family narrates. The child may keep a trip journal and write or dictate thoughts and feelings, draw pictures, and collect photos and postcards. The child might e-mail the class while traveling. Encourage families to take trips connected with classroom studies.

36. **Family Field Trips, School-Initiated.** Plan a field trip in the evening when the whole family can participate. Bring the family along. The Sea Scholar Program in Virginia Beach, Virginia, is an example. Twenty-three buses filled with families and faculty arrived at the Virginia Marine Science Museum for family night where students, their families, and their teachers explored the museum together. The trip gave parents an opportunity to participate in their children's learning. And it built a sense of community among all the participants.

37. **Farm and Ranch Stores.** Visit equipment dealers or shows to look at tractors. Compare children's height to that of tires, and ask to see tractors doing work.

38. **Farmers' Markets.** Interview farmers. Ask why we have farmers' markets in addition to grocery stores. How do farmers' markets help customers and farmers? Learn about a movement in the food world today for people to eat locally and in season, for better freshness and flavor. Find out why eating foods grown close to home appeals to the environmentally conscious, including saving energy required for transporting food thousands of miles. Find out where the farmers live, what makes their booth special, what difficulties

they have, and what they like and dislike about what they do. See the variety. Buy fresh food, and then prepare a meal back at school. Learn about the slow food movement, an international organization whose aim is to "protect the pleasures of the table from the homogenization of modern fast food and life . . . it develops taste education, conserves agricultural biodiversity and protects traditional foods at risk of extinction" (www.slowfood.com).

39. **Farms.** Try to find a traditional farm with a barn and farm animals. Ask the farmer to show equipment and feed. Taste fresh apples and/or apple cider. Get gourds and Indian corn for fall decorations. Each farm is unique. Some farms have hay bale mazes, country crafts for sale, petting zoos, dried flowers, or even a mini-train to ride. Call your county extension office to see if it has a listing of farms in your area that sell fresh produce and welcome groups.

40. **Feed Stores, Farm and Ranch Supply Companies.** Learn about tack, saddles, animal medicines, ropes, calf bottles, and feed.

41. **Fire Departments.** See trucks, living quarters, maps, and equipment. Listen to a fire safety talk. Find out who is volunteering and who is a regular. Why do they like their job? How many false alarms do they get? Has the fire department ever come to your house?

42. **Fish Hatcheries.** Ask specifically for a close-up look at eggs and other parts of the process that shows how fish grow.

43. **Flea Markets.** Find out how a flea market is a form of recycling. Ask people there how flea markets help those who are buying and those who are selling. Have a flea market project. Find out how much students can stretch their dollars to make the classroom more interesting. Each group of students might get a particular part of the classroom to improve and come to agreement on a purchase.

44. **Florist Shops.** Learn about different kinds of flowers. See the cooler where flowers are stored. Enjoy a florist's demonstration on flower arrangement. Arrange some flowers yourselves.

45. **Food Banks.** Bring donations. Collect coupons to get good deals on the donations. Do the math to learn how to get the most for your money. See how the food is sorted and find out how the items get to the people who need them.

46. **Forts.** Learn the purpose of the fort and why it is in this particular location. How did people get their food and water? What was it built of and who built it? Can your class do a reenactment of what happened at that fort? What is the shape of the fort and why? How might an enemy have attempted to storm the fort? Did they use ladders? catapults? tunneling? Once my class had an overnight at a fort

where the ranger had us take turns keeping watch all night, walking the parapet with wooden guns, to experience what the soldiers endured in the 1800s.

47. **Fossil Digs.** Find out what a fossil is and how it is formed. Discover the kinds of fossils that can be found in this particular spot. Why are they often deep in the ground? What happened so that we can find them (erosion, mining)? Collect some fossils if it is allowed. Use books and experts to identify your finds.

48. **Garbage Dumps.** These make a lasting impression when the children see the dump and watch the truck unload. Discuss ecology and recycling.

49. **Gas Stations.** Learn how the gasoline gets to the station, the differences among various types and grades of gas, and how gasoline enables cars and trucks to operate. Find out how the price of gas is determined at this station.

50. **Government Facilities.** Find out what the government is doing in relation to your community and your school—safety, repairs, lunches, testing. Tour the area, compare facilities of your city with those of the state, or compare your state government with the federal government.

51. **Greenhouses.** Find out what they do, how they work, and how they are made. Learn about hydroponics. Some countries use greenhouses for much of their food. For instance in Iceland most food is grown in greenhouses with geothermal energy. The Netherlands also does a lot with greenhouses.

52. **Grocery Stores.** Ask for a tour that includes the freezer, produce area storage, meat market, warehouse area, bakery, and office. Ask if the store has any one-way mirrors. Find out if your grocery store includes lessons on healthful eating. Have a math lesson and perform a service as you collect coupons and buy foods for the hungry (see page 92). Donate to your local food bank.

53. **Hardware Stores.** Look at different kinds of tools and compare sizes of nuts and bolts. Watch a spare key being made, and identify replacement parts for lamps and plumbing fixtures.

54. **Herb Shops/Farms.** Learn about how herbs grow and their many uses such as teas for enjoyment and remedies for health problems. Which parts are used—seeds, roots, leaves, stems, flowers? Which herbs do students know of and use already? How do native people of North America, South America, and Central America use herbs? How do herbs and spices relate to history and culture—Asian-Indian, Mexican, European, and Colonial American?

55. **Historic Homes.** Discover what a home and its contents reveal about the people who lived there and the time they lived in.

56. **Historical Societies.** Learn about the history of people, places, or items. Enjoy reenactments of events.

57. **Home Businesses.** Discover what it takes to be an entrepreneur. How are the family members a part of the business? What do they do to help? Who has a family member with a home business?

58. **Homeless Shelters.** Bring donations. Tutor the children. How and why do people get there? What could happen to make any of us homeless?

59. **Hospitals.** See the ambulance entrance, an X-ray machine, and the maternity ward. Visit a baby nursery. Take a tour, if possible. Principal Miriam Kronish says that taking young children to a hospital to demystify the experience for the future is one of her favorite field trips!

60. **Houses of Worship: Churches, Synagogues, Mosques, and Temples.** Learn about the art and architecture. What does this building say about the religion, its principles, and beliefs? What do people do there? How is this building similar to and different from other places of worship?

61. **Humane Societies.** Take a tour of the animal shelter and learn about owning pets.

62. **Infant Stores.** Compare sizes of clothing, chairs, car seats, and dishes. What is the purpose of the car seat or bed buffers? What products are designed to keep the babies safe, clean, calm, relaxed, or entertained? If you were a parent, which would you buy?

63. **Junkyards.** These need special safety considerations but will often donate pieces of cars and appliances that can be made into a group sculpture.

64. **Kite Stores.** Learn about all kinds of kites. What makes them fly? See a kite-flying demonstration.

65. **Land and Water Forms Tours.** Take a bus tour around your community, observing examples of landforms (hills, cliffs, valleys, peninsulas, islands) and water forms (rivers, lakes, ponds, marshes, seas).

66. **Libraries.** Visit a library regularly to select a book, look at magazines, or cruise the Internet. Or go for a special event such as a puppet show or author talk.

67. **Lighthouses.** Learn their purpose, where they needed to be, and who lived there. Why don't people live in lighthouses anymore? Are some still used today? Why are they less essential today than they

were 100 years ago? Imagine growing up in a lighthouse. Find stories about lighthouses. Learn about foghorns.

68. **Livestock Shows.** Take extra helpers and stress safety. These shows allow city children to see, hear, and smell farm animals.

69. **Manicure Shops.** Find out what is involved in a manicure and pedicure. Learn some of the science behind these services. Our nails are like horses' hooves. Compare human nails with pet nails. Learn about the changing styles for shaping nails.

70. **Manufacturing Plants.** Learn how the product is made, packaged, and delivered.

71. **Marine Science Museums.** See if you can get a behind-the-scenes tour of how the organisms are cared for.

72. **Martial Arts Studios.** See exhibitions. Visit in the context of learning about Asian culture. Compare martial arts with Western modes of combat such as boxing and fencing. Consider how martial arts reflect the cultures they come from.

73. **Mechanic Shops.** These may allow you to observe workers through a window. Observe cars, boats, computers, or other electrical appliances being repaired.

74. **Music Stores.** Compare sounds of instruments. Compare the instruments used for different musical genres. Look at unusual instruments such as instruments from different cultures. Find out about reading sheet music. (See Concerts, page 45.)

75. **Music Studios.** Observe the soundproof rooms where music is recorded. Note how musicians can make layers of tracks on a recording. Perhaps students can be recorded and hear themselves.

76. **Native American Powwows.** Learn the purpose of and what happens at a powwow. See how the first Americans continue their cultures in the present day. How are their cultures and philosophies similar and different from each other and from other cultures?

77. **Newspapers.** See the advertising offices, reporters at work, and huge printing presses. Find out how the news gets to the printed page. Learn about career opportunities.

78. **Nursing Homes.** Make cards, sing songs, or take oral histories of people in retirement.

79. **Optometrist Offices.** Learn about the structure of the eye, eye care, and safety.

80. **Orchards.** Choose among fruit and nut orchards, and go at blossom or harvest time. Learn about the life cycles of the fruits or nuts. Compare these with other life cycles.

81. **Parents' Workplaces.** Learn about what the parents do at work. What is the contribution their work makes to the community? Interview parents and their coworkers. Students can "shadow" their parents and report what they learn to their classmates.

82. **Parks.** Learn about the plants, animals, and nonliving things in the park. Look for signs of animals. Where do they live? What do they eat? How is the park maintained? Who uses it and why? Keep track of people's paths of movement through the park. Make a map of the park. Note interesting places. Note where interesting sounds are. Is there some form of water in the park? Who is attracted to it?

83. **Pet Stores.** Learn from the clerks about the needs of pets and how to select appropriate pets. Compare sizes of doghouses. Look at pet medicine, grooming equipment, and cages. Depending on the age of your students, use the store to teach about animal body coverings, animal classification, or adaptations.

84. **Petting Farms.** Learn about the different kinds of animals. Use the senses. How do the animals look, sound, smell, feel? How are they alike and different? What do they need to live?

85. **Photo Processing Centers.** Find out how pictures taken of or by the students transform from film to photographs. Compare with digital photography.

86. **Pizza Shops.** Learn about how the shop operates. These may allow children to make their own pizza. What are the ingredients? How is the dough made?

87. **Plant Nurseries.** Take along a gardener to identify plants native to the area, fruit trees, bedding plants, and shrubs. Observe water gardens and pottery. Ask for a talk on the importance of plants and trees, or tips on planting a children's garden.

88. **Plays.** Prepare for the play by acting out the plot in advance. After the play, go backstage and interview the performers, if possible. Write reviews for the school newspaper.

89. **Playgrounds.** Learn physics principles and theories such as gravity and momentum from swings and friction from sliding boards. Learn about a simple machine called a lever by studying how a seesaw works. Make hypotheses and test them. Focus on safety. (http://teacher.scholastic.com/products/instructor/Aug04_playground.htm)

90. **Pools.** Learn about pool safety and the chemistry involved in keeping the pool clean. Learn how to swim.

91. **Post Offices.** Ask if they will allow you to follow a bright letter from the mail slot to the delivery truck.

92. **Potters' Studios.** Watch a potter make a pot on a wheel. Learn about the chemistry of glazes. Make and glaze pinch pots and have them fired. When my students were studying Japan, they made raku pots and watched the potter fire them by moving the pots from a kiln to a trashcan with burning leaves. This raku process gives the pots an opalescent effect. Raku pots are used in the Japanese tea ceremony.

93. **Poultry Farms.** In addition to chicken and turkey hatcheries, look for duck, emu, and ostrich farms. How are the animals cared for? What products come from the animals? Are they breeding farms where they raise poultry for meat or layer farms where they produce eggs?

94. **Power Plants.** Tour the electric utility or gas company. Ask for a talk and demonstrations about different sources of energy, how electricity is made, and how it gets to homes. Discuss conservation.

95. **Preschools.** Learn about how the children are cared for. Read to them, play games with them, tutor them, and learn from them.

96. **Printing Shops.** Learn about different kinds of printing—offset printing; newspaper printing; screen printing onto cups, T-shirts, boxes, etc.; book printing; xerography; and digital laser printing. What are the similarities and differences among different types of printing? What is the process for printing in color?

97. **Pumpkin Patches.** Learn how the pumpkins grow. Pick favorite pumpkins. Take a hay ride while there, if possible.

98. **Quarries.** Observe the soil and rock layers of the earth. Old abandoned quarry areas can show the negative effects of destroying the earth's surface.

99. **Radio Stations.** Tour the on-air studio with its console, microphones, computers, and CD players. Observe the production studio where commercials are assembled, music is recorded, and promotional announcements are created. Where are the transmitter and broadcast towers? They could be as much as 30 miles away. Syndicated radio shows may be transmitted by satellite. Perhaps your students could sing a song or present a message to the community on a radio show (http://radio.about.com/library/station tour/blstationtour12.htm).

100. **Ranches.** Find out how ranchers herd horses, cows, or sheep. What is life like on the ranch for the people who work there?

101. **Recycling Centers.** Ask for a talk and tour of the largest facility in your area because it will be recycling the most products. What gets recycled? What happens to the materials collected for recycling?

102. **Renaissance Festivals.** Find out what the Renaissance was and when and where it happened. Experience the events at a Renaissance festival. Are there jousting demonstrations and puppet shows? Are there people in costume? What did people wear in the time of the Renaissance? How many outfits might they have had and how might they have gotten their clothes? Have students make and wear something that represents the Renaissance on the trip. Have some Renaissance-style food. Explore where food came from and how it was prepared during the Renaissance.

103. **Restaurants.** Visit a restaurant with food of the country you are studying. Note the types of food and how the food is cooked and served. Meet the cooks and waiters from that country. Find out in advance if your group can tour the kitchen. How does this food reflect the culture of the country you are studying?

104. **Schools for Blind or Deaf.** Learn about alternative methods of communication such as Braille for the blind and sign language for the deaf. In advance of the trip blindfold students so that they have a taste of what it is like not to be able to see.

105. **Senior Citizen Centers.** Plan your visit carefully with the activity director. Suggest activities that residents and children can do together such as painting a picture, reading a book, or planting flowers in a pot. Do the students have any relatives in Senior Citizen Centers?

106. **Shell Shops.** Identify different types of shells and the creatures that lived in them. Use the shells to make art projects.

107. **Soup Kitchens.** Help make and serve food to those in need.

108. **Sporting Events.** According to Ron Fairchild, Johns Hopkins Director of Summer Learning, there are fun and easy ways to reinforce math with field trips involving sports. For instance with bowling, even young children can learn to tally by keeping track of balls and strikes. At baseball games students can compute baseball statistics. They can compare the cost per ounce of a soda at a ball park with a two-liter bottle of soda from a grocery store. Students can learn about careers, not just of the athletes, but the coaches, broadcasters, advertisers, and others who make the games happen.

109. **Stables.** Ask for a demonstration of how to groom, feed, and ride a horse.

110. **Stars.** Have a family night or overnight camping trip in a place away from city lights with a good view of the stars. Look through telescopes. Pick out the Milky Way, the North Star, and the constella-

tions. Look at the craters on the moon. Or visit a planetarium and enjoy a show there.

111. **Strawberry Fields.** Learn how strawberries grow and why they are called "straw" berries. Pick and eat the strawberries. What are some different ways that strawberries can be prepared?

112. **Teleconferences.** These may require a short trip to your local high school or community college, somewhere that has the dedicated bandwidth for teleconferencing. Some schools have their own tele-conferencing capabilities through software, such as CU-Seeme from Cornell University, available free. There are many state muse-ums and other institutions that have teleconferencing programs for elementary students. Go to www.kn.pacbell.com/wired/vidconf/adventures.html for a "yellow pages" listing of teleconferenced field trips in history, science, art, and other subjects from institutions all over the United States. Or, check www.gsn.org for teleconferencing involving schools and worldwide experts. (See Global School Net described on page 79.) In some cases the teleconferenced field trip can even be a hands-on experience. For instance, the Museum of Natural Sciences in Raleigh, North Carolina (www.natural sciences.org/education/distance.html) sends materials for students to study such as box turtle shells, coral, and animal eggs to learn about the North Carolina coast and real spices for the teleconfer-ence on the tropical rain forest. At the teleconference the students are able to ask questions and answer the docent's questions. Students actively participate throughout the program and can see and hear responses from students at other participation sites, get-ting a taste of the high-tech environment of today's workplace.

113. **Telephone Companies.** Ask how telephones work, talk to a repair person, look at equipment, and see an employee ride the bucket on a repair truck.

114. **Television Stations.** Look at the satellite dish, visit the anchor desk where the nightly news is broadcast, and try out a video camera.

115. **Uniform Shops.** Observe and discuss the different uniforms worn by community helpers. Why do people wear uniforms?

116. **Veterinary Offices.** Learn how animals are cared for. How are vet-erinarians' practices similar to and different from doctors' offices for people? Veterinary offices may be very different from each other, depending on whether you visit a small animal practice with grooming rooms or a farm animal practice.

117.   **Water Treatment Plants.** Learn where the water in our faucets comes from, how it is treated, and how it gets to our homes. Ask for a talk on conserving water and the importance of clean water.

118.   **Wildlife Refuge and Nature Areas.** These often require several hours. Take a fanny pack, first-aid kit, and water. Arrange for a guide if possible. Take time for unexpected finds. Encourage a sense of wonder of the beauty of nature.

119.   **X-ray Labs.** See X-ray equipment and X-rays of different parts of the body.

120.   **Yogurt Shops.** Get a tour and free samples. Learn the science behind making yogurt. How do yogurt bacteria transform a liquid (milk) into a solid or semisolid (yogurt)? When are bacteria helpful and when are they harmful?

121.   **Zoos.** These often have educational programs for children that fit well with curriculum units. Ask if scholarships or grants are available for admissions and programs.

This list was adapted from *Field Trip Planning Made Easy* by Jo Ann Lohl Spears, with permission from *Texas Child Care*, a quarterly newspaper published by the Texas Workforce Commission (www.parentinginformation.org/fieldtripplanning.htm). Additions were made with the help of Mardy Burgess. Carol Ryan and her friends John and Sarah Bishop and Marjorie Lockwood (www.lessontutor.com/crfield.html) also contributed.

Summer Program Field Trips

When I was teaching in Baton Rouge, Louisiana, I wrote a grant proposal for a summer program, which the school system accepted. It was a three-week program for third graders with a theme of "Our Community." The program included field trips to places that contribute to our community in different ways such as the post office, the fire station, government offices, and the bank.

One trip we took was to our local fire station. The students had walked by this fire station every day, but they never really had any idea about how it worked inside. They hadn't known that there was a dormitory filled with beds or a big TV where the firefighters wait for the call. The students got to dress up in fire clothes; they hadn't known how heavy the clothes were or how hard it was to climb up the truck. They got a better picture of the life of their own local fire officers.

We also went to a local bank, which students found very interesting. For most, their only prior experience with banking had been ATM machines. Students got to see the bank teller and the safety deposit boxes. We met the president and sat in a conference room with big leather chairs. These students got an inside look at corporate America. They were able to experience nice people who wore suits and were service oriented.

One message was, "Here is something you might do in the future." Before our field trip, they hadn't had any idea of banking. So students got to see other jobs that are out there. Previously the only career possibilities some of these children knew about were what their parents do. One benefit of these field trips was that they start the students thinking about careers and their future, what they might want to be when they grow up.

For follow-up, we wrote thank-you notes to all the people we visited. We also built our own community in the classroom. We had a neat computer program called "Community Construction Kit" from Scholastic.* The children designed buildings, printed them, cut them out, folded them into three dimensions, and put the buildings together with parks as a part of a bigger community they invented. Each student chose a building to write about, including the services provided in that building, who worked there, and why the building was important.

Then we did a presentation for the principal and other teachers. The children could speak intelligently about the community. The students felt smart because they were able to share information that even the adults didn't know. They had learned a lot and they got a picture of their own community that they hadn't had before.

—Jennifer Smith, teacher, Baton Rouge, Louisiana

* software by Tom Snyder, neighborhood map machine published by Scholastic (www.teachtsp.com/ products/product.asp?SKU=CCKCCK).

Learning Through Nature

Just a few miles from the urban streets these students called home, there was a mysterious, almost untouched wilderness on an island in the Potomac River. The students were delighted to travel to the island in a new way by a raft with a hand-pulled rope pulley. These children, some of whom had never even been in the woods before, were fascinated with every aspect of the island.

The students used all their senses exploring the island. They put their fingers into deer prints in the mud and felt the peeling bark of sycamore trees. They ran their hands over the tree stumps the beavers had sawed off and smelled the wild flowers and examined them with magnifiers. As they listened to the water slipping around the rocks, they watched the movements of Canada geese, cormorants, and mallard ducks, and saw a turtle sunning itself on a rock. Some who wanted to climb used fallen trees to serve as nature's jungle gyms.

A few students walked through nettles and found their legs itching. Near the nettles was another plant called jewelweed; they rubbed it on their itching legs to find it eased the irritation. We discovered that nature provided nettles and an antidote to the nettles nearby.

The students made their own artwork from the materials that nature provided. They made collages by gluing nut shells; twigs; and moss, leaves, or other greenery onto a sycamore bark base.

They used their mathematical skills as they paced off the island in several directions to measure the area. They found the height of a tree when they measured the tree's shadow, the height and shadow length of a pencil, and then set up a proportion. The length of the pencil's shadow was to the height of the pencil as the length of the tree's shadow was to the height of the tree:

$$\text{tree length} \div \text{tree shadow} = \text{pencil length} \div \text{pencil shadow}$$
$$\text{or (using algebra)}$$

$$\text{tree length} = (\text{pencil length} \div \text{pencil shadow}) \times \text{tree shadow}$$

Students learned about Native Americans who had lived on the adjacent island thousands of years ago. There had been an archeological excavation where ancient spears, arrowheads, and pottery shards were found. The students found plants that grew on the island that Native Americans were known to use to dye their clothes. They also learned about the farmers who lived on that island many centuries later and the troubles they had when storms blew in, the river rose, and the island flooded.

As we sat along the bank of the river, watching the blue sky and shimmering water, the children listened to a Native American creation story of how the earth was formed. Sky Woman had fallen. She was caught by Swan and placed on Turtle's back until Muskrat dove down deep to find mud to extend Turtle's back to make land. The children, in turn, imagined and wrote their own creation stories such as how seeds became "popping seeds," how Spider got his long legs, and how Great Blue Heron created Sycamore Island. Some wrote poems such as the following:

Sycamore Island
Forest—Woody
Exciting—Adventurous—Interesting
Where the fun is
Beautiful!

On this trip into nature, the students gained knowledge of science, practiced math, made art, took part in physical education, learned some history, and wrote stories and poems. They did this all in a spirit of joy and fun. And they began to grow a sense of awe and wonder about the natural world.

—Dr. Mardy Burgess, educational consultant, Annapolis, MD, and Kathleen Carroll, Washington, DC

Faraway Trips

Trips to faraway places make the world the classroom in the grandest sense. These trips are generally reserved for upper elementary-aged students and older students. Whether the visit is to a city in another state, a national park, or a foreign country, a great deal goes into planning for faraway trips. Sometimes it works best to have an agency help with the logistical planning. Chapter 5 includes suggestions for logistical planning and fund-raising.

Trips to distant places often provide unique benefits. They can open students to whole new worlds. They often show children that the way they have always lived is not the only way to live. Even if students visit a place within their own country, they may experience accents, music, dress codes, and many other aspects of life that are different from their own. The landscape and climate may be different. Of course, all of these differences are magnified in other countries. Students also get to learn the many ways that all people are alike. These trips sometimes lead to ongoing pen pal relationships with other students.

To get the full value from faraway trips, students need to be well prepared. Particularly if they are visiting another country, students need to be prepared for a different culture. This includes teaching them proper etiquette for the culture they will visit.

Our Africa Connection

Our urban elementary school had exchanges with African schools in Kenya and Dakar for 10 years. One year we would take our students to Africa and another year the African students would be our guests here in Washington, DC. We took our trip during spring break.

Our students' families don't have a lot of money. Fortunately the children's airline tickets were half-price. Since the children became a part of the African family they visited, they didn't have to pay for food and lodging. Some churches around our school donated money to help defray the costs of the trip. We also made popcorn and sold it at lunchtime to raise money. One requirement was that if one of our students took the trip, his or her family would need to commit to hosting two African students the following year.

Our students had a lot of preconceptions about Africa that were dispelled. Some of them thought that they would be staying in a tent or a hut. "Why, I have my own bed here!" one child exclaimed to me. "At home I have to share the bed with my two sisters."

Our students were impressed with the studiousness of the students in Africa. I remember one of our little girls pulling me by the hand to look in on a class. She was amazed that the students were all quiet and working diligently, even though their teacher wasn't in the room!

In between trips our students connected with the African students through a pen pal program. Some children couldn't think of anything to write about, so I bought a lot of packages of seeds and had our children send some packages of seeds to their pen pals in Africa. Both pen pals would plant the same kinds of seeds at the same time. Then they would compare how tall their plants were on day 10 for instance. They drew pictures of their plants and made graphs. It worked very well.

Having pen pals was good for developing writing skills, too. You know how kids get annoyed when they have to redo their written work? These kids didn't. They wanted to get their letters right because their pen pals were going to read them.

Discipline was good, too, when we were having the Africa trips. We would tell them that you need to behave if we are going to take you out of the country; they started being good at the beginning of the school year!

We took our students to the dollar store so that when they went to Africa, they could bring along little gifts like bags of pens or pencils or pencil cases. The staff at the African school would provide snacks, and they would visit with their pen pal and present their gifts.

Most of our students had never been to another city, much less another continent. Very few had flown before on a plane. Some had never been on a train. We changed planes in New York City. We had a special waiting room there. I remember what a thrill it was for them to look out at the New York skyline.

For many of our students our Africa connection was the highlight of their elementary school years. It brought learning to life for our students, our school, and our community. You don't have to be in a rich school to do a trip abroad, but you do need to have vision, commitment, and perseverance. That type of experience pays off in so many ways.

—Margaret Jackson, teacher, Washington, DC

Quebec City—Fostering Student Independence

We live in a rural area where children are always driven places because everything is far away. Our field trips to Quebec are perfect for our students because Quebec is a walled city. The children are free to walk around and do their own discovering. They are safe. I can say, "Meet me back at the town square."

Pre-adolescence is a time when children want to begin to experience some independence, and Quebec is a place where it can happen. I'm trying to let them have the experience of being on their own and figuring it out, whether it's changing money or getting a lemonade. Being on their own gives them the motivation to expand. The trip gives them a feeling of confidence as they learn that they are able to solve the problems that come up.

Another benefit in going to Quebec is that it is in another country. Here is Canada, our neighbor, and we don't know anything about it! As soon as you cross the border, you know you are in another country. The red of the roofs are different; the houses are different. The children begin to get a sense of what makes a nation by experiencing one that is different from their own. How does Canada deal with its diversity? What are the Separatist issues? It's an experience of another culture.

That's the advantage for us who live in Maine. It is not far to go, yet you are in another world with the French language and different ways. The money, based on the metric system, provides some great math opportunities.

Quebec City is the closest one can get to being in Europe. It has the oldest streets in North America. Students get a sense of the past when they are in a place with buildings that are 300 years old. It's difficult to do that in the United States. A trip to Quebec helps children understand the early history and the founding of North America.

Our trip to Quebec is an important experience for my students. They write about it in their journals and put their photo albums together. They learn about history; they learn about another country. And they learn something new about themselves through their response to that first glimmer of independence.

—Catherine Razi, teacher, Blue Hill, Maine

Field Trips in the Neighborhood

There are many advantages to taking field trips in the school's neighborhood. While you may need permission, you don't have the hassle of arranging transportation and reservations for the field trip site. These are among the easiest field trips to arrange and they offer a wealth of information. An added advantage is that students get to know and appreciate their own community. Encourage students to focus all their senses during the trip.

Themes for walks might be shadows, insects, trees, plants, gardens, structures, colors, shapes, and more! The following are some suggestions for neighborhood field trips and associated projects:

1. **Animal Locomotion Walks.** Take a walk around the neighborhood with tally sheets to record the types of animal locomotion you observe. Look for flying animals such as birds and insects; walking animals, such as dogs and cats; climbing animals such as squirrels and chipmunks; and (by digging a little and looking closely) crawling animals such as snails and worms.

2. **Bird Walks.** Tally and graph the different kinds of birds in your neighborhood. If no one knows a bird's name, say "small brown bird." My students have been amazed at all the birds in their neighborhood that they had never noticed before their bird walk.

3. **Buildings: Business or Residential.** Note the kinds of businesses and the kinds of residences: Are they apartments? townhouses? detached houses?

4. **Community Design.** Take a walk for background information for students to design their own community by hand, or use software such as a computer program called "Community Construction Kit" from Scholastic. (See Summer Program Field Trips, page 56.)

5. **Construction of a Home, Building, or Street.** Observe and record changes over time.

6. **Counting Vehicles at a Corner.** Tally and graph the kinds or colors of vehicles that pass by.

7. **History of Neighborhood.** Interview people, especially older residents, about the history of their neighborhood.

8. **Improvement of the Neighborhood.** Walk around the neighborhood, noting what needs improvement. Depending on the school's neighborhood, students might call and have abandoned vehicles and bulk trash removed. At a school where I taught, students wrote to government officials to have missing tree boxes replaced. In return they not only got trees, they also got to adopt them! Students received official printouts stating that Tommy Jones had adopted a maple tree on V Street, 36 feet from 13th Street. Interestingly, 19 of the 20 trees planted stayed alive, a survival rate that was unheard of in that poor urban area.

9. **Map of the Neighborhood.** Walk around the block and make a map of streets, alleys, buildings, trees, etc. Note street signs, directions, distances, and time. Depending on their age and readiness, students might start with a simple outline map of the neighborhood that

they fill in, or they can make their own from scratch. There is also technology available where students can input to computers, add digital pictures, and even pinpoint their location on satellite pictures (see chapter 4, page 203).

10. **Parks.** Adopt a park that you visit often.

11. **Runoff.** Observe runoff after rains. How does the water leave the street? Research and find out where the water goes eventually. How do oil, pesticides, and other foreign materials affect our waterways?

12. **Seasonal Walks.** Look for signs of spring, winter, or fall. Make bark and leaf rubbings. Collect acorns, leaves, and other objects for hands-on classification and other science and art projects. Identify leafless trees by their shapes and bark. Identify spring flowers. Press plants. Observe—look, listen, smell, and feel changes in nature. Take a camera or drawing materials to compare the changes of the seasons over time in the same location. Have stopping points to note temperature, the amount of traffic observed, wildlife seen or heard, etc.

13. **Service.** Clean up older people's houses and/or yards. Bring food and good cheer to neighborhood shut-ins.

14. **Traffic.** Collect data on types, colors, or state license plates of cars in the parking lot or driving down the streets. Observe pedestrian and vehicle traffic flow. Develop safety guidelines.

15. **Trash Cleanup.** With disposable gloves, remove trash from around the block. Warn students to avoid hazardous materials such as broken glass or other sharp objects. Learn how long it takes different materials to decompose. Collect data on the amount and kinds of trash. Graph findings. Recycle the trash into art. Write a story about one piece of trash.

16. **Writing Campaigns.** Write to city managers with suggestions about how to improve unattractive areas. Find out if they will work with students to improve the sites.

Thanks to Portland, Oregon, walking-tour guide Peter Chausse for contributing to the suggestions above.

Taking It to the Streets

A class of fourth graders in San Diego, California, integrated science, math, language arts, and social service in a study about cars driving past their school. The students had prior knowledge of a relationship between distance and speed. Students knew that in a race to a finish line the distance is the same for everybody, but the time varies with different contestants. In a game like "Red Light, Green Light" the time is the same for everyone playing, but the distance varies. The students learned how to measure distance and time and how those measurements are influenced as speeds increase.

In an experiment on the school grounds, students saw a raw egg cracked when a driver was at a speed where he unable to slow down fast enough to save it. They found that just adding 10 miles per hour to the speed doubled the time it took the car to stop.

Then they applied that learning to the cars speeding in front of their school. They invited an officer who had a radar gun, and the officer was able to clock the speed of passing cars. Even with a police officer and a whole class of children watching, 86 percent of the cars passing by in a half hour's time were exceeding the speed limit. The children realized that just as in the egg experiment, speeding cars might not be able to slow down fast enough to avoid hitting them when they cross the street.

The children wrote letters to the city council, their parents, and other adults to slow down in school zones. They also recognized the dangers of jaywalking, which some had indulged in previously, and began to cross the street more carefully themselves. Word got out in the community, and the students were asked to repeat their experiments on live TV with the police officer for 90 minutes.

Thanks to Randy Yerrick, San Diego State University; Chris Schmidt, fourth grade teacher; and Bob Jones, principal. (http://ali.apple.com/ali_sites/ali/exhibits/1001420/The_Lesson.html)

The Power of a Walk Around the Block

When my students were learning map skills, we would take a walk around the block at school. The students drew maps of the neighborhood, filled in streets and buildings, and made a compass rose. I remember one boy who had been retained. He didn't have a very positive self-image as a student. But when he went to work on the map, he was amazing! He filled in every street, every back alley, and every detail accurately. I realized that his spatial intelligence was a lot stronger than mine! I think that was a beginning of his turnaround. By the time he graduated from the sixth grade, he was one of the star pupils.

When we were learning the parts of plants, we would go outside and study weeds. We were in an urban school where most of the children were on free lunch, but there were plenty of weeds! And that proved to be an easy, interesting, and relevant way to see the variety of roots, stems, leaves, flowers, and fruits that can grow in an area. We also came to appreciate the strength and resilience of the little dandelions and other plants who manage to push their way up through cracks in the sidewalk. They manage to bloom under the toughest conditions. (Some of my students were like that, too.)

Adopting a tree presents an opportunity for ongoing short field trips that can relate to a thematic curriculum. If you live in an area with deciduous trees, fall or spring are ideal for observation because a tree changes from week to week. As a preassessment, have students draw a tree and a leaf before they begin the study. For science, students study the roots, bark, changing leaves, flowers, insects, and other animals that live on the tree. For math, they measure its height, width, and leaf variations. For social studies, students might learn about traditional uses of tree parts for building, medicine, and food and whether the tree is native or exotic. If the tree is native to another country, where did it come from? Did immigrants bring it to their new land, and if so, why?

For language arts, students keep journals about the tree, write poems, and communicate with other students as they compare their findings. For art, they sketch the tree from varying distances at different times of the year. Students compare similarities and differences among their trees and other students' trees, including changes throughout the seasons. As a culmination students become "docents," describing their trees to parents or other classes.

—Kathleen Carroll

Field Trips on Your School Grounds

In many schools the school grounds provide an easily accessible way to give students real-world learning experiences. A field trip on the school grounds also gives students practice with how to be outside the classroom at the beginning of the school year to prepare them for the longer trips to come. For their own safety, Sylvia Shugrue, science teacher and former president of the National Science Teachers Association (NSTA), liked to help students develop a pattern of behavior for field trips. At the beginning of the school year, she would start with a simple trip that didn't involve buses or money; students would take a trip to the school's playground. Before going outside, she helped students become very clear about why they were going and how to behave.

Suppose they went out on the playground to study simple machines. The students needed to realize that in this case they were not there for their usual patterns of behavior, to play on the seesaw. Instead they were on the playground to see how the seesaw works as a fulcrum and lever. They were there to experience how the pulley makes it easier to raise the flag and how the ramp allows a wheelchair to move easily up a hill and into the building. The field trip to the playground gave students time to get used to the idea that certain signals from the teacher meant for them to group around her.

Shugrue was helping the children distinguish between the patterns of behavior that are appropriate for free play and the patterns of behavior appropriate for field trips. Once students became accustomed to the patterns of behavior needed for field trips, they were ready for trips away from school.

Trips to the playground can also have value in their own right. For one thing, these trips are convenient. Students can take these trips outside anytime without the logistical burdens required of trips away from school. Remind students to focus on their senses while on the trip. The following are some ideas for field trips right outside your school building:

1. **Study Air Pollution.** Place glass slides or other materials covered with petroleum jelly in strategic places around the schoolyard and near the parking lot. In a few days collect the specimens and use magnifying glasses to observe particles collected from the air. Did some areas collect more particles than others? What might your findings suggest about air pollution?

2. **Observe Birds.** Make or buy bird feeders. Hang them right outside the classroom window. Students make graphs of how many of each kind of bird visits the feeder.

3. **Identify Birdsongs.** Listen for birdsongs around the schoolyard. Use tapes of birdsongs or experts to identify the kinds of birds who make the songs.

4. **Study Butterflies.** Observe and find out which flowers in your neighborhood attract butterflies. Students help to plant those varieties in the schoolyard. Keep track of which butterflies visit your garden for the nectar from the flowers. In addition plant milkweed, the only plants that monarch caterpillars can eat. Observe the life cycle of the monarch.

5. **Classify Objects.** Take out a hanger or meter-long piece of string and magnifying glasses for each student or small group of students. Students place their hanger or string tied in a circle on a plot of lawn or under a tree. They observe carefully and come up with ways to classify what they find by putting the objects they find in groups. Originally, I expected students to classify the objects as plants, animals, and nonliving things. However, they often come up with many different and unusual classifications that are perfectly logical! This shows students that there is more than one way to classify. This activity can serve as a basis for descriptive writing.

6. **Learn About Clouds.** Keep a sky journal. Study the different kinds of clouds. Students look for how accurately they can predict the weather from the types of clouds that are present. Students use their imaginations to see shapes in the clouds. They sketch the clouds and write poems and other reflections.

7. **Write Eco-Mysteries.** Read an eco-mystery by Jean Craig George. An eco-mystery is a mystery based on a real environmental problem. Finding the cause(s) of the problem becomes the mystery to be solved. Students find an environmental problem around their school grounds and write their own mystery (Carroll 2000).

8. **Create Field Guides.** Make a student-designed field guide of the schoolyard. Take photographs or make drawings of interesting plants, animals, or geological areas and provide information about each. Other classes in the school can test the guide and let your class know if some parts are confusing so that your class can make improvements. Share the field guide with the rest of the school (Carroll 2000; Booth 1999).

9. **Plant Flowers.** Take a field trip right outside your window. Students learn what is required for plants to grow by planting and taking care of the plants. They also learn about helping to make their surroundings more beautiful.

10. **Make Habitats for Wildlife.** Plant shrubs and plants that provide wildlife with food all year. Provide a bird bath, pond, or water dish. Replace the water everyday to avoid bacteria buildup. Provide shrubs, trees, and nest boxes for cover and to raise young (www.nwf.org). Students compare the number and kinds of wildlife before and after. Students learn to be stewards for the environment (Carroll 2000).

11. **Observe and Listen.** Go outside and invite students to stand very still with their eyes closed and have them intently listen. Each student holds up one finger on the right hand for each mechanical sound he or she hears and one finger on the left hand for each natural sound the student hears. Then students open their eyes and discuss their observations (Carroll 1999).

12. **Observe and Look.** Walk around the schoolyard with a magnifying glass. Study walls, weeds in cracks in the pavement, lawns, trees, or bugs.

13. **Measure Plants.** Measure and label trees, shrubs, flowers. Plant new ones.

14. **Make Maps.** Map the playground or school grounds. Learn the cardinal directions. Find the perimeter and area of the school building. Science consultant Sylvia Shugrue told me of a first grade class that

mapped the playground. Afterward students cross-stitched the map on burlap with colorful thread as an art activity.

15. **Observe Cars in Parking Lots.** Inventory the cars on the parking lot. Graph by color, two doors vs. four doors, make of cars, etc.

16. **Take a Poll About Playground Equipment.** Survey which equipment on the playground is most popular.

17. **Measure Shadows.** Take young children out to the playground at different times on a sunny day. Observe and/or measure how the shadows change their size and directions. Students might hypothesize what makes shadows and why they change. Upper elementary students can learn about the rotation of the earth each day and the revolution of the earth around the sun over time by observing how shadows change. Go to www.nsta.org/301/ and read the units called "Astronomy with a Stick" by Sylvia Shugrue for step-by-step instructions on how to do these and other astronomy projects on your school's playground. Currently students from different religions and cultures in the Middle East are learning to connect with one another by sharing data they collect with these astronomy projects.

18. **Solo Spots.** Pick a special spot outside as a "solo spot." Each student sits quietly at his or her own solo spot and observes regularly, perhaps once a week. Look, listen, feel, and smell for patterns, collect data, and note changes over time. Use this activity as a basis for writing activities (Carroll 2000).

19. **Study Over Time.** Study a tree or a plot of earth as it changes with the seasons. Write and draw observations.

20. **Grow Vegetable Gardens at School.** Plant vegetables and herbs. Learn to care for the garden and prepare and eat the vegetables. Vegetable gardens help children become more receptive to healthful eating.

21. **Use Weather Instruments.** Take daily readings. Graph findings. Use data for word problems.

22. **Study Weeds.** Find weeds growing in the schoolyard. Learn their names and possible uses. For example, dandelions were brought to the United States from Europe for salads, soups, and as a coffee substitute. Lamb's quarters, a weed that can be found in many lawns, makes a good substitute for spinach. Even if they don't learn the names of the weeds, students can draw and label the roots, stems, leaves, and flowers (if present) of the weed and compare the similarities and differences among different varieties.

Thanks to Portland, Oregon, walking-tour guide Peter Chausse for contributing to the suggestions above.

Sky Gazing

The sky field trips take place just outside the school building, on the playground, sitting on a rock, or on a carpet sample. Each person finds a special place apart from the other students—sky journal in hand. These trips take place throughout the school year. The students look up and learn. They open up to the natural world with their senses and put down their thoughts.

In the words of Drew Prairie, age 10, Vista Grande School, Danville, California (Kronish and Abelmann 1989):

Life is like a room.
You learn math, a door opens in your room. Yet, I dislike rooms.
I like to be free outside, and now I am.
For the door to the sky was opened for me.

Students write poetry and prose, sometimes adorning their pages with sketches. Descriptive writing, expository writing, reflective pieces—all are included in our sky journals, while in the classroom students are learning about weather, cloud formations, how to construct weather instruments, and much, much more.

The wonderful aspect to these field trips is that they are free of cost and accessible everywhere. The sky's the limit!

—Miriam Kronish, principal, Needham, Massachusetts

Healthful Learning, Healthful Living

American children need to change their eating habits and level of exercise. The U.S. Centers for Disease Control and Prevention states that the percentage of young people who are overweight has more than tripled since 1980. The implications on health are disastrous. Heart problems, Type Two diabetes, strokes, sleep apnea, and high blood pressure are appearing among younger and younger children. How might we counter the junk food culture?

Here is one solution that can improve children's nutrition and increase exercise while helping them enjoy learning about science, math, history, and ecology. It will also make the school grounds more beautiful. Chef Alice Waters calls it the "Edible Schoolyard" (www.edibleschoolyard.org).

With the Edible Schoolyard, children grow vegetables in a school garden and learn to use what they grow to make healthful and delicious meals. The idea is to get permission to take part of the school grounds for children to grow a vegetable garden.

Growing a garden gives students a full sensory experience as they learn a variety of subjects:

- ▶ **Science**. Students learn about where their food comes from, how plants grow, and how to live in harmony with the cycle of seasons.
- ▶ **Nutrition**. Students learn about organic food, what it takes to eat well, and the health advantages of eating in season. They learn how to cook fresh and nourishing foods.
- ▶ **Mathematics**. Students learn how to measure the garden plots, graph plants' growth over time, and compare different vegetables and the size of the harvest.
- ▶ **Geography**. Students can grow and learn to eat foods from the countries they study.
- ▶ **History**. Students can grow and learn to prepare and eat foods eaten in ancient Mesopotamia, Egypt, Greece, China, the Incan and Aztec empires, or during colonial times.
- ▶ **Physical Education**. Students are physically active as they plant, weed, and harvest their vegetables.
- ▶ **Ecology**. Students learn about the interdependence of plants, animals, and the rest of the environment. They learn how eating locally grown food in season not only tastes better, but also saves the environment from the energy consumption and pollution generated by transporting food thousands of miles. Just compare how delicious a locally grown tomato is to an out-of-season tomato flown or trucked in from far away.

According to Chelsea Chapman (conversation at the Smithsonian Folk Life Festival, 6-30-05), who teaches with the Edible Schoolyard Program:

> Our goal is to educate children about nutrition through sensory education—to see, smell, and eat healthful beautiful fruits, vegetables, and herbs. Students love tasting as we walk through the garden. You can start with a couple of raised beds or box beds right on the asphalt.
>
> For the cooking, if you don't have room for a garden you can use local farmers' markets. We have a cooking class for every child at school. In the cooking classes we use everything that grows in the garden. Students make salsa, stir fry, soup, and pizza. Gardening and cooking are incredible community-builders. Food is something we all have in common. Kids eat what they have grown and cooked. We are eating "civically" as a group, talking about ideas. Many families don't sit down to eat together that way anymore.

Alice Water's next step is "The School Lunch Initiative." Its purpose is to educate youngsters enculturated with fast-food values with new values of wellness and stewardship for the environment.

Here are some comments from students who participate in the Edible Schoolyard Program:

The garden and kitchen have shown us that nature is beautiful (as if we didn't already know) and we should treat it with respect because although some things may not seem important, they can be used in great and useful ways.

I like it when I'm cooking and gardening because it's fun. You get to hang out with your friends and have fun.

At the turn of the 20th century, school gardens were everywhere. Wouldn't it be wonderful to have them return?

Field Trips in Your School Building

Field trips right in your school building can provide real-life applications of the curriculum and introduce students to career possibilities. The following are a few ideas:

1. **Look at Blueprints.** Ask for the blueprints of the school building. Students might use the blueprints to help them map their classrooms or the school, or to compare blueprints with the maps they have made themselves of their classroom, school, or school grounds.
2. **Tour the Boiler Room.** Ask the custodian to take your class on a trip to the boiler room. Learn about what kind of fuel is used, how the fuel is transferred to heat, and how energy-efficient your school is. Plan ways to help make the school more energy-efficient by informing others of ways to save energy such as turning off lights.
3. **Explore the Cafeteria.** Learn from the cafeteria workers where students' food comes from and how it is prepared each day. How are the menus planned?
4. **Visit Classrooms.** Visit the classrooms of older students so kids can see what is coming. Visit classrooms of younger children. Your students might read stories they have written to the younger students or tutor them.
5. **Celebrate Cultural Diversity.** Learn about the different cultural backgrounds of staff and students.
6. **Interview Graduates.** Talk to graduates of the school to discover what they are doing now. Ask students with relatives who have graduated from the school, or ask the teacher who has been around the longest, to refer you to graduates.

7. **Create a Staff Map.** Interview staff and find out where each person was born. Keep track on a classroom map or map in the school hall.

8. **Research Building Materials.** What materials were used to construct the school building?

9. **Visit with Maintenance Workers.** Learn what goes into keeping the school building and grounds clean. What can students do to help?

10. **Explore the Metric System.** Measure objects in and around your school using English and metric units.

11. **Make Mileposts.** Make posts that show direction and distances in paces within the school or direction and distances to field trips students have taken (see pages 166–167).

12. **Construct Models.** Make three-dimensional models of the school and grounds.

13. **Create a School Newspaper.** "It was all happening at our school at 9:30 A.M." Students visit classrooms and take notes. Then they report on what was happening concurrently at a particular day and time.

14. **Visit the Nurse's Office.** Visit the health room. Learn about the duties of the school nurse and the instruments he or she uses.

15. **Visit the Main Office.** Interview the principal, assistant principal, administrative aide, and/or counselor. Find out what their work consists of and what kinds of education and skills are needed to perform that work.

16. **Host an Overnight Event.** Have a sleepover at school inside or in tents on the school grounds. As teacher Catherine Razi noted, "One of the most wonderful things to observe was students spending the night in the backyard of school. There they were at school with their little stuffed animals. The overnight didn't start until after three. But, from the moment they brought their things to school in the morning, the relationship they had formed with the space that they know so well changed. It's a state of mind."

17. **Study School Organization.** Obtain data from each classroom, including the numbers of boys, girls, and total number of students. Then make bar graphs and use the data to work out mathematical problems.

18. **Explore Shapes.** Observe and keep track of lights, windows, doors, drinking fountains, electronic devices, etc.

19. **Hold a Trivia Contest.** Design a trivia contest for the rest of the school: How much do you know about your school?

Thanks to Portland, Oregon, walking-tour guide Peter Chausse for contributing to the suggestions above.

An Overnight at School

The third grade has an overnight at school every year when we are studying Colonial times. We have these wonderful linen costumes for the students that were made by parents and teachers years ago. The students wear these costumes on our Colonial Day. (Even if you don't have costumes for your trip, just putting on a scarf can bring the experience for students.)

Each year they make pouches to go around the waist before the overnight. In Colonial days, people didn't have pockets in their clothes. The kids make clay marbles in advance, and carry them in their pockets on the day of their overnight.

Making lanterns is another pre-overnight activity for our children. The students make lanterns out of tall #10 juice cans. We provide one can of juice per child. We put water in the can and freeze it. When the water is frozen, we put the cans on their side. Students make holes all around the cans by pounding big roofing nails into the cans. The ice keeps the can expanded. During the overnight we put tea lights into the lanterns and place the lanterns in a circle.

In the afternoon we divide the children into groups for craft activities. Boys and girls embroidered initials on linen handkerchiefs with cross-stitch embroidery. Kids made butter from heavy cream by shaking it in jars. There were stations where students would make the food with the help of parents. Students would make cornbread, gingerbread, and stew. It was exhausting for us adults, though!

We have changed the overnight some over the years to make it a little easier on the adults. We have had to simplify to avoid teacher burnout. For instance, now we take the students to a museum instead of doing all the crafts ourselves. The students wear the costumes to the museum. The director of the museum does a spinning demonstration and shows the students how to play games from Colonial times.

And now we order food in instead of organizing the students to cook the meal. We order chicken, corn, and applesauce with carrots and celery. We still make the cornbread and gingerbread, so we have that, too. The parents help get the meal ready. Each student has chores, either for the dinner set up or clean up. They get to play Colonial games and Native American games—Colonial children might have learned these games from their Native American friends.

A man comes from the Maryland Historical Society for an hour. He pretends to be a miller who lived 200 years ago. He is dressed for the part and has artifacts in his sack. He tells the children about his life, family, and what he does for a living.

Then we have a square dance. Someone plays the fiddle and someone calls. The parents and teachers participate. After the square dance, the kids have apple juice. We light the tea lights in the lanterns the children made before. We sing songs around our circle of lights. It looks beautiful.

The students are in groups. Each group has a name reminiscent of some occupation from Colonial times. Groups may be called by names such as the Blacksmiths, the Bakers, the Apothecaries, or the Carpenters.

When the children get ready for bed, I pass out Native American folktales for the adults to read to the children to settle them down. We have found it best to spread out the students among classrooms with four students to one adult. The goal is to actually sleep. (I don't like to have the teachers supervise a group. The teachers lock up.) The next morning everyone packs up and eats breakfast. The children are gone by 8:00 A.M.

For the follow-up, we ask our students, "How does your life compare with a child's from Colonial days?" Their homework is to write a story in two paragraphs describing what they did and their feelings about it—what they enjoyed and what was hard. For some children, not being home is hard. We think the children might take pleasure in reading about these memories when they are older.

—Anne Fretz, Kensington, Maryland

Field Trips in the Classroom: Bring the World to You!

Taking students out, whether that means going for a walk, riding a bus, or flying to an exotic destination by plane, gives children rich, memorable sensory learning experiences. But it is also possible to get some of the benefits of field trips right in the classroom. One way to bring a field trip to you is to have an expert come to your classroom. This person can bring equipment, dress in uniform, give a demonstration, show a video, and answer children's questions. These options are educational, avoid the hassle of transportation, and permit several groups of children to enjoy the event. While older students can benefit from these in-class field trips, they are especially well suited to young children.

Living Creatures Make Learning Exciting

I used to have field trips in the classroom with a focus on animals, thanks to the local pet store. The owner of the pet store was kind enough to lend me hermit crabs, feeder goldfish, a frog, a small lizard, and a hamster. (The pet store owner was reluctant to lend me a bird, since the birds were a little more delicate and sensitive to changes in temperature. Sometimes I would borrow a pet bird that was already acclimatized to the school. Other times I used a stuffed bird.)

The animals became the focal point of stations in my classroom. Each table had a terrarium or aquarium with the animal, along with photographs of other animals in that group. The stations also had other artifacts: the table with the hermit crabs had other shells; the table with the lizard had a snake skin; and the table with the hamster had other examples of fur. Written materials rounded out the stations.

I was the science resource teacher so I saw all the children from early childhood through sixth grade. The youngest students visited the stations to learn about animal body coverings. Third graders focused on animal adaptations, the required standard for their grade level. Older students used the stations to develop an understanding of the scientific classification system of invertebrates and the five classes of vertebrates: fish, amphibians, reptiles, birds, and mammals. The students learned inductively, from examples to idea, by looking at what the animals and the pictures of animals at each table had in common.

Each child received a booklet of blank pages stapled together. They took a page or two for each station. They drew the animal and wrote down their observations and sometimes their inferences, based on their observations. Often fifth or six graders acted as docents at the stations for small groups of younger children, pointing out what to observe. Groups of students had a certain amount of time at each station. I would ring a bell when it was time to move on to the next station.

Students got to look, listen, touch, discuss, and move. Whenever we had this lesson, all students were fully engaged, even the squirmiest. Students developed new concepts by using all their senses and by experiencing many examples.

—Kathleen Carroll

Experts you can have visit your classroom include

1. **Animal Shelter Employees.** Ask employees to help students find out about the animals' daily care and how they are adopted.
2. **Artists.** See the artists in action. See their works. Encourage students to ask questions. Students can use the artists' work as their inspiration as they make their own art.
3. **Beekeepers.** Ask the beekeeper to bring an empty hive and beekeeper clothing for children to try on. Discuss the many ways bees help us and safety around bees, and taste samples of honey.
4. **Boat Owners.** Ask a parent or boat shop owner to bring a boat the children can explore. It is great to observe a sailboat, rubber raft, canoe, and motorboat on the same day. Students look for similarities and differences among the different kinds of boats.
5. **Clowns.** Watch a clown demonstrate how to put on makeup, dress in costume, and do some tricks. Clowns can show they are just people dressed in funny clothes.
6. **Conservation Specialists.** Learn about litter, pollution, and various kinds of conservation (soil, water, energy). Call the local agricultural extension service, university, or environmental group about special programs for children.

7. **Disabled People.** Massachusetts principal Miriam Kronish says, "We invited handicapped people to come to each grade level and interact with the children. They included learning disabled, mentally impaired, blind, deaf, and physically handicapped. We had the grade levels meet together with the guest and then have a question-and-answer period afterward. It made a huge impact on both the speaker and his or her audience. The program was called AVID—Appreciating and Valuing Individual Differences. We gave a stipend to the speakers and the program was coordinated by a parent."

8. **Elders.** Learn from the knowledge, wisdom, experience, and memories of the elders in the community.

9. **Emergency Medical Technicians (EMTs).** They will often bring an ambulance, give talks about emergencies, and reassure children about hospitals.

10. **Farmers.** If they can get a tractor on the playground, have a demonstration. Farmers can give advice about planning a spring garden. Winter is off-season and a convenient time for farmers to talk about what they do.

11. **Firefighters.** These community helpers will often bring a truck, give a safety talk, and demonstrate how to use a fire hose.

12. **Gardeners.** Gardeners, landscape architects, and plant nursery owners will often share plants, seeds, and pictures and will help plan and plant gardens for children.

13. **Geologists.** Consider a wide range of people knowledgeable about rocks, minerals, and gems, including jewelers and rock hounds. They can provide wonderful specimens of rocks, books, posters, and tools.

14. **Judges and Lawyers.** They can explain about courts, trials, and how our judicial system works.

15. **Lifeguards.** Ask for programs on water safety.

16. **Mail Carriers.** In addition to talking to the children about how mail can come to children's homes from almost anywhere in the world, they sometimes allow students to look into their mail trucks or cars.

17. **Marine Biologists.** They usually have specimens to show in the classroom and can explain the importance of keeping the beach and water clean. Ask for a demonstration of how the food chain works.

18. **Medical Professionals.** Nurses, doctors, dentists, and optometrists can do many programs on health, safety, and related topics. They can bring medical tools and tell stories about their experiences.

Make sure they come in a uniform, and be careful to avoid sex stereotyping (invite male nurses and female doctors, for example).

19. **Parents and Grandparents.** Survey children's families about hobbies, travels, culture, and occupations. Invite them to share their knowledge and skills with the children.

20. **Park Service Rangers.** Ask the rangers to share their daily duties. They may be able to bring in animals. If they are historians, they may be able to bring an aspect of history in your curriculum alive.

21. **Pest Control People.** They often have insect collections or pictures to share. They will discuss helpful and harmful insects, poison safety, and equipment.

22. **Pet Shop Owners.** They usually stress the responsibilities involved in owning pets, considerations in pet selection, and needs of different animals. One pet store owner allowed me to borrow animals from his pet store. Younger students studied animal coverings. Older students classified the animals into fish, amphibians, reptiles, birds, and mammals. Another class used the same animals to study adaptations. Students made booklets: at each station students sketched the animals, wrote down their observations, and wrote other pertinent facts about the animals.

23. **Pilots.** These can be commercial airplane pilots, military pilots, amateurs, and hot-air balloonists. They might be able to demonstrate setting up a hot-air balloon or bring an ultralight plane to the playground.

24. **Police Officers.** In addition to giving a talk, they may bring a police car and let children sit in it. Some police may be able to show children a police robot or a dog in a K-9 Unit who helps police sniff out crimes. Some police may be able to help students learn about fingerprinting.

25. **Radio and Television Hosts.** These are always favorites with the children. They usually talk about the importance of being able to communicate effectively.

26. **Ranchers.** Invite a rancher or rodeo performer to demonstrate roping, cattle calling, or branding. Ask for a talk about clothing and equipment. A rancher might be able to bring a calf or horse.

27. **Scuba Divers.** They will dress in wet suits and demonstrate their equipment. They may have slides or videos to share.

28. **Shell Shop Owners.** They will bring a collection of shells and talk about marine life.

29. **Skin Care or Hair Care Professionals.** Ask a beautician to show students how best to keep their skin and hair clean and healthy.

30. **Teachers of the Deaf.** They can help students understand the challenges and abilities of the deaf. They may teach children a song or verse in sign language.

31. **Telephone Repair Workers.** They will show how they climb poles and the tools on their trucks.

32. **Veterans.** Invite a war veteran who remembers World War II, Korea, or Vietnam or who has traveled to the country being studied.

33. **Veterinarians.** These professionals and their assistants can do programs on pets, especially health, care, and safety.

34. **Weather Forecasters.** TV forecasters are big hits. School-aged children may be motivated to track temperature and rain, learn about storms, and learn how weather affects daily life. Ask the expert to come in for a talk about hurricanes or natural disasters that affect your area: what to do, what to expect, how to prepare, etc.

35. **Zoo Personnel.** Zoos often have outreach programs to bring animals and programs into schools.

Adapted from *Field Trip Planning Made Easy* by Jo Ann Lohl Spears with permission from *Texas Child Care*, a quarterly newspaper published by the Texas Workforce Commission (www.parentinginformation.org/fieldtrip planning.htm). Additions with the help of Mardy Burgess. Carol Ryan and her friends John and Sarah Bishop and Marjorie Lockwood (www.lessontutor.com/crfield.html) also contributed.

Sharing a Passion

Our local TV weatherman Bob Ryan often talked about weather information he got around the region from volunteer weather watchers. When I heard about a particular volunteer, Floyd Abell, I called him and asked him if he would be willing to come to our school and share his knowledge with my students, who were learning about the weather. He was delighted and brought samples of the many weather instruments he keeps in his home and yard.

Abell showed us how he keeps track of the temperature and barometric pressure, as well as the wind speed and direction with his various instruments—all as a hobby. He told us how storms form and described how he had accurately predicted a major snow storm, a "crippling northeaster" as he called it, before the professionals did. He described how he had begun his hobby when he was the same age as the fifth graders he was talking to.

The students were fascinated. Abell's knowledge and enthusiasm helped the students learn and remember the weather instruments and how they work, as well as some of the basic concepts of weather. His visit to our class definitely helped my students meet the science standards on weather.

—Kathleen Carroll

Web-Based Virtual Field Trips

With access to the World Wide Web, the possibilities for field trips become almost unlimited! Web-based virtual field trips can bring experiences to students that they might never have without technology. Students can tour the Louvre in Paris (www.paris.org/Musees/Louvre), travel across a desert in Australia, journey to J. R. R. Tolkein's Middle Earth, or go back in history to the Westward Expansion, all from their own classroom. They can also team up with students around the world to engage in educational and service-oriented projects.

Designing Webquests

In designing Webquests for my second graders, I either hear of or find a Web site that correlates with what I am teaching (science), then I check it out. If it is a site that could easily be managed by students, then I will go through and create some questions that can only be answered by navigating through the site. They are usually fill-in-the-blank questions. I make those in Word format and print them out so the students have them to write on in the computer lab. This becomes their activity sheet for this lesson.

Then I construct a "page" that has the link to the site and a picture of some sort that matches the topic. This page is then placed in the appropriate grade level folder on the computer where students can access it. (They have usually been given instruction on how to access this page by now. All pages from previous Web activities are also there to access at any time.)

To begin the lesson, I have the students sit together, and I use the TV or SMART Board to show them how to navigate to this new page and then introduce the site. I will point out some important things they need to look for and usually go over the first two questions on their activity sheet.

Students will usually work in pairs (higher/lower students together). Each student has his or her own activity sheet, but they can discuss the answers and share the task of navigating through the site.

Our lab times last year ran about 50 minutes, so they usually had plenty of time to complete this activity. If not, we would finish up during the following lesson.

—Jennifer Pavol, Sterling, Virginia

The following are some examples of Web sites for virtual field trips in a variety of subjects:

Artsonia

www.artsonia.com

This is a site with children's art from over 100 countries around the world. You can post your students' art there. You can also help your students learn about the cultures in other countries by studying children's artwork. Art lesson plans are available too.

ArtEdventures

www.sanford-artedventures.com

ArtEdventures are interactive online games for teachers and students. In these activities, students discover how great artists made their famous works—while learning tips and techniques for creating their own art.

Global SchoolNet Foundation

www.gsn.org

Global SchoolNet Foundation is a nonprofit organization that has reached over a million students in 194 countries. GSN's stated mission is to:

> Identify, support, and encourage effective practices and programs that engage students in meaningful content and personal exchanges with people around the world to develop basic and advanced literacy and communication skills, create multicultural understanding, and prepare them for full participation as productive and effective citizens in an increasing global economy. GSN partners with organizations around the world to achieve these ends.

The following are examples of resources provided by GSN:

Clearinghouse. Get access to more than 2,000 online collaborative projects, organized by topic, grade, and project date. You can find partners or join projects from around the globe.

Newswire. Your students can write articles for the whole world to see. They can also download articles from other schools and include them in their own newspaper.

Video Conferencing Connections. GSN puts you in touch with schools around the world that have video-conferencing capabilities over the Internet. CU-SeeMe, free software developed at Cornell University, allows you to video-conference with schools and experts. A mailing list lets you know about upcoming events and opportunities for schools to participate in live video conferences with schools, scientists, authors, athletes, and government, business, and community leaders. The GSN Foundation maintains a directory of K–12 schools with the capability for using CU-SeeMe.

Travel Buddy Projects. Students can have fun as they make meaningful connections with students around the world. At the same time students will increase science, math, social studies, or literacy skills. One class sends a stuffed animal or puppet to a class in another country. The class that receives the guest photographs the stuffed animal with students on field trips and during projects. Sometimes the two schools focus on a particular subject at the same time such as weather, habitats, or community. The visit may include pen pal relationships among students (www.gsn.org/programs/travelbuddies). For teachers who like the idea but find the mailing too difficult, Traveling Techno Teddy is an Internet-based variation on the travel buddy theme.

Online Expeditions. Students can take part in expeditions to remote parts of the world as they happen. For instance American Wave Vidmar walked, skied, and swam solo and unsupported to the North Pole, while thousands of students around the world tracked his journey. When he reached the North Pole, students in three schools were able to speak with him live via satellite phone. There is an inspiring video at the GSN Web site of students from a school in Israel who sang the Beatles tune "From Me, To You" to him during the satellite phone call at the North Pole.

Service Projects. GSN is sponsoring service projects, such as the Uganda Project, where schools learn about life in Uganda and help the schools there. GSN sponsored students in San Diego, California, who made a Web site showcasing the plight of homeless children in their city.

The New York Times on the Web LearningNetwork Web Explorer
www.nytimes.com/learning/students/explorer/
The Web Explorer provides guided Web tours of sites related to important topics of the day. New explorations are added each month. Topics include American history, global history, civics, language arts, math, economics, science, health, fine arts, social studies, geography, and technology.

Peace Corps Kids World
www.peacecorps.gov/kids
At this site, students learn about faraway countries and the people who live there. They also learn about how Peace Corps volunteers are helping.

Tramline

www.tramline.com

This site was developed as a free resource to K–12 educators everywhere. The following are some examples of its resources:

Baking Bread (www.tramline.com/sci/bake/). This field trip offers a convenient way to introduce scientific research to your students through measuring the results of their bread-making experiments.

Deserts (www.tramline.com/sci/desert/). Students will be introduced to deserts in a number of environments, including Africa, North America, South America, and Australia.

Dinosaurs (www.tramline.com/sci/dino/). Students can develop in all areas of the curriculum as they delve into the mystery of dinosaurs, their amazing existence, and their extinction.

Fierce Creatures (www.tramline.com/sci/fierce/). Students explore creatures that have evolved elaborate means of defense.

Getting Green (www.tramline.com/sci/green/). Students learn about simple things we all can do to reduce waste and minimize a negative impact on our planet.

Oceans (www.tramline.com/sci/oceank/). Students will be taken to various Web sites where they can research information about oceans.

Rain Forests (www.tramline.com/sci/rainforest/). This field trip takes a look at what a rain forest is, why it is an important ecosystem, the animals and peoples of the rain forest, and differing types of rain forests. The Web site also provides some ways that students can actively participate in protecting the remaining rain forests.

Beach (www.tramline.com/sci/salt/). Students will be introduced to the coastal environment through participation in a field study of the beach, dunes, estuary, and salt marsh habitats.

Sharks (www.tramline.com/sci/sharks/). Sharks are found in all the oceans of the world, but there are only four species that are considered dangerous. Students will be introduced to sharks and their environment.

Field Trips Through the Imagination

It is possible to take students on a field trip with little or no logistical preparation. This is a field trip students take in their imaginations as the teacher tells or reads an instructional story. Sometimes quiet music is played in the background. Field trips through the imagination are best told using rich, sensory descriptions—as if the students were actually in the story.

Children today are continually exposed to external sensory stimuli from TV, DVDs, computers, and electronic games. Developing their ability to make internal pictures can benefit children in many ways. The ability to make internal images is needed for reading comprehension, mathematical thinking, creative writing, and problem solving. Field trips through the imagination provide simple and engaging ways to reinforce the vocabulary, skills, and concepts in the curriculum.

Here are some suggestions for designing your own field trips through the imagination:

1. Decide on the vocabulary, skills, and/or concepts you will use
2. Choose a destination
3. Prepare students for distractions such as bells or announcements; have them ready to resume the story at the place where it was interrupted
4. Have students imagine they are people in history, world explorers, visitors to "Mathland," or molecules or enzymes
5. Ask students to sit back, relax, and picture in their minds the story they are about to hear (Sometimes I invite students to act out the imaginary journey physically as they crouch down and pretend to be tiny seeds and then slowly come to a standing position as the plant grows. Students might imagine themselves as molecules of oxygen, as they physically move around the classroom pretending to travel through the windpipe, heart, lung, and arteries, eventually reaching a cell where they help make energy.)
6. Immediately and continuously involve all the senses (Example: You are on a scientific expedition to study the tropical rain forest in Brazil. Look at the tall canopy of trees blocking the sun above you. Feel the warmth and wetness around your body. Listen to the insects and an occasional bird around you. You are very focused. You intend to . . .)
7. Give students time to reorient themselves after the imaginary field trip
8. Have students share or write about their experiences (Many teachers have found this to be an effective way to elicit exciting creative writing from students. Students who had previously claimed that they couldn't write have eagerly written stories based on their imaginary field trips.)

You may also want to take students on an imaginary field trip in preparation for a real field trip. In the imaginary field trip prior to the real trip, students envision the appropriate behavior. They might picture themselves using their senses and their minds to learn as much as they can. This rehearsal increases the likelihood that students will get the greatest value from the trip.

Gifts from the Imagination

I taught students in my third grade classroom about the Eskimos and their way of life. We learned that one of their favorite foods is muktuk (whale blubber). This tidbit of information was met with groans and "yuck, gross . . ." Later the students in the class imagined becoming an Eskimo; they created their own adventure in their own minds. When they were ready, they came back to the classroom and wrote a story about their adventure or drew a picture, or both. As usual, they went through this whole process joyfully. Their writing and drawings were creative and beautiful, accomplished with ease and enthusiasm. I found this method to be the best way to facilitate creative writing.

After the stories and pictures were finished, at least three of the students told about eating muktuk while they were Eskimos. They elaborated on how "good" it tasted to them . . . the same students that were saying "yuck" and "gross."

What a wonderful way to see through another's eyes and taste through another's taste buds! The possibilities of reducing prejudice are thought provoking (www.winwenger.com/wallace.htm).

—Rosella Wallace, teacher, Anchor Point, Alaska

An Imaginary Field Trip Through the Water Cycle

After helping my students learn the water cycle vocabulary through hands-on experiments, we would take an imaginary field trip with background music—from the point of view of a drop of water. Using their imaginations in this way helped my students to understand the water cycle from the inside out and retain the learning. A description of our imaginary trip follows:

Relax, get comfortable, and imagine you are a drop of water in the vast blue ocean. There you are, on a wave, moving up and down, up and down. The sun shines warm upon you. After a while you begin to get hot, for the sun is giving you energy. Suddenly you pop into the air, evaporating. You are water vapor, invisible and free.

You float around for a long time. An updraft comes along and pushes you higher and higher, up into the atmosphere where it is cool. You move together with some other water vapor molecules. You condense back into water and become the rain. You fall gently to the earth.

You soak into the ground and find yourself being sucked up by the roots of a tree. Up, up you flow through the trunk, and then out the leaves in transpiration. You are water vapor again.

Now it is night; the air is cool and you condense and become the dew. Later it rains and you flow into a stream, and the stream flows into a river, and the river to the vast blue ocean where you are a drop of water in a wave, moving up and down, up and down, and the sun shines warm upon you (Carroll 1999).

Students reinforced their understanding of the water cycle by writing their own stories. I remember one fifth grade girl who ended her story by describing herself as rain that dropped into a reservoir, got swooshed into someone's faucet, poured into an ice tray, and ended up melting in a glass of grape soda!

—Kathleen Carroll

Field trips help make the world your classroom. The possible destinations for meaningful field trips are limited only by the imagination. With thoughtful planning, students can take meaningful field trips to almost anywhere in your community or faraway places.

Checklist: The World as the Classroom

You can give students engaging field trips in the local neighborhood, on the schoolyard, and even inside the school building. You can also bring the field trip right into your classroom by inviting experts, using the Internet, and taking imaginary trips.

- ☐ Local Community Trips
- ☐ Trips to Faraway Cities or Countries
- ☐ Neighborhood Walks
- ☐ School Building and Grounds Field Trips
- ☐ Teleconferencing
- ☐ Experts in Your Classroom
- ☐ Virtual Field Trips (Online, Software, DVDs)
- ☐ Field Trips Through the Imagination

References

Booth, B. et al. "High, Wide, and Windswept." *Science and Children*, March 1999, 33–40.

Carroll, K. 2000. *Science for Every Learner: Brain-Compatible Pathways to Scientific Literacy*. Chicago: Zephyr Press.

Carroll, K. 1999. *Sing a Song of Science*. Chicago: Zephyr Press.

Chapman, C. 2005. Interview by Kathleen Carroll. Conversation on June 30. Washington, DC. Smithsonial Folk Life Festival.

Kronish, M., and J. Abelmann. 1989. *Focus on Fine Arts—Elementary*. Washington, DC: National Education Association.

Spears, J. *Field Trip Planning Made Easy*. Texas Child Care. www.parentinginformation.org/fieldtripplanning.htm (accessed August 26, 2005).

3

Caring and Curiosity

The Foundations of Field Trips

"The habits we form from childhood make no small difference, but rather they make all the difference."

—ARISTOTLE

What is more important on a field trip than having students who care about themselves, other people, and the environment, and are curious and eager to learn? Caring and curiosity are the foundations of successful field trips. Both are expressions of emotional intelligence. Just as IQ (intelligence quotient) is used when referring to cognitive intelligence, EQ (emotional quotient) is used when referring to emotional intelligence.

Psychologist Daniel Goleman has stated that EQ is even more important than IQ for success in life. EQ reflects a set of competencies such as self-control, the ability to control one's impulses, self-awareness, empathy, altruism, social skills, and self-motivation. It is a two-way street. Field trips work best when students are caring and curious—when they have the basics of EQ. On the other hand, field trips help students develop their EQ further as they interact with others and their environment in ways not usually possible in the regular school day. The first part of chapter 3 focuses on the cultivation of caring, and the second part presents a number of strategies to help spark students' curiosity.

Cultivate Caring

In this section, we will address ways for students to develop habits of personal responsibility and caring in the classroom and on field trips. This section also presents ways to encourage students to think about appropriate behavior and help design a code of conduct for the trip. How students conduct themselves on the field trip is an aspect of their EQ. Of course teachers and group leaders want students to behave well for the students' safety and because their behavior reflects on your school or organization. But equally important is the fact that the students' behavior reflects on who they are inside and what kind of human beings they are becoming.

Caring includes respecting the cultural norms of the places we visit on field trips. This section will consider the need to introduce students to unfamiliar behaviors they may need on field trips such as when to clap and when not to clap during a symphony, or how to eat with chopsticks.

Just as a sense of service and personal responsibility are values to encourage in students, caring about one another is another value that will make all the difference in the classroom and on field trips. This section presents a number of ways to build a caring community of students.

Caring needs to extend beyond the classroom to people in need in our community and around the world, as well as to other species and their habitats. We will discuss how field trips can help students develop empathy toward those in need and help them become stewards of the environment. There are suggestions for your class to show their appreciation to the guides, chaperones, and others who help make the field trip a success.

There are also suggestions for bringing caring right into the curriculum. For learning to last, children need an emotional connection to the curriculum. Emotional connections emerge when feelings of empathy, concern, or fascination fix the learning in the mind. Field trips offer opportunities for students to grow socially and personally, and to become good citizens, lifelong learners, and, most importantly, caring human beings.

The second section of chapter 3 will provide structured methods for students to follow their curiosity and ask and find answers to their own questions. EQ skills, such as self-awareness and self-motivation, develop more fully when we allow students to learn about what they are most interested in.

Developing Student Responsibility Through Service

Students' behavior on field trips reflects their day-to-day behavior in the classroom. When students are accustomed to following agreed-upon ways of behaving and of respecting one another and their surroundings, they will do the same on field trips.

Responsibility is an expression of caring. Dr. Jeannette Vos, coauthor of *The Learning Revolution*, told me about the Puma School in New Zealand where teachers focus on the following four aspects of caring:

- "I care for myself" means I respect myself and the unique ways that I contribute.
- "I care for others" means that I notice what others need and how they feel. I do my best to respect and feel empathy for those needs and feelings.
- "I care for property" means I will work to keep my own and others' living space safe, clean, and beautiful.
- "I care for the environment" means that I understand our connection with the natural world. I will do my best to protect the environment for our own well being and for generations to come (Dryden and Vos 2001, 187).

Victoria Mansuri, a fourth grade teacher in Baltimore, Maryland, has never heard of the Puma School, but she lives its precepts. Victoria puts special focus on developing a sense of community responsibility in her classroom every day. This sense of community responsibility relates to the EQ trait of altruism, of moving from self-centeredness to the realization that other people have needs, that our community as a whole has needs, and that it is up to each of us to contribute to our community.

Students Caring About Their Communities

Children will do what you expect of them. I continually find this to be true.

I grew up in an environment where life always included helping others, building a sense of personal responsibility for community sustainment. So when I became a teacher, community responsibility became an integral part of my classroom.

My students have daily chores. They don't just clean up after themselves; for example, they must water the plants, straighten *all* of the desks, or wash *all* of the painting boards (not just their own). All this is in an effort to maintain a classroom that everyone will enjoy.

When we took our first extended field trip in third grade, this theme of community service continued. We went to a farm in upstate New York for a week. On the farm, everyone was responsible for different chores. Every morning at 5:00 A.M. a group of children got up to feed the animals. This was a coveted chore. Surprisingly, these children did not return sleepy-eyed, but refreshed and rosy-cheeked. Another group made bread and butter every day for dinner each night. Other jobs included chopping wood, weeding the garden, collecting eggs, and herding the cows. There was also a group to set up and clean up after each meal. Of course, this was all interspersed with playtime, horseback riding, hiking, and quiet time.

In fourth grade, our field trip was a three-day camping trip to Point Lookout State Park. While on the trip we had three chore groups, which rotated between preparing breakfast and dinner, gathering firewood, or cleaning up after meals. In addition, the children had to set up and take down their own tents (we had practiced this at school), and each child had to make his or her own lunch and wash his or her own dishes. Above and beyond the maintenance of daily chores, the children also collected trash on our two-mile hike to Point Lookout. When we returned, we did community service for the Park Service directed by the park ranger. The children used hoes, rakes, and shovels to smooth the earth in a construction site, cover it with crushed gravel, and smooth the gravel out. They sang while they worked and told jokes and stories.

After this full day, which included a four-mile walk, playing on the beach in the sun, and moving soil and gravel, the children were pooped; but they were not too tired to play on the playground. It was also nearing dinnertime, so one group had to prep for dinner. I was sure this group would complain, "Oh can't we play, too?" But they didn't. They went to prep for the meal willingly, without a word of protest.

On the last night as we sat around the campfire, we each shared our favorite part of the trip. One of the parent chaperones said that the part she enjoyed most was seeing how well the children worked together. The teacher in charge of the meals also said that what she appreciated most was having so much willing help.

The park ranger and parents who accompanied us were amazed at the children's ability, cooperative nature, and readiness to take on the responsibilities asked of them. Some parents also realized that their children were willing to do more at school, where this level of responsibility was expected of them, than at home, where it wasn't—all too poignantly proving the point that children will do what you expect of them. I expect the children in my class to actively care for the environment and their community, and they do.

—Victoria Mansuri, teacher, Baltimore, Maryland

When students have opportunities to perform service for others, EQ traits of empathy and altruism are nurtured. Even if your field trip is a trip to the zoo or a museum, in what ways might you bring in some element of service? How might your group make the site a little better for the next group who arrives? Are there other members of your community who might enjoy learning about what you have learned?

With some field trips, the service may be the main focus. For example, my students, who lived in an urban environment, filled 20 window boxes with flowers at our school. The neighbors were so inspired by the school's beautiful flowers that they put out window boxes too, and the whole neighborhood was filled with flowers. The students were recognized by the city for their contributions to the beauty of their community. These same students sometimes donned plastic gloves and picked up trash in the neighborhood. We estimated how long it would take the trash to break down if left in the open, graphed the kinds of trash we found, and inferred who might have put the trash there. Students informed the police about abandoned cars in the neighborhood. Students learned a sense of community responsibility at the same time as they learned science, math, and how the community services work. They also saw the police as partners rather than adversaries.

Here is another example. Every December a group of homeless children who live at the Community of Hope in Washington, DC, sings carols at a nursing home. From October on, the children prepare for this service by practicing songs and making cards for the residents and staff of the nursing home. When the big day arrives and the children perform, the old people are often brought to tears by the sweetness and generosity of these children. It is a rare privilege for these children, who have so little, to be able to give to someone else. As a society, we often think that homeless children need to be given to, and this is true. But they also need ways to give to others.

All children need opportunities to be of service. Brain researcher Dr. Paul MacLean, formerly of the National Institute of Mental Health, has said that young people need opportunities to be of service in order to develop the frontal lobes of the brain properly. The frontal lobes are sometimes called the Executive Function. In addition to allowing us to control our impulses and to plan for the future, the Executive Function reflects our ability to extend our caring beyond ourselves and our group, to the rest of the world. Developing this aspect of ourselves as humans may well be necessary for the continued survival of our species.

Take a Service Field Trip to Your Grocery Store

Children will have fun as they do some real-world mathematical problem solving, learn about budgeting, and take a field trip to the local grocery store with this service project to help hungry people in your community. Students will collect coupons and plan the best way to stretch their dollars to help your local food bank or other charity. Here are some ideas for planning the project:

1. **Help students learn about hunger in their community.** Most of us don't realize that 1 in 12 Americans receives help with food and other basics from private charities.

2. **Find out what kinds of items to buy.** According to www.couponmom.com, the items charities need most are:
   - Canned protein sources (stews, chili, tuna, meats, beans)
   - Pasta sauces, canned tomatoes
   - Peanut butter, macaroni and cheese, pastas, rice
   - Toilet paper, shampoo, deodorant, toothpaste/toothbrushes
   - Cereals including boxed and hot items like oatmeal
   - Diapers in sizes larger than newborn

3. **Collect coupons for the appropriate items**. Look in newspapers and online at sites such as www.couponmom.com.

4. **Prepare to pay for the items**. Collect two dollars from each child or have a fund-raiser. (See page pages 225–230 in chapter 5 for fund-raising ideas.)

5. **Calculate which purchases will help your class stretch their dollars the farthest.** Small groups might work out their own solutions to the problem and then compare their results.

6. **Call the grocery store manager.** Ask for a tour and make sure the store has the items in stock that you plan to purchase.

7. **Have small groups of students learn about each section of the grocery store.** Each group gets to pick up certain items for the purchase.

8. **Report to the children how many families they helped with their donations.** One way to do this is to divide the total number of food items—the number at the bottom of the grocery store receipt—by 15, which is the average number of items given to a food bank client.

9. **Invite children to help their parents.** Students can help collect coupons to save money on their parents' grocery bills.

Stewards of the Earth

Students also need to have experiences that help them bond with and care for nature. Most children today don't have the same opportunities to play outside after school that children had in previous generations. The forests and meadows are covered with houses and pavement, and children's lives are filled with scheduled activities, TV, and computer games.

In addition, certain cultural norms may make it difficult for children to bond with nature. How many times have I seen adult responses teach children that the slug plying its way along the ground leaving its iridescent trail and the worms enriching our soil as they tunnel through the earth are disgusting? Children need experiences with nature that turn on their sense of awe and wonder and give them a visceral connection with the earth and the creatures that inhabit the earth. Many teachers need to transcend their own negative programming to be able to provide these experiences.

Some researchers avow that middle childhood may be a crucial time for people to bond with the natural world, just as six months through six years is a crucial time for children to bond with other people (Carroll 2000). Naturalist Edward Wilson has called this human need for bonding with nature the "biophilia hypothesis." According to Wilson, "Biophilia, if it exists, and I believe it exists, is the innately emotional affiliation of human beings to other living organisms" (Kellert and Wilson 1993). Giving children experiences of nature right in their own schoolyard and neighborhoods, in a beautiful setting in the woods, or by the water can help them make the connections that will naturally lead them to become stewards of the earth, rather than mere consumers of it.

The Preciousness of Life

We gave our students all kinds of firsthand experiences with living things. For instance, for a bird-watching walk in the area of the school, our younger students made their own "binoculars" out of the cardboard centers of toilet paper rolls. They decorated the rolls with crayons, attached them together with a brass fastener, attached a piece of wool to the rolls so they could wear their "binoculars" around their necks, and took off to see the birds. The binoculars helped them narrow their field of vision and focus on the birds. We saw cardinals, blue jays, robins, sparrows, finches, crows, and some birds we couldn't immediately identify. The kids used the binoculars to help them focus; they felt very scientific.

We saw other animals, too. Once we found a fish on our bird walk when we stumbled upon a pond. The kids were so excited. We turned over logs and looked under leaves to have macro and a micro vision.

Think about walking through the woods. What is your filter? A detective looks for clues and an artist looks for colors and shapes. A farmer looks at the soil to see if it is arable. Lovers look for a shady place to sit down together. What does a scientist look for? A scientist keeps his or her eyes open for everything! Let the children be scientists. Take a magnifying glass and look at everything.

Sometimes we took "buggy field trips" to a conservation area. All the students in grades K–3 came and each was given a little plastic jar with a cover that had tiny holes. Their charge was to gather bugs and place them in a huge terrarium. The terrarium had a top so the bugs couldn't fly out. The children collected hundreds of specimens and after about a half hour, we all came together and learned about the kinds of insects they had found. What was lovely about this experience was that they "forgot" to be afraid of bugs and just delighted in seeing how many they could find. We liberated the bugs before we got back on the bus and sang insect songs all the way back.

For a follow-up, the children got to have a firsthand experience of insect metamorphosis. The children had mini-terrariums around their necks with a mealworm in each one. The kids got to watch the whole process as their mealworm changed from a worm-like creature, to an unmoving pupa, to an adult beetle. All this was to teach the preciousness of life, the kind of sensibility that if you find a bug in the house, you use a saucer and glass to let it go. You can never know who is going to rise to be most fascinated, but these experiences may lead to some child's career.

—Miriam Kronish, retired principal, Needham, Massachusetts

Ground Rules for Good Behavior on a Field Trip

Actress Julie Andrews has said, "I think of discipline as a kind of order that sets me free to fly." Students want boundaries. The boundaries provide a safe container in which they can express their freedom.

Students can accept boundaries most fully when they understand and agree with why the rules exist. It might help if students understand how their behavior may reflect on their school, age group, and any other group to which they belong. It may also help if students understand that these rules are necessary to keep everyone in the class safe and help everyone learn as much as possible, while having a good time. It is most important for students to absorb worthy values; this occurs when, throughout the school year, students have been encouraged to care about themselves, others, personal and community property, and the environment.

Visualize the Field Trip in Advance

Students may need a visual image of appropriate behavior on this particular field trip. One way to provide the vision is to tell a story of a real or imaginary group of students who behaved appropriately, learned a lot, and enjoyed themselves. Another way is by having your students visualize how they will be when they take the trip.

Even if our field trip involved taking 10 minutes out to study the furnace in the school's basement or observe the effects of erosion on the school grounds, I used visualization to prepare students for the trip. Students would either close their eyes or just not look around and I would describe how we were going to tiptoe through the corridor so that other classes wouldn't be disturbed. (Sometimes we would pretend to be ninjas, so quiet that no one would know that they were there.) Then I would describe what the students would do on the field trip and how they would do it so that they would get the most value from the trip. Educators sometimes call this visualization technique "future pacing." Future pacing makes neurological connections, pathways that increase the likelihood that the images visualized will happen in reality. When students imagine certain behaviors in their minds first, they are more likely to manifest those behaviors when the time comes during the field trip.

Careful Observers

Field trip time was approaching. I wanted to take my class to the museum. I had taken other classes to the museum and knew that it could be a rich experience. But this time I was a bit worried. I had four children who were behavior problems. Since it was a large class (35 students), I knew that they all needed to know how to conduct themselves or the trip would not be successful.

In order to deal with these potential problems, in advance I used a method I learned from Dr. Win Wenger, a pioneer in creativity and mind development. Each student, in his or her imagination, "put on the head" of an especially sensitive, intent observer, who was able to see and feel with all the senses. They loved using the observer's eyes, senses, and mind to perceive the same scenes as richly as the observer sees it. They *became* that observer.

I repeated this procedure, this time in the context of preparing for the museum trip, after a bit of modeling the ideal decorum that would be expected of the students during the trip. I had the students become that "observer," going through the various exhibits, noticing things to discuss when the trip was over, and not wanting to "miss a thing." I told them "As this observer, you can describe what you are seeing softly to yourself while you wander through the museum. I'll be silent now so you can do this. When I ring the chime, bring your awareness back to the classroom, and tell your partner what you saw as this observer."

On the actual field trip, the manner in which that potential problem class embarked upon the bus, and then disembarked at the museum, was orderly, polite, and impressive. I was delighted to hear the children describing softly to their peers what they were seeing. Win Wenger states, "What you describe aloud while observing it, you discover more about," and "The more you describe your perceptions, the more perceptive you become."

The tour guide quickly took a cue from me and became a resource person to answer questions, rather than a lecturer to do all of the talking. Her comment was, "They are noticing things that I hadn't even noticed before!" and "They ask the most interesting questions I have ever heard from such a young group."

The next day back in class was as educational and enjoyable as the actual visit. I had taken other classes to the same museum before, without this preparation, because those classes were not so large or problematic, so I had a clear comparison. I can honestly say that though this was the class that I was worried about because of the size and behavior problems, this class was the best behaved and got the most out of the field trip. I know it was because of the advanced preview of the museum trip through the "careful observer" experience. An added bonus was that we were always able to return to the museum and see in our mind's eye what the whale bones looked like when we were studying about whales, or see the octopus in the aquarium during our sea week project.

—Rosella R. Wallace, teacher, Anchor Point, Alaska

Note: See more of Win Wenger's creativity and mind development techniques at www.winwenger.com.

Students Help Make the Ground Rules

Children may take more responsibility for their personal behavior on a field trip if they help make the ground rules. Making the rules helps students care about following them as it enhances these EQ traits:

- **Self-awareness.** Students discover their own thinking about the rules by writing and/or talking about which rules make sense to them and why.

- **Self-motivation.** Students will be more motivated to abide by rules of their own making.
- **Self-control.** When students have made the rules, they will be more likely to internalize them and remember them when challenging circumstances arise.
- **Social skills.** Students develop the ability to express themselves, listen to others, problem solve, and negotiate when they work together to make the rules.

While most children already have a basic sense of suitable behavior, their ability to think of apt rules for this particular field trip may be enhanced if they have already heard the story or the visualization about an ideal trip (see Careful Observers on page 95).

If students are too young to write, you can list their ideas on a sheet of chart paper, and then add any that they didn't think of. Children can act out each agreed-upon rule first as a class, mimicking you, and then in small groups or individually. They can even act out the entire trip.

Another way for students to help make the rules is to use what cooperative learning expert Spencer Kagan calls "Rally Robin" (1994). Students in pairs take turns sharing suitable rules with each other for a few minutes. (These rules can either be written or verbal, depending on your students' ease with writing.) Then all students stand. The teacher or group leader calls on a student to share his or her idea and writes it on the board or on chart paper. Then the teacher calls on another student. When all of a particular student's ideas have been written down, that student sits down. Continue until all students are seated. The teacher adds any important rules that students have left out. The class discusses the advantages and disadvantages of each idea. Then the teacher takes a tally of students' choices and the class agrees on consequences for noncompliance.

A third, very quick way to gather students' ideas is to use a technique from Total Quality Management, a movement from the corporate world whose purpose is to increase efficiency and effectiveness in organizations. This technique is called the Affinity Chart.

Steps to Creating an Affinity Chart for Field Trip Rules

1. Groups of five or six students get a stack of sticky notes.
2. Each student in the group silently puts one idea on each sticky note, using just a few words. (Magic markers and block printing show up better than pencils and script.)
3. Then the group places the sticky notes on a sheet of paper on a wall where everyone in the class can see them.

4. Next, everyone in the group stands up and silently moves the sticky notes into categories. If there is any disagreement about the categories, that can be discussed in the next step.

5. Now members of the group can talk to one another. They decide on a title for each grouping.

6. The instructor or group leader consolidates lists from each group and adds rules if any important ones were missed.

7. The class discusses the ideas listed and agrees on field trip rules. (It is best if the rules are stated in the positive, rather than the negative, e.g., "Walk" instead of "Don't run.")

8. Students agree on consequences for breaking the rules by repeating the Affinity Chart process or through discussion.

Once the field trip rules and guidelines are established, it may be appropriate for some or all students attending the field trip to sign a contract: an agreement to abide by the rules and guidelines. A contract introduces students to a means used in the adult world to formalize agreements. The contract helps both students and parents to be clear about expectations. It teaches students to care about the importance of keeping their word.

Sample Contract

Memo

To: _____

From: _____

Re: Student Contract to Follow the Field Trip Rules and Guidelines

Date: _____

As a class we have come up with the following ground rules for our field trip:

_____

_____

_____

_____

_____

While on our field trip, I agree to abide by these rules. If I do not abide by these rules, I will accept the consequences that we have agreed upon.

Student Signature:

_____

Teacher Signature:

_____

Parent/Guardian Signature:

_____

Caring About Each Other

Perhaps the most valuable gift a teacher can give a student is to build a classroom community where students care about each other. This sense of care on the part of all students can also be a key to keeping everyone safe and happy on a trip.

One way to foster a supportive classroom community without taking any extra time from academics is to use cooperative learning consistently (Kagan 1994). When teachers use cooperative learning as it is meant to be used and not just as unstructured group work, students build their EQ by developing:

- **Self-awareness.** Students find out their own perspectives by listening to themselves talk.
- **Self-control.** Students wait their turn to speak and act in the group.
- **Self-motivation.** Students are allowed to talk to each other, an activity that human beings are designed to do and naturally motivated by, rather than requiring rigid silence.
- **Empathy.** Students learn to listen to others' perspectives.
- **Altruism** (its Latin root *alter* means "other"). As children learn to listen to and understand the thoughts and feelings of others, they are likely to become less self-involved and more caring about the well-being of other children.
- **Social skills.** By learning how to participate equally in groups, learning to take turns, learning to disagree agreeably, and learning to communicate more effectively, children develop empathy by beginning to understand other children's perspectives.

The emergence of leadership may be a by-product of the EQ skills students develop through cooperative learning. In a workshop Spencer Kagan gave on character education, he told the audience about a school he spoke at, halfway around the world in Korea. Kagan described how Korean schools typically have desks in rows and shun physically disabled students. This school adopted both inclusion and cooperative learning. Helping each other has become a natural aspect of the school day there. An interesting result has been that although the school has never explicitly taught the character virtue of leadership, this school has produced presidents of the student council in 30 of its 39 feeder schools.

A good way to introduce cooperative learning to students is by a simple cooperative learning structure called Think-Pair-Share (Lyman 2003). In this structure, students think by themselves, then pair with a partner, and finally share with the whole group on some agreed-upon topic. Think-Pair-Share is a good place to begin practicing cooperative learning since it is simple and involves only two children at a time. As a student develops his or her social skills with one other child, eventually he or she will be ready to work with groups of three or four students. The Think-Pair-Share cooperative learning structure is particularly well designed for field trips because students are usually in pairs for field trips. Teachers can design Think-Pair-Share questions for the bus trip to the destination, during the trip itself, and on the way home. Some examples are:

Think-Pair-Share Sample Questions

On the Way to the Destination

Think: Observe the bus route as you ride and write directions from your school to the destination.

Pair: See if you and your partner agree about the directions.

Share: When you arrive at the destination, compare your directions with those of other classmates and with a map to the site.

At the Site

Think: Observe some aspect of the field trip with your partner.

Pair: Listen to your partner's observations, and tell your partner what you heard. Find out from your partner if you heard correctly. Then have your partner do the same for you.

Share: Report your partner's observations to the whole group.

On the Way Home

Think-Pair-Share . . .

- Your partner shares about what the class did on the trip, and then you add on. Then your partner adds more, and so on.
- Take turns sharing the most important parts or new learning from the trip.
- Pretend to be a person, animal, or object that you learned about on the field trip. Then share with a partner as if you were that person, animal, or object.
- Think-Write-Pair-Share. Write in your journal about the trip, and then share your writing with a partner.

Think-Pair-Share

Think	Pair	Share
Predict what will be the best part of the trip. Why?	Add to a partner's story. Then the partner adds more.	Share your answer verbally.
Imagine yourself as an observer of the location.	Take turns sharing observations, one observation at a time.	Show your finished product or answer.
Pretend to be a person, animal, or object related to the trip.	Paraphrase. Restate in other words.	Act out the situation or answer.
Remember the order of the events in your trip.	Prepare to share your partner's ideas.	Vote on alternatives as a class— thumbs up, down, or sideways.
Create a Mind Map, Venn diagram, graph, or cluster.	Defend the opposite of your true viewpoint.	Present data and conclusions.
Write in your journal.	Ask each other questions.	Find alternative methods for the task.
	Use metacognition. Think about your thinking. Tell how you used your thinking time.	Speak in unison on cue.

About Think-Pair-Share

Designed by Dr. Frank Lyman, University of Maryland instructor and educational consultant, the Think-Pair-Share strategy has become a foundational tool in cooperative learning. In many classrooms, workshops, and training rooms, when the facilitator asks the group a question, the same few people answer while the rest sit by passively. Think-Pair-Share provides "think time" or "wait time" for everyone to formulate an answer to the question *and* time to think about the meaning of each person's response. "Pair time" gives everyone a chance to respond orally or rehearse for sharing. Think-Pair-Share enhances the engagement of all learners with the subject matter and gives the facilitator time to make better decisions. At the same time, it helps develop communication skills. This strategy can also be used at a distance with e-mails and chat rooms (2003).

Think-Pair-Share

Why to Use Think-Pair-Share

- To increase learning and achievement
- To improve the quality of thinking by providing "wait" or "think time" and by giving every learner an opportunity to respond
- To improve social skills
- To increase learners' knowledge and acceptance of others, including ethnically different, special education, and handicapped peers
- To improve class climate by creating a community of learners
- To increase participation of all learners
- To improve students' observation and communications skills
- To get more value from a field trip

How to Use Think-Pair-Share

1. **Listen**. Learners listen to the facilitator's question. (The facilitator can be the teacher or a student.) Each of the suggested modes on page 101 can be used with any others.
2. **Think**. Learners think (for at least three to five seconds), visualize, write, or map about their responses silently. Think mode only works if it is specially cued with hands down. (Cueing can be with voice, hand signals, or cueing devices.)
3. **Pair**. Learners share their responses with a partner freely or in a structured way. Each has a chance to speak while the other listens silently. Structures can be timed and can have alternating speakers. Partners can be varied and predetermined. To end the pair talk, the facilitator should use a sound cue (e.g., a clap or bell) or a kinesthetic cue (e.g., all raise hands).
4. **Share**. Learners share their individual or mutual responses with a team or the whole group. Think time after each response encourages learners to reflect on others' answers or reactions. The share time can be shorter since all students have had response time.

Variations

Think-Pair-Square-Share. Each pair speaks with another pair (the square) before sharing with the whole group. This offers more protection and increases interaction.

Think-Pair-Think-Share. Learners are cued directly to share after thinking about their interaction.

When to Use Think-Pair-Share

This strategy can be appropriate at any time with any level and any subject matter. If time is a constraint, the facilitator can make the decision to pair and/or share.

For more information, go to kagononline.com for Frank Lyman's Think-Pair-Share Smart Card (2003).

Kagan has designed a number of content-free structures for cooperative learning that can be used with any subject matter. Good resources for cooperative learning in general, and teambuilding in particular, can be found at Spencer Kagan's Web site, www.kagononline.com.

The following are some other trust-building activities that enhance a sense of caring and can take place before or during a trip:

- **Trust Walk.** Before beginning this activity, discuss the importance of trustworthiness, of keeping one another safe. In the activity, one student is blindfolded; the other carefully guides the blindfolded student on a walk around the classroom or, better yet, on the grounds outside. To debrief, discuss whether students preferred being the guide or the blindfolded one. Discuss what it is like to have to count on and trust another person so completely. Talk about how this need for trust relates to partners on a field trip.

- **Camera/Photographer.** One student becomes the "camera." She closes her eyes while her partner the "photographer" leads her to an interesting "photo opportunity." When the photographer gently pulls on the "camera's" ear, the "camera" opens her eyes. The photographer may place the "camera's" head for a close-up, right next to a flower, for instance, or gently move the head from left to right for a panoramic photo of the sky or tree line. The debriefing may include everything from how it felt to trust another person to what it was like to see the surroundings through another's eyes to how a game like this helps us notice beauty and details, which we usually miss when seeing in ordinary ways.

- **Find a Tree.** One student is blindfolded. The other student leads the blindfolded student in a circuitous path to a tree. The blindfolded student feels the circumference of the trunk, bark, roots, branches, and leaves, if possible, in order to identify the tree later. Then the leader takes the blindfolded student back to the starting place by way of an intentionally confusing route. The student who was led removes the blindfold and attempts to find his tree. Then students swap roles. Once both students have had a turn, I often invite them to sit by their tree and write a poem about it. The debriefing can be about the experience of trust. It can also be about connecting with and caring for our environment.

All of the above activities require training for the students who act as leaders. The leaders need to know how to stay focused and anticipate each step their partners take. They need to take seriously their responsibility for keeping their partners safe. Young children love leading adults around in this way. Leading gives little children a sense of power that they rarely experience in their lives (Cornell 1998).

Fostering a Culture of Caring

For some years I was an instructor at SuperCamp, a 10-day academic and personal growth camp students attend during their school vacations. SuperCamp has camps all over the world especially designed for elementary, secondary, and even college students. SuperCamp has documented amazing academic improvements in students. Most students with grade averages of C or lower improve a whole letter grade after SuperCamp. Before students begin to learn techniques to improve their academics, though, a culture of caring is instilled in the camp. One way is through a ropes course.

A ropes course is a program where students are challenged physically, emotionally, and socially in increasingly difficult activities, some of which involve height. In many ropes course programs the focus is on the participants moving beyond their perceived physical limits in the challenges. At SuperCamp, however, the focus is even more on how well each student can support whichever team member is facing the challenge. For instance consider the trust fall, where one person falls back as the other members of the team catch her. Each team member must realize that his focus and care is essential to the safety of the person who is falling. Each teammate must be centered and grounded, with the full intention that the person falling is safe. Many students have never experienced that kind of responsibility before; rising to that level of responsibility is empowering. It is up to the leader of the activity to have the highest intention that each student gets the message fully because another person's safety is at stake.

Even when the teammates aren't responsible for each other's safety, they are responsible for rooting for whoever is facing a challenge, letting that child know that the rest of the team is giving their full support to that child's success in the activity. Some activities involve team members as a group solving problems such as getting every member of the team over a wall or some other hurdle with no one left out. A sense of community responsibility comes out of this kind of activity.

How did this culture of caring translate into a SuperCamp classroom when the students learned academics? Here are some examples. When one student would shyly stand to read a poem or essay he had written, other students would cheer him on with the same gusto they had on the ropes course. Cliques broke down. Students began to develop empathy for others who were not as good looking or popular. Students began to appreciate each other's uniqueness rather than banding together only with others who were like themselves. A commitment developed in classes to help everyone learn, to help everyone get through. Teachers can build the same kind of culture of caring in their own classrooms. Preparing for field trips can be an impetus, just as the ropes course is at SuperCamp (www.supercamp.com).

—Kathleen Carroll, former SuperCamp Instructor, Washington, DC

Learning New Behaviors for Field Trips

We need to care enough to learn cultural norms. In planning the field trip, consider whether there are certain social behaviors that some or all of your students may not be familiar with. An example is going to restaurants. When students study about foreign countries, it can be highly motivating and culturally broadening to experience the cuisine of that place. If the students are learning about Italy and go to an Italian restaurant, do they need to learn the proper etiquette for using their knives and forks? If they are studying an Asian country and attending an Asian restaurant, would it be good to learn how to use chopsticks? For an Ethiopian or Afghani restaurant, they may need to learn how to eat appropriately with the hand (and make sure it is the *right* hand, at that! I am left-handed. Once I sat down to eat a meal in the Sudan, where everyone uses their hands and eats together from the same plate. My hosts were shocked when I touched the food with my left hand. In their culture the right hand is the eating hand and the left hand is the wiping hand! I learned from experience that it is important to learn the cultural norms of the places we visit.)

There are other cultural norms, even with groups within our own country. Do your students need to be taught how to introduce someone to an older person? If they are visiting a government function, are there certain titles they need to learn when addressing government officials? Do students need to dress in a certain way or speak at a certain voice level to fit the cultural expectations?

Depending on the trip, the learning can extend beyond cultural norms to how to conduct themselves in an outdoor environment. When students are visiting a park, studying a pond, or hiking through the woods it's important to know the behaviors that protect the environment and that keep everyone safe in the environment. Do they know how to move to minimize any negative effect on the earth and maximize the likelihood of hearing and seeing birds and other animals? Can they identify rash-inducing plants, such as poison ivy or poison oak, and their antidote, jewel weed? Do they know which cactus plants produce an itch when touched and which don't?

Expressing Thanks

Field trips help students expand the EQ trait of empathy and their social skills when students take time to express their appreciation to the chaperones, guides, bus drivers, and other people who contribute to the field trip. In order to send thank-you notes, get each person's address during the trip to save time later. Encourage students to think of specific incidents either of that person's helpfulness or examples of new learning that the students enjoyed because of the trip that person helped make possible.

Students will enhance their social skills by writing thank you notes. They will practice the skills of summarizing and finding the essence. They will review their learning from the field trip. They will also have a real-world reason to further develop and use their writing skills.

In addition to writing, encourage students to thank their chaperones, guides, and others who help them during the trip in person. For example, Victoria Mansuri's whole fourth grade class recited a poem as an expression of appreciation to the ranger at the park where they camped (see page 89).

Bring Caring into the Curriculum

Caring is not just about students' personal and social development. Caring is also necessary for academic mastery. The only way that learning will last is if there is an emotional connection. Robert Sylwester, expert on the brain and learning, points out that emotion drives attention and attention drives learning (1998). If we try to memorize nonsense syllables, the memory won't last because there is no meaning. Emotional connections make hooks to the learning by enhancing a child's personal association with the material through adventure, mystery, humor, surprise, or real-world relevance (Carroll 2000).

Stories of the lives of historical characters, of people who live in distant countries, or even of animals, plants, and places can arouse our caring and compassion. Primary sources, such as letters, journal entries, and photographs, can also help. Music and songs that relate to the learning often elicit that heart connection. One of the great advantages of learning through the multiple intelligences, which is described at length in chapter 4, is that it infuses the curriculum with the arts, and the arts link us to our hearts.

A field trip that is designed for this purpose is one of the best ways to inspire emotional connections and the caring that accompanies those connections. In chapter 1, Dr. Frank Lyman applied this concept to field trips. "Field trips," he said, "Need some emotional charge. Students have to be feeling the experience or they won't bother to learn. They need to know why it is important. For instance in going to a battlefield, such as Gettysburg, there needs to be emotion. Students need to learn in advance about that battle and its effects, about war and what war is. Otherwise all they see is a green field and a gift shop" (see page 15).

Similarly, when children have opportunities to spend time in nature, and when the adults around them model a sense of wonder, children are inspired to care for and become stewards of the environment. That is why frequent field trips right in the schoolyard are so valuable.

As homeschooler mother and author Teri Brown says of her own children, "I want them to know that children have always made mud pies; they just wore different clothes while doing it. Before they can care about the important events in history, children must first realize that these events involved real people. Historical day trips to interactive museums or reenactments do more to foster this perspective than any textbook could."

Curiosity also engenders powerful emotions that produce lasting memories. The next section provides a number of ways to ignite curiosity and give real-world relevance through field trips.

Spark Their Curiosity!

Curiosity goes hand-in-hand with caring as a foundation for field trips. In a way curiosity *is* a form of caring. Curiosity implies caring enough about your own inner questions to be motivated to answer them! It means caring enough about this amazing world we live in to *want* to learn about it.

A question may arise, "How can students follow their own curiosity and learn through discovery when the standards dictate what they are supposed to learn?" Chapter 4 provides details on how to align field trips with standards. In considering alignment, we recognize that some standards do involve processes such as making and testing hypotheses and collecting data. But you can even teach content standards through discovery.

When students follow their curiosity, at the same time as they learn the required content, students will also develop ways to do research, think creatively and critically, and solve problems and generate new questions that will serve them well for life. In the rest of the chapter, we will address some techniques that provide structured ways for students to become interested in what they are required to learn and to learn by following their own interests.

Spark Curiosity Through Exploration

One way to whet students' curiosity and inspire their questions about the subject matter is through an exploratory trip to the field trip site at the beginning of the unit and/or exposure to books, pictures, brochures, and Web sites. Teacher and educational consultant Sarah Shellow describes the process well when she says, "As a teacher, I scaffold the students' learning by setting up situations that will evoke the very questions from the children themselves that I deem important for them to learn while simultaneously allowing the space for them to explore questions I have not anticipated. At the same time they are taking in generally agreed-upon knowledge, they are learning to become life-long learners, full of curiosity with the skills they need to satisfy that curiosity."

The K-W-H-L-N Chart for Responsible Learning

Many teachers use the K-W-L approach, listing what students already know (K) about a subject or field trip, what (W) they want to find out, and, later, what they learned (L). A variation on that idea that places more responsibility on the student is the K-W-H-L-N chart, where students list what they know (K) or think they know, what they wish (W) to find out, how (H) they will find out, what they learned (L), and, finally, new (N) wonderings—new questions that arise from the learning.

The wish list (W) can be made in advance of the trip and serve as a focus for the field trip. How (H) students plan to find out might involve the following:

- Pre-trip preparations, such as visiting the Web site; looking at photographs or videos; reading books, brochures, or articles; checking Internet sources; interviewing experts; and doing their own experiments
- During the field trip students might make observations, do experiments, and/or interview experts who are at the field trip site
- After the field trip, students write down what they learned and how they were able to answer their questions; the students compare notes and share their findings; students might begin a whole new K-W-H-L-N chart based on the new questions that arise

K-W-H-L-N Chart for a Field Trip to _____

Student's Name _____

K	W	H	L	N
What Do I **K**now? Do I know this for sure or do I think I know it?	What Do I **W**ish to Know?	**H**ow Will I Find Out? Web site? Videos? Books? Articles? Internet? Experiments? Will I find out before, during, or after the trip?	What Did I **L**earn?	What Is Something **N**ew That I Wish to Know? What new questions do I have from what I have learned? Do I wish to make a new chart?

The K-W-H-L-N Chart gives students the tools they need to satisfy their curiosity and create new questions in an ongoing quest for understanding. These are tools they can draw from and expand on for the rest of their lives.

Essential Questions

The use of Essential Questions is a practice that is closely related to the K-W-H-L-N approach. It takes the "What Do I Wish to Know" column up a notch by helping each student, or a small group of students, or the whole class to craft "big questions," Essential Questions that go far beyond the simple recall of facts. An Essential Question often implies action such as "What can I do to help save the monarch butterflies?" "How can I get the most value from my trip to a museum?" or "How can I keep healthy?" Essential Questions may also dig under our unexamined assumptions to ask questions like "What are museums for, especially the one we are about to visit?" "What is health?" "What does it mean to be alive?" or "What is freedom?" In choosing and working with Essential Questions, students are likely to become engaged with some of the most fundamental questions that humans have.

Essential Questions are questions that are at the heart of a discipline. They are questions that matter. An Essential Question will lead to more questions. An Essential Question doesn't have one simple, right answer but can be studied in greater and greater depth over time. More than answers, the good Essential Question generates more questions. For example, a child who is trying to figure out why zoos exist will inevitably be led to other questions such as why so many animals are now in danger or need protection, why habitats are being lost, or why elephants are hunted. Essential Questions enable students to delve into subjects, following their own curiosity. Sometimes addressing the Essential Question can be a lifetime endeavor.

How do you come up with an Essential Question? An Essential Question is a question that must be formulated in the student's own words, is meaningful to the student now, and will be worth knowing as an adult. The actual crafting of an Essential Question will probably benefit from and require the support of an adult. Durango, Colorado, educational consultant and media specialist Bliss Bruen has immersed herself in helping students develop their own Essential Questions for extended field trips. She warns that an Essential Question will fizzle out for the student when the question is too forced or is beyond the student. She suggests that a first step in working with Essential Questions can be to brainstorm possible questions with the class on the general topic and then have students work on their chosen question in small groups, dividing the work of starting to answer the big question.

In her work the teachers also form their own personal Essential Questions, making it easier for the class as a whole to see the value. Little by little the teachers share their own refinement and/or process of coming to terms with a question that is so large and important that it could last a lifetime. When the teacher has an Essential Question, she models curiosity and a sense of wonder. Teachers and students become curious, probing, discovering lifelong learners together. This breaks down the great divide—the idea that learners who know nothing stand on one side of a huge chasm, looking across a distance to the teacher, who is expected to know everything. Instead, as they collaborate on a set of connected questions, they may find that

- the best teachers are the ones who help them generate the most interesting questions, not necessarily the most ("right") answers.
- these teachers respect the students' knowledge, experience, and unique perspectives.
- teaching and learning are two sides of the same coin.
- learning can be a joint endeavor, a partnership with an enthusiastic teacher.
- questions will never end.

According to Bruen, developing individual Essential Questions is a process that takes place over time. It requires patience and probing on the part of the teacher and the student. Each child's uniqueness begins to emerge, though, as he or she forms individual and authentic Essential Questions. One way to help students develop their own Essential Questions is through the Taxonomy for Discovery described below. With the Taxonomy for Discovery, students start freely exploring and eventually develop their own theories or hypotheses. Those theories may become Essential Questions.

Essential Questions make field trips meaningful to students because the questions matter in real life. The learning becomes even more significant when individuals, groups, or the whole class share their findings and perspectives with others.

Taxonomy for Discovery

A teacher recently said to me, "Suppose you take a child who has never been to a museum before on a field trip. If, instead of letting him look around to find out what this resource in his or her community is, you make him or her concentrate on a worksheet about dinosaurs right away, you aren't doing the child any favors." This teacher was pointing out the problem that can arise from over-focusing too soon. Students need to get the big picture of the field trip site before they narrow down to the details. Following their own curiosity, at least some of the time, will make the trip more enjoyable. One of the values of field trips is that they help students learn about the resources available in their community. If they go to a museum or art gallery, the experience should be so enjoyable that they want to return.

How can we make a balance between a child's need to follow his or her own curiosity about a field trip site and the teacher's need for order and the attainment of the required standards? How can we balance structure and freedom?

The Taxonomy for Discovery is one solution. Based on the doctoral thesis of Dr. Robert Cohen of the University of the District of Columbia, the Taxonomy for Discovery provides an organized strategy to make this possible. The Taxonomy for Discovery is a structured way to allow children to have fun as they explore what interests them most in a new environment or with new materials. First students explore the place or materials freely, limited only by the confines of safety and care for themselves, others, and the environment. Gradually they take note of their observations, organize their observations in some way and look for patterns, share their findings with others, and finally process their findings in a large group and begin to develop hypotheses or theories that they can explore further. Students can follow up these explorations with a K-W-H-L-N chart or by developing Essential Questions or other questions to explore further, based on their findings with the Taxonomy for Discovery. A student might also follow up with that dinosaur sheet, once the child has satisfied his or her initial curiosity about what a museum is.

W. Edwards Deming, the initiator of the Total Quality Management movement, stated that everyone is born with intrinsic motivation (1993). Learners bring that intrinsic motivation to education when the learning experience is in keeping with how their brains work naturally. Brain researchers agree that when learning experiences are truly effective, learners construct personal meaning (Jensen 1995). Researcher Numela Caine has pointed out that the brain is designed to make and detect patterns, which in turn make meaning (www.cainelearning.com).

The Taxonomy for Discovery is brain friendly, because it allows the student's brain to do what it is designed to do: observe and experience what attracts the individual, find patterns, and make meaning. The Taxonomy for Discovery encourages learners to satisfy their curiosity by becoming observers, pattern finders, and theorizers in any content area.

The Taxonomy for Discovery

1 Experiencing: Do-Observe-Record

- **Doing.** Learners freely explore. Facilitator asks action-oriented questions such as "What would happen if . . . ? Can you figure out how to . . . ?"
- **Observing.** Facilitator asks attention-focusing questions as simple as "What do you observe?" If some learners begin to get discouraged, ask "What are you noticing about . . . ? How does it look, feel, smell?" Ask measuring and counting questions such as "How many . . . ? How much . . . ? How long . . . ? How often . . . ?"
- **Writing.** Facilitator encourages learners to write every observation, listing anything that might be important. Let them know that there is no need to organize yet.

2 Organizing: Categorize— Look for Patterns

- **Learners look** for patterns in the data they have collected and come up with ways to organize the data into groupings.
- **Learners present** the groupings in charts, tables, graphs, or other formats.
- **The facilitator supports** the organizing stage by asking learners to analyze and classify. "How are _____ similar or different? What goes together? How do they go together?" Technology can be a tool for organizing through spreadsheets, computer-made graphs and Mind Maps, e-videos, and slide presentations.

3 Sharing: Compare Findings and Ways of Organizing

Learners work together as a community of researchers. Learners develop skills in speaking and listening. Learners write comments and suggestions to the other individual or group. Learners are often fascinated to see the differences in what other people notice and how they organize their findings.

The facilitator supports the Sharing Stage by

- **encouraging learners** to articulate their findings clearly and listen well enough to restate the other's findings and write helpful comments and suggestions.
- **having learners notice differences** in data. If there are disagreements, inform learners that this is exactly what happens when professionals share their findings. Inform learners of the value of disagreeing agreeably. Encourage learners to observe together to resolve differences.
- **asking learners to see** which ways of organizing yield better results than others. This supports learners in developing discernment.

4 Processing: Share with Whole Class and Journal Your Thoughts

Learners integrate the data and synthesize their findings through whole group discussions and journal writing. Learners formulate hypotheses or theories they test using the four steps of the taxonomy. The facilitator may

- **encourage discussions**, including reasoning and clarifying questions. "Why do you think . . . ? Challenge the thinking of other learners. "Do you agree with . . . ? Why or why not?"
- **relate learners' findings** to currently agreed-upon understandings.
- **assist learners** in verbalizing their budding hypotheses: "What happens if . . . ?" "Invent a rule for . . . "
- **suggest questions** to reflect and journalize on paper or computer: "What did you learn from your data?" "What did you learn about organizing data?" "What did you learn about your own skills as an observer and organizer?"

About The Taxonomy for Discovery

The 21st century needs learners who do more than passively take in and parrot back information. Educators around the world recognize that learners need to ask their own questions and develop skills to answer their questions effectively, no matter what the subject matter. The Taxonomy for Discovery, an alternative to Bloom's Taxonomy, was based on a doctoral dissertation by Dr. Robert Cohen, a mathematics professor in Washington, DC. The taxonomy provides a step-by-step method to transform "cookbook-style," highly-directed lessons into real inquiry.

The Taxonomy for Discovery

Why Use the Taxonomy for Discovery?

- To hone inquiry skills
- To improve powers of observation and ability to interact with new information (experiencing)
- To develop skills in pattern finding and organizing data (organizing)
- To verbalize their thinking with others, so students can begin to clarify their understandings and make tentative generalizations about principles (sharing)
- To reflect on the subject, thoughtfully construct meaning from the new experiences, integrate new understandings with previous knowledge, hypothesize, and predict future outcomes (processing)
- To acquire richer and more lasting learning as students discover new concepts themselves, rather than being told
- To uproot deeply held misconceptions, which remain intact with passive approaches to learning
- To develop lifelong learning skills that will advance careers and build more responsible citizenship
- To think metacognitively; students begin to have insight into their own thinking

Ways to Use the Taxonomy for Discovery

Science. Students use the Taxonomy to develop hypotheses. Then, they go through the steps of the taxonomy a second time to test the hypotheses. (This is the Scientific Method.) This strategy changes highly directive science activities to true inquiry by allowing learners to ask their own questions, rather than giving them the questions. Learners design their own ways to organize the data ratner than filling in premade data tables. During the sharing and processing phases, students discover for themselves the value of following good experimental procedures.

Mathematics. Students solve mathematical problems. The taxonomy is particularly helpful when the mathematical discoveries involve manipulatives. Students observe, collect data, and analyze—then discover the thinking of others. They learn that there is more than one way to solve a problem. The process gives students metacognitive insight into their own approaches to problem solving.

Social Studies. Students gather information from primary sources, books, magazines, the Internet, personal interviews, and surveys in the experiencing phase. They organize their findings, learn from others' findings, and synthesize the discoveries into new understandings.

Literature. Students develop skills in appreciating and understanding literature by making and collecting their own observations, organizing their observations and finding patterns, and sharing and processing the literature they read.

When to Use the Taxonomy for Discovery

- On field trips
- As the discovery phase in a learning experience
- Any time there is a desire to base an educational experience on *educare* (Latin, meaning "draw forth learning") rather than to pour learning in

For more information, refer to *Science for Every Learner: Brain-Compatible Approaches to Scientific Literacy* by Kathleen Carroll. The book contains five science units based on the Taxonomy for Discovery.

Depending on the goals for the trip, a use of the Taxonomy for Discovery on a field trip might look like this:

Experiencing

Do. Students are instructed to find out as much as they can about this particular room in the museum, exhibit at the zoo, or space in the park. Safety regulations and rules for protecting the area are presented at this time.

Observe. Students begin to take note of their findings.

Write. Students write or draw their observations.

Organizing

Alone or in pairs, students decide on a way to organize or categorize their findings, putting their observations into groups based on similarities. They might use graphic organizers such as Mind Maps, charts, or Venn diagrams. Or they may make up an entirely original way to organize their findings.

Sharing

Individual or pairs of students share their observations and ways of organizing their observations with another individual or pair of students.

Processing

A class discussion ensues, based on students' observations and their unique ways of and reasons for organizing their observations the way they did. The whole class may go to see particularly interesting findings. Questions for further inquiry arise from the students themselves. These questions may become the Essential Questions for the field trip.

Using the Taxonomy for Discovery

A few years ago when I was consulting in a school, the teachers wanted to observe me teach a lesson. They chose a class of fifth graders, notorious for their rowdiness and misbehavior. The class was kept in a trailer outside of the school building. I entered the trailer with more than a little trepidation. It was after lunch. Teachers were sitting around the edge of the room, watching. The unruly students came bounding into the classroom. At first the students seemed wary, but they soon became engaged in designing and sharing their own tests for paper whirligigs—little paper helicopters the students made. The whirligigs were part of a lesson to introduce the Taxonomy for

Discovery. Students eagerly shared their experiments and thinking behind their discoveries.

One student blurted out, "My hypothesis is that if I put the whirligig in a steamy bathroom with the shower running, it will turn more slowly. I'm going to try it at home tonight!"

After that comment, students popped up with one creative hypothesis after another, as the level of permission for thinking increased moment by moment. At the end of the lesson, the students thanked me profusely. Some students came up and hugged me. Their enthusiasm came from the nature of the Taxonomy for Discovery—experience, organize, share, process—a strategy that may be ideal for your field trips. It was new for these students to have their ideas listened to and respected. The respect they experienced may have been reflected in the improvement in behavior and the respect they showed for others. Instead of students becoming discipline problems, with the Taxonomy for Discovery, they became fully engaged in learning as they satisfied their curiosity and constructed personal meaning.

In addition, these students were learning to work with data, look for patterns, and develop theories. They were inquiring, making hypotheses, analyzing, synthesizing, and discerning. They were developing their ability to think—scientifically and creatively—as they followed their own curiosity. The Taxonomy for Discovery is a tool that teaches students how to learn, not just what to learn—a skill students will need to thrive in an unknown future.

—Kathleen Carroll

Toward Lifelong Learning

The first instinct in humans is one of exploration. Children need time to explore without the constraints of specific questioning or filling out papers. The subject of the inquiry then becomes a combination of the children's genuine interests with what the teacher feels is important to learn about the topic. As a teacher, I scaffold the students' learning by setting up situations that will evoke the very questions from them that I deem important while simultaneously allowing the space for them to explore questions I have not anticipated. At the same time they are taking in generally agreed-upon knowledge, they are learning to become lifelong learners full of curiosity with skills they need to satisfy that curiosity.

When I am preparing for a field trip, I go through a process similar to the one I ask the students to use. I use the following steps:

I begin by exploring my topic by immersing myself in literature, photos, stories and objects. Then I come up with Essential Questions that percolate out of my explorations.

I come up with theories about the answers to my questions based on my prior knowledge and explorations. After that, I research the topic further to try to answer my questions.

For example, when my fifth and sixth grade combination class was studying Mayan art, I began developing my curriculum by visiting the Museum of Natural History in New York. I started by walking through the Mayan art exhibit and jotting down my observations and questions. Then, I went into the research library of the museum and poured over books, photos, and slides of Mayan art and history. Some of these would be available to take back to my classroom and do previsit lessons. With my new knowledge, I took myself through the exhibit once more, this time categorizing my observations and questions into themes that I could explore easily with the students. For example, the Mayans believed that the gods influenced the success of their harvest; therefore, much of their art and ceremonies were based on this concept.

With the children, I followed the same process. I began the study with a quick museum visit during which the students took clipboards and wrote down their observations of and questions concerning Mayan art, with an emphasis on generating their own reactions rather than focusing on the captions. Then in class, I assigned the children to partners and I distributed a photograph of a piece of Mayan art to one student in each pair. The students sat back to back. One child described the piece of artwork in detail based on his or her observations while the other, who could not see the photograph, drew the artwork based on the other student's description. The child describing the artwork had to use descriptive and specific language for the other child to be able to draw accurately. The student drawing needed to use his or her best listening skills and ask for more specific detail when necessary.

I always like to have a self-confidence and community-building element in my teaching. We displayed the photographs and the children's drawings and celebrated how closely the students' drawings resembled the artwork. My goals in this activity were for the children to become careful observers of artwork and begin to recognize specific symbols that the Mayans used in their artwork. We later would discuss these symbols and others they had not noticed through readings and slide shows. We continued to go through the process of coming up with our own ideas and theories and then researching to learn more. Our culminating activity was to go back to the Mayan art exhibit and experience the artwork with more expert eyes—this time reading the captions, recognizing things we knew, and filling in the gaps with new knowledge. Experiencing an art or museum exhibit in this multilayered way (observing/exploring—questioning—theorizing—researching) is a process for lifelong learning.

—Sarah Shellow, educational consultant, New York

Discrepant events, weird facts, and puzzling problems are some other ways to inspire curiosity about the subject matter. "In any field, find the strangest thing and explore it!" This advice from John Wheeler (who proved black holes exist) provides the key to one of the best ways to turn students on to learning. Make a dissonance or a cognitive incongruity through information or experiences that run counter to expectations. Piaget called this experience a "disequilibrium," which compels the learner to try to understand the unexpected phenomena (1962). It helps students uncover their unexamined assumptions and misconceptions and replace them with more accurate understandings. Discrepant events, weird facts, and puzzling problems, addressed through problem-based learning (PBL), motivate the most disengaged learners to want to learn. They can serve as the starting points for inquiry and a basis for Essential Questions. (See page 111 for Essential Questions.) They also serve as a catalyst for teaching thinking. Have students examine their thinking as they make analogies, hypothesize, classify, articulate previous misconceptions, and evaluate new understandings. Arousing students' curiosity is like an itch that must be scratched. These strategies can provide the fuel for learning the standards.

Discrepant Events

Discrepant events relate to students' prior knowledge where the outcome runs counter to the students' previous experience, intuition, or prior learning. Discrepant events give students an internal need to find out why it happened that way. For instance, suppose you are going on a field trip to the airport and you would like students to be curious about what makes a heavier-than-air plane fly. For a discrepant event you might

1. give each student a 1″ × 6″ strip of paper and have him or her fold one end.
2. invite the student to predict what would happen and why if he or she were to hold the strip by the folded end and blow under the strip. Most students will expect the strips to rise because the air would lift the papers.
3. have each student predict what would happen and why if he or she put the folded end next to his or her chin and blew over the strip. Most students will predict that the strips will fall because they would expect their breath to push the papers down.
4. note the importance of having them predict what will happen and give their reasons why. If you miss this step, the students may not notice that the discrepant event took place!

5. explain Bernoulli's principle. When each student sees that the paper rises when he or she blows over it, there is an opening for him or her to learn about Bernoulli's principle. Stationary air exerts pressure on all sides. When a person blows on the strip, there is a faster moving flow of air above the strip. The faster the flow of air, the lower the pressure it exerts. The higher pressure on the bottom of the strip makes the paper lift.

6. research and ask experts how the Bernoulli principle relates to airplanes. The students might experiment with the principle themselves by making and testing different styles of paper airplanes. They will witness the principle at the airport as they watch the airplanes lift off the ground.

The key ingredients of a discrepant event are that something unexpected happens and that children realize that the event is unexpected. Then they will naturally be moved to find out why it happened that way. Well-presented discrepant events help children begin to change their intuitive misconceptions to more accurate concepts. See Tik Liem's book, *Invitations to Science Inquiry* (1992), for hundreds of examples of discrepant events or do an Internet search under "Discrepant Events." Topics in Liem's book include air, weather, matter, chemicals, energy, heat, magnetism, electricity, light, sound, the earth, space, the moon, plants, and the human body.

Weird Facts

You can find them everywhere! Weird facts pop out from the newspaper, Internet, books, articles, and even the teaching materials sent to you from your field trip site contact.

Students love to collect weird facts and use them to amaze their friends and families. Students can collect weird facts before the field trip, and they can pick up more during the field trip. (This can serve as an incentive to listen to the guide and read the captions with care.) Then they can share their findings with parents and other students, on school bulletin boards, in classroom blogs (see page 198), podcasts (see page 199), and in other projects they design after the field trip.

Here are some examples:

Are you studying ancient Egypt?

- ● The nylon-bristle toothbrush is a descendant of the "chew stick," a twig with a frayed end of soft fibers that was rubbed against the teeth to clean them. Chew sticks have been found in Egyptian tombs dating to 3000 B.C.
- ● In 1890 more than 18,000 mummified cats were sold in Liverpool,

England. Everyone wanted to own one. There were so many that the auctioneer used one instead of a hammer. Twenty tons of them were shipped from Egypt where they were discovered in a 2,000-year-old tomb.

Are you taking a trip to Thomas Jefferson's home in Virginia? That place is full of weird facts! Invite students to collect them on their live tour or at www.monticello.org.

- ⏵ The dome on Monticello, Thomas Jefferson's home, conceals a billiards room. In Jefferson's day, billiards were illegal in Virginia.
- ⏵ Jefferson designed a great clock to keep his plantation on schedule. The clock gives hours, minutes, and seconds. The weights show the day of the week, with Sunday at the top. Since the clock was too big, Jefferson had a hole made in the floor of the main entrance to make space for the weights. Saturday is in the basement.

Are you taking a field trip to the zoo? Do a Google search for weird facts on animals and collect weird facts about the animals you will see. Students can collect weird facts at the zoo to amaze their friends and family. Here are a few:

- ⏵ Experts say that crocodiles may be the closest living relatives of Tyrannosaurus rex; if so, crocodiles have been around for nearly 195,000,000 years.
- ⏵ The prairie dog makes burrows which are known as "towns"; one town may contain 1,000 animals and stretch under the ground for miles.

Is your class going to the planetarium? There are many weird facts to collect about the solar system. Here is one I came across today:

- ⏵ *New Horizons*, a small spacecraft traveling more than three billion miles to the planet Pluto, uses less electrical power than two light bulbs.

Are you taking a walk through your city? See what you can learn from this fact:

- ⏵ If a statue in the park of a person on a horse has both front legs in the air, the person died in battle; if the horse has one front leg in the air, the person died as a result of wounds received in battle; if the horse has all four legs on the ground, the person died of natural causes.

Students may want to learn more about the people represented in statues in their town or city.

Some teachers have a permanent learning center for weird facts, with magazines, books, and learner-created collections to record, analyze, and hypothesize and inquire about.

It is very gratifying to a child who sees other peoples' looks of awe and surprise when he or she shares some unusual pieces of information. Weird facts increase class community, raise self-esteem, and can elevate a child's status among his or her peers. Whether they are looking face-to-face at live sharks and stingrays at the marine aquarium, walking through a replica of a colonial farm, or studying dinosaurs at the natural history museum, kids have more fun learning through weird facts.

Cognitively, there can be some differences in the need-to-know factor between discrepant events and weird facts. Discrepant events are counterintuitive. They impel us to find a new understanding. Unless a student is in the habit of questioning, though, a weird fact could be no more than a piece of trivia. How can we use weird facts to inspire inquiry?

Questioning Skills

Dr. Frank Lyman shared the fact with me that scallops have 32 eyes. You could stop there and say "That's weird." Or you could get curious about that fact. You might ask, for example:

 I've read about them before somewhere. What *are* scallops anyway?

 How is the way a scallop sees similar to the way a human sees?

 How is the way it sees different from the way a human sees?

 How would 32 eyes help a scallop to survive?

 What are some examples of other animals with many eyes?

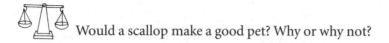 Scallops and oysters belong to the same group. What is the name of that group?

Would a scallop make a good pet? Why or why not?

Each of the previous questions considers a weird fact about scallops through a different lens. The questions are based on a question/response method called ThinkTrix, designed by Frank Lyman to help teachers and students develop the habit of questioning from different levels and perspectives. In some classrooms, questions rarely rise above the level of recall of basic knowledge. ThinkTrix encourages teachers and students to develop thinking skills by getting in the habit of questioning from many points of view.

ThinkTrix provides graphic anchors to help learners from kindergarten through graduate school develop the mental muscles for different kinds of critical thinking. Primary teacher Nancy Koza describes how she helped young children understand different ways to think. Her students learned about similarity and difference by looking for ways that two bears were alike and unlike. They labeled natural questions that arose on field trips as cause/effect type thinking. Learners of all ages eventually are able to use the ThinkTrix anchors to help them think about their thinking, discriminate between types of thinking, discern what is being asked of them, and develop their own higher-level thinking. At the same time, using ThinkTrix can help rekindle students' curiosity.

Over thirty-five years ago Neil Postman, coauthor of *Teaching as a Subversive Activity*, noted that children "enter school as question marks and leave as periods" (Dryden and Vos 2001). In many schools that judgment is as true today as it was then.

We are all naturally curious learners and explorers from the moment we are born. When this natural curiosity is fostered, we become lifelong learners. When this natural ability is stifled, learning in school can become irrelevant. ThinkTrix helps turn that period back into a question mark as it renews curiosity and encourages the habit of questioning.

ThinkTrix

Recall
repeat, describe, list, detail

Cause/ Effect
postulate, consider motive, infer, predict, hypothesize

Similarity
make analogy, compare, find common attributes, set intersection

Difference
contrast, compare, distinguish, differentiate, discern

Example to Idea
classify, induce, conclude, generalize, find essence, summarize, identify the theme

Idea to Example
categorize, deduce, substantiate, make analogy, support

Evaluation
consider ethics, evaluate, judge, rate, weigh evidence

About ThinkTrix

Nobel Prize winner Isidor I. Rabi considered his mother the source of his success. Every day after school his mother inquired not "What did you learn?" but "Izzy, what good question did you ask today?" (www.kidsource.com/kidsource/content/learnscience.html).

ThinkTrix is a question/response method formulated by University of Maryland instructor and consultant Dr. Frank Lyman to teach children and adults how to ask good questions. It is used successfully in many classrooms around the United States. In some classrooms, questioning tends to stay at the level of basic knowledge. ThinkTrix encourages students to extend their thinking and questioning using seven fundamental types of thinking. Each type of thinking is cued by a different icon. The brain is wired for an almost instantaneous response to icons and symbols (2005). The knowledge that the icons represent is a form of metacognition. Students will know how they know.

ThinkTrix

Why Use ThinkTrix?

- To encourage students' curiosity
- To give an impetus for students to design their own varied, higher-level questions
- To provide simple graphic icons, or anchors, to remind teachers and students to use a variety of types of thinking on a regular basis
- To offer a metacognitive device, a means for students and teachers to think about their thinking; i.e., to recognize the type of thinking required in particular circumstances or with certain processes
- To help students to understand how their minds work in any given thinking task
- To help students improve performance on standardized tests, specifically by teaching them how their minds should work to answer the question or solve the problem

How to Use ThinkTrix

Understand ThinkTrix yourself. Practice all the uses you will require of your students.

Post the anchors on the wall. Do this a few days before you introduce the anchors to pique curiosity. When asked, call the anchors your "secret thinking code."

Use the ThinkTrix anchors to engage in discourse. Do this at a variety of levels, in addition to the recall level.

Introduce the anchors. Students guess what kind of thinking each represents.

Teach with examples. Use examples along the continuum from recall to evaluation. Students identify the types and begin to make their own examples.

Use a variety of graphic organizers. Expand students' understanding of each type of thinking. "All thought has shape" as Lyman says. Find or design a variety of graphic organizers that reflect each of the seven thinking types.

As students become familiar with the different patterns of thinking represented by the ThinkTrix anchors, they become more discerning about asking and answering questions, solving problems, and taking tests.

When to Use ThinkTrix

Use ThinkTrix to expand the range of possibility when forming Essential Questions or when brainstorming questions to ask the field trip guide.

After the field trip, students might use ThinkTrix to devise questions about the field trip as a review. Partners might help each other design the questions. The class might form concentric circles with the partners, facing each other, with each student holding his or her set of questions. When the music begins, the outside circle moves in a clockwise direction while the inside circle stays put. When the music stops, new partners face each other and take turns asking each other ThinkTrix questions about the trip. Continue the partner changing and questioning as long as time and interest allow. Just make sure that the original partners don't become questioning partners since they have the same sets of questions. Later, you might draw from the students' questions for a posttrip test.

For more information, look for Frank Lyman's ThinkTrix Smart Card at www.kagononline.com.

Expanding Curiosity; Expanding Perspectives

In many ways our education system limits students' perspective. As creativity expert Roger von Oech states: "By the time the average person finishes college he or she will have taken over 2,600 tests, quizzes, and exams. The 'right answer' approach becomes deeply ingrained in our thinking. This may be fine for some mathematical problems, where there is in fact only one right answer. The difficulty is that most of life isn't that way. Life is ambiguous; there are many right answers—all depending on what you are looking for. But if you think there is only one right answer, then you'll stop looking as soon as you find one" (von Oech 1983, 21).

The Six Thinking Hats process gets beyond the one-right-answer fixation by providing ways to examine an issue from many different perspectives. All members of a group use the same perspective at the same time, rather than in opposition. The following variation on a familiar story illustrates the idea:

Once upon a time, a group of blind mice came upon something strange in their midst. Each mouse went off alone to explore the strange something and came back to report.

"It is huge, rough, and round," declared one. "I am sure it is a tree."

"How ridiculous," said another. "It is long and slinky. It must be a snake."

"No, no, no! It's wide and floppy! It's a great big lily pad!"

"How can you say that? It's short and spirally. It's a corkscrew!"

As you can see, the mice couldn't agree at all. Finally one very wise mouse said, "Let's examine this something together."

So all of the mice used their little paws and whiskers together at the same time and discovered that the something was huge, rough, and round like a tree. It was long and slinky like a snake. It was wide and floppy like a lily pad. It was short and spirally like a snake. And it was clear to all that the something was an elephant!

The moral of the story is that every issue can be considered from many points of view. Six Thinking Hats helps a group consider the different points of view together, at the same time, rather than arguing about them. Six Thinking Hats also keeps us from deciding on one right answer or the rightness of one point of view without considering the many facets of the issue.

The Six Thinking Hats process helps us get out of the box of narrow thinking and sparks our curiosity about different perspectives. The process can be used in problem solving or decision making, evaluating an experience, and delving more deeply into subject matter. The process can be an activity for a whole class, small group, or individual. A class might use Six Thinking Hats when deciding which field trip to take; in evaluating the field trip after it is taken; in assessing themselves, their behavior and/or learning on the field trip; and in solving conflicts. Students can also use Six Thinking Hats in exploring the complexities inherent in the subject matter they are studying. As students explore the subject from many perspectives, the learning becomes deeper and more connected with the students' life experience. Some examples of using Six Thinking Hats with subject matter could be:

Would you like to take a trip to the moon?
Is it right to keep animals in zoos?
What was the Lewis and Clark expedition like?
Should we plant a butterfly garden on the school grounds?
How should a family prepare for a hurricane?

The Six Thinking Hats strategy helps us get beyond knee-jerk reactions to a fuller view. Students were taught the Six Thinking Hats strategy at a school for violent youth in London. Twenty years later they had one-tenth the rate of criminal activity of students who were not taught thinking skills (www.edwarddebono.com). Thinking skills are tools that will last a lifetime.

Edward de Bono's
Six Thinking Hats®

White Hat
Information

- Information we know
- Information we would like to know
- Information we need
- Information that is missing
- How are we going to get that information
- Includes hard facts to doubtful information

Red Hat
Feelings, Intuition, Emotions

- Permission to express feelings
- No need to justify
- Represents feeling right now
- Keep it short
- A key ingredient in decision making

Black Hat
Logical Negative

- The pessimistic view
- Reasons must be given
- Points out thinking that does not fit the facts, experience, regulations, strategy, values
- Points out potential problems
- The most useful hat

Yellow Hat
Logical Positive

- The optimistic view
- Reasons must be given
- Needs more effort than the black hat
- Looks for the concept behind the idea

Green Hat
New Ideas, Possibilities

- Creative thinking
- Seeking alternatives and possibilities
- Removing faults
- Doesn't have to be logical
- Generates new concepts

Blue Hat
Managing the Thinking

- "Control" hat
- Organizes the thinking
- Sets the focus and agenda
- Summarizes and concludes
- Ensures that the rules are observed

www.micaworld.com

Six Thinking Hats

Curriculum Example

Would I like to have been a child on an early Colonial farm?

- ▶ **White Hat—Information.** They worked in fields, cared for animals, made soap, cooked, and spun. The whole family worked hard to survive.
- ▶ **Yellow Hat—Logical Positives.** There were homemade toys, games like cat's cradle, and shoo-fly pie.
- ▶ **Red Hat—Feelings, Intuitions, Emotions.** They were glad to have land. They expected that life would be better than in the old country. They may have been lonely for friends and family who stayed in the old country.
- ▶ **Black Hat—Logical Negatives.** Illnesses were frequent in families. Children had to stand and be silent at dinner.
- ▶ **Green Hat—Possibilities.** A Colonial child might have had a Native American child as a friend. Spring would have brought warmth and fresh food.
- ▶ **Blue Hat—Manage the Thinking.** Colonial life was hard, but the people had more choices than in the old country. I'm glad to live in the world of today!

Class Problem-Solving Example

How can our class get along with one another better on our field trip?

- ▶ **White Hat—Information.** There are some cliques. Some students don't want to sit next to other students. Some students get along with everybody.
- ▶ **Red Hat—Feelings, Intuitions, Emotions.** There is anger and fear from those who are excluded and lack of ease from others.
- ▶ **Yellow Hat—Logical Positives.** If we get along with one another, we will have more fun. No one will feel left out.
- ▶ **Black Hat—Logical Negatives.** Excluders may not want to give up their power. But no one in the group feels safe when some are excluded. It could happen to me next.
- ▶ **Green Hat—Possibilities.** We could get to know one another better by having lots of different partners in class beforehand.
- ▶ **Blue Hat—Manage the Thinking.** People in our classroom and in the world need to get along better. I'll find one person in class I don't usually partner with to get to know today.

Connect with Current Events

Diana Ramsey, co-director of Regional Training Center, a New Jersey–based teacher-training organization, extols the virtues of connecting field trips and other learning with current events. Students are more likely to become curious when the field trip relates to something that is already meaningful in their lives. Following are some of Ramsey's examples of connections with current events.

If the field trip is related to:	Connect with current events on:
History	legislation, elections, war, summit talks, political figures
Music	music awards, local performances, television programming
Art	local art exhibits, photography in print media, computers, network news
Science	weather extremes, planet discoveries, space travel, medical discoveries, environmental issues, extinction
Health	medical findings (nutrition, fitness, wellness, drugs, smoking)
Sport Events	local, national, and world competitions; wellness and fitness issues
Language Arts	local performances of theater and poetry; author visits; print news; television shows; films
Social Studies	cultural events, political events, famous people from the country being studied

It can work both ways: events in the news make students curious about the field trip, and the field trip can make students more interested in current events.

Problem-Based Learning (PBL)

Problem-based learning (PBL) takes the idea of connecting the content with current events to a new level. While connecting with current events gives a link to the real world, with PBL the learning *is* the real world (Esch, 1998). The Caines' precepts for dynamic knowledge described earlier (see page 15) are in keeping with a PBL approach to education. With PBL, students learn the content required of the standards as dynamic knowledge, by grappling with messy, ill-structured, real-world problems. Solving real problems that matter makes learning meaningful and memorable and helps students learn for life, rather than just to pass tests. At the same time that students are learning content, they are also learning how to think creatively and critically, deal with complexity, be responsible members of their communities, and problem solve. In addition they learn how to work on teams and communicate more effectively. PBL focuses on the long-term well-being of young people by preparing them for the future.

A problem-based learning approach is currently helping people around the world solve their own problems. MIT professor Dr. Neil Gershenfeld is a founder of Fab Labs, where he teaches a course called "How to Make (Almost) Anything." At the Fab Lab—laboratories that are fabulous or for fabrication—technically inclined students and students with no technical background alike use their passion and inventiveness with high-level tools in what he calls "personal fabrication." For example, one student designed an alarm clock you have to wrestle with to make sure you really wake up. Even Gershenfeld's six-year-old sons use the Fab Lab to make their own toys.

Fab Labs have now been set up to solve serious survival problems in places, such as rural India, where machines are being designed to figure out when milk is starting to go bad. At the top of Norway, nomads are using Fab Labs to make radio collars to track their herds. In Ghana, people are making car parts, jewelry, and solar-powered items in Fab Labs.

Neil Gershenfeld says that we are approaching the ability to make one machine that can make any machine. He believes that just as personal computers brought about a digital revolution, we are about to embark on a personal fabrication revolution where ordinary people will be able to make customized products to meet their needs (www.economist.com/science/displayStory.cfm?story_id=3786368).

Now why are we telling you about Fab Labs in a book about field trips? Neil Gershenfeld expresses a viewpoint that relates directly to teaching through PBL. He says, "You can view a lot of MIT's instruction as offering just-in-case education; you learn lots of stuff in case you eventually need it. What I'm talking about is really just-in-time education. You let people solve the problems they want to solve, and you provide supporting material they can draw on as they progress" (www.edge.org/3rd_culture/gershenfeld03/gershenfeld_index.html).

Neil Gershenfeld's observation is as relevant to primary students as it is to graduate students. It is even more relevant to people in poor, developing countries than it is to people in rich countries. PBL is based on just-in-time learning.

How do you design a PBL experience for your classroom or your field trip? There are a number of different problem-solving methods to choose from. Check out *How to Use Problem-Based Learning in the Classroom* by Robert Delisle and *Problems As Possibilities: Problem-Based Learning for K–16*

Education (second edition) by Linda Torp and Sara Sage. Go to the Center for Problem-Based Learning's Web site (www2.imsa.edu/programs/pbl/cpbl.html) for some resources and real-world examples of problem-based learning.

Following are some guidelines that most upholders of PBL would agree with:

1. Begin with an issue. The issue may come from the organizers at the field trip site such as this:

    ● Students are asked to take a field trip (either virtual or actual) to discover what species are in jeopardy in their community and what resources are in place to save the population. Students use technology to communicate with experts and research the most current statistics. The ultimate goal of the mission is to adopt an endangered species and disseminate relevant information about the species to the neighboring community. This project, which took place at the Indiana Dunes National Lakeshore, can be used as a model to investigate any community's endangered species and provide the community with information (http://ed.fnal.gov).

Or the issue may start with the students and then turn into field trips such as these:

● Students want a class pet. They research the care of various pets and then take a field trip to the pet store to choose the most appropriate pet. This experience gives students "dynamic knowledge" as they address the standards about animal needs.

● Students observe mud sliding down the hill onto the playground each time it rains. When they notice the erosion on the hillside, they research to find the most likely causes, then make and execute a plan to stop the erosion. Students meet the standards on earth studies and scientific experimentation while they solve their playground problem.

● Students in the class of Mary Ann Jones in Richmond, Virginia, wanted their cafeteria to be more attractive. Students toured the cafeteria and filled out their ideas for improvements on maps of the cafeteria. They wrote letters to the administrators and PTA president. Now the cafeteria tables have flowers and the walls have become a showcase for student artwork. The students have addressed the standards of organizing and summarizing group reports and letter writing in authentic ways.

The issue for PBL can be teacher-initiated as in this example:

> ● Dr. John Grassi of Cambridge College in Massachusetts had his
> class test water from sources all around their town. The students
> found unacceptable levels of *E. coli* in the drinking fountain in
> their park. Their findings were verified and corrected by officials.

Or someone else's problem may become the source of the PBL:

> ● Linda Torp and Sara Sage tell of an elementary school in
> Arlington Heights, Illinois, that has used PBL for years. This
> problem was investigated by first through fifth graders. The
> students' former principal was having difficulty maintaining a
> healthy flower garden at home. The students studied her soil,
> learned about which flowers grow best in their climate,
> conducted plant experiments, checked on the Internet, consulted
> experts, and helped her to make a more beautiful garden (2002).

2. Students brainstorm what they know and what they need to learn
    about the issue. In this way they gradually get to the crux of the
    problem.
3. They research the problem, perhaps through books, articles, the
    Internet, surveys, interviews, and/or consulting with experts and
    mentors. Sometimes the research may be based on the students
    own observations and experiments. Sometimes they might divide
    the problem up so that different groups can research different
    aspects of the problem.
4. Students come back together as a class and, based on their research,
    they make a plan to address the problem.
5. Students take part in Performance Tasks (see page 158–159) to
    address the problem. While formative assessments have taken place
    throughout the process, the Performance Task is the summative or
    final assessment.

Teachers at the school in Arlington Heights, Illinois, say that they can tell
when students have been though several PBL experiences. They are the students who solve conflicts in the lunchroom. They are the students who hold
on to their questions until they are sure they understand the issues thor-
oughly. They are even known to assign themselves homework to satisfy their
curiosity (Torp and Sage 2002)! A special education teacher added that while
all students benefit from PBL, this process is especially valuable to special education students because it shows them the reason for learning, allows them to

use their own learning preferences, and offers choice in assessment such as oral presentations, debates, or posters.

The term PBL is also used for a somewhat different approach called project-based learning. Problem-based and project-based learning are similar in that both are authentic, real-world approaches that allow open-ended avenues to developing dynamic knowledge. A difference is that while problem-based learning is about dealing with a real problem or opportunity, project-based learning is about making a product. When students design their own in-school museum (see page 194), make a podcast (see page 199), or write a book about the field trip for younger children, they are making products. These products lend themselves to authentic, performance assessment. Both problem-based learning and project-based learning extend the value of field trips.

Discover Learning's Essence Through Dance

How would you like a discovery-based follow-up to a field trip that is fun, expands learning, cements memory, elicits empathy, improves vocabulary, teaches math, develops teamwork, enhances class cohesion, promotes body awareness, and provides students with physical exercise? Try dance!

Traditionally the assumption was that students learn best when they stay in their seats, sit still, and either listen to the teacher's lecture or do their worksheets. That fit with our culture's old beliefs that the body and mind are separate and that using the body is of a lower order than using the mind. But neurological research is reporting strong links between whole body movement and learning (Jensen 1998). The cerebellum, or "little brain," as it is sometimes called, has long been associated with coordination and movement. Eric Jensen, who has written a number of books on the brain and learning, points out that the cerebellum contains over half the brain's neurons and that those neurons connect to all areas of the brain. He quotes research indicating that the link between movement and thinking is inescapable. One example is a study in Seattle, Washington. Third grade students who learned language arts concepts through dance activities boosted their reading scores by 13 percent over six months, while the test scores of their sedentary counterparts decreased by two percent (Jensen 1998).

Educational consultant Sarah Shellow has studied the Laban Movement method and has used dance as an extension to field trips. She points out that dance can become a medium of discovery about a subject. The term *education* is derived from the Latin word *educare*, which means to "draw forth from within." Discovery through dance encourages children to draw forth the essence of the learning from within. At the same time, children are enhancing sensory integration.

Shellow helped me think through a sequence for children to learn how to make their own dances. Following are three different ways that children might enhance their learning from a field trip through dance.

○ **Design a dance.** The first idea is to make a sequence of movements that symbolize the trip, and then put the movements to music. Here is a way to sequence the dance experience:

Before the Trip

1. Prepare students by building a movement vocabulary. Students might walk in a circle or randomly around the room as the teacher calls out directions for ways to make movements with their bodies such as fast/slow, high/low, smooth/jagged, small/big, shrinking/growing, pushing/pulling, or straight/round/spiraling.

2. Prepare students by introducing four- and eight-count patterns. Clap out or beat a drum to a count of four. Then nod heads to a count of four, raise arms to a count of four, and kick legs to a count of four. Do the same with an eight-count pattern (Benzwei 1987). This sense of patterning will help later when students put their movements to music, since much music lends itself to an eight-count beat. The patterning sequence also helps with math by reinforcing number sense in the students' bodies.

3. Next, put the movement vocabulary and pattern counting together as students perform all different kinds of movements to the count of eight.

During the Trip

Encourage students to look for and write down shapes and movements as they see them, such as machine movements on a city tour, animal movements at the zoo, or shapes observed in paintings at the art gallery.

After the Trip

1. Make a list of shapes and movements students observed during the trip. A list like this can increase students' vocabulary. Students can make a movement phrase out of one item on the list or combine several ideas into one movement phrase. Sarah Shellow suggests that the teacher might help with questions such as "Remember your visit to the aquarium; in your mind's eye, in your memory, think of one of the fish you saw there.

a. What shape is your fish in the water? With your body, show how your fish takes up space in the water. Is it fat or skinny, long or short? How can you make your body look like the fish?

b. What color is your fish? Using movements as your language, show what the colors of your fish look like. For example, what does the color 'red' look like in movement? How is it different from blue? Can you combine the color movements of your fish?

c. Does your fish have a pattern on its scales? Pick a point across the room and walk to that point like the pattern of your fish. How will you translate lines, zigzags, or dots into movement?

d. Can you remember how your fish took up space in water? Now let's go back to the color. Blend your shape and color phrase together. Add your pattern phrase. Make a movement sentence that combines all of these different things you have learned about your fish. Can you pull the essence or heart out of all your phrases and make one expression for your fish?"

2. One student designs an eight-count movement for an item on the list (or the "essence") described above.

3. Pairs teach each other the movement. Now each pair has 2 eight-count movements.

4. Two pairs teach each other their movements. Now there are 4 eight-count movements. This will be the dance.

5. Groups of four practice putting their dance to a drumbeat or metronome sound on a keyboard and then to music. The music might be chosen by the teacher or by the students.

6. Each group presents their dance to the rest of the class.

7. The audience observes and interprets what the movements represent.

8. Then the dancers say what they were thinking and feeling and what they learned about the topic.

○ **Improvise a dance.** A second way to incorporate dance is simpler and requires less time. While you may want to give students a movement vocabulary as described above in the "Before the Trip" section of "Design a dance," with "Improvise a dance," students simply make up their movements to your suggestions in the moment. Choose music that you consider appropriate for the subject. Spread out students around the room then suggest ways for them to move. For instance, with the aquarium trip, Sarah Shellow gave her students the following dance ideas as they moved like fish: "You see your favorite food in the water.

How will you move to get it? You sense a predator coming up from behind. How will you respond? Now you are all fish in the sea together. Look around you at these other fish. Are you a fish that swims in a school? Are you a fish that swims alone? What does your fish do around other fish? When I say, 'go,' move yourself the way the fish would move in this group."

⚫ **Add movements to songs.** Here is a third way to incorporate dance. After making a song or rap that shows the sequence or summarizes the main learning from the trip, make hand motions and/or steps that reinforce the words of the song. Alternatively, choose a song that teaches and add movements to it. Physical movements added to songs make more neurological connections, which enhance the memory of the words or sequence. When students choose the words and/or movements themselves, the learning is even more memorable.

As Carla Hannaford, author of *Smart Moves: Why Learning Is Not All in Your Head*, puts it, "Every time we move in an organized, graceful manner, full brain activation and integration occurs, and the door to learning opens naturally. . . . movement is essential to learning" (1995, 96–97).

Reflecting

In following one's curiosity, there are two sides of the coin: active and reflective. The active side is when students delve into what they wonder about. They make observations, ask questions, research in books and online, talk with experts, or even dance about the topic. The reflective part is when they sit back and digest their findings. We don't just learn from experience; we learn from experience *and* reflection. As students reflect, they begin to find patterns and make connections with their prior knowledge and experience. As they reflect, they evaluate their experience and come to the essence of the learning. New questions emerge from reflection. Think-Pair-Share discussions with other students (see pages 100–103), journal writing, portfolios, and myriad posttrip activities suggested in chapter 4 all contribute to the reflection that is a key to lasting learning.

In conclusion, caring and curiosity, characteristics of emotional intelligence (EQ), are the foundations for successful field trips. Well-designed field trips serve as a vehicle for developing students' EQ. Field trips are a natural way for students to increase their self-awareness, self-control, self-motivation, empathy, altruism, and social skills. You will find a checklist for this chapter on the next page to help you remember to use the ideas or techniques that are most relevant to your situation.

Checklist: Caring and Curiosity

Look at the list below and check off the ideas or activities that you would like to incorporate into your field trip:

Have I structured the field trip to develop students' caring by employing or encouraging the following?

- ☐ Altruism through service to others, the community, or the environment
- ☐ Envisioning ideal ways to be on the trip through story or future pacing, a guided visualization about the field trip to come
- ☐ Students' ability to help make the ground rules
- ☐ Self-control with a contract for behavior
- ☐ Caring for one another through cooperative learning
- ☐ Self-awareness and empathy through trust-building activities
- ☐ Think-Pair-Share activities, other cooperative learning, and trust-building
- ☐ Social behaviors they may need for the trip
- ☐ Caring behaviors toward the environment
- ☐ Empathy and social skills by writing thank you notes
- ☐ Emotional connections—caring about the curriculum

Have I structured the field trip to develop students' curiosity by employing or encouraging the following?

- ☐ Exploration
- ☐ K-W-H-L-N Charts
- ☐ Essential Questions
- ☐ Taxonomy for Discovery
- ☐ Discrepant events
- ☐ Weird facts
- ☐ Questioning skills—ThinkTrix
- ☐ Expanding perspectives with Six Thinking Hats
- ☐ Connecting with current events
- ☐ Problem-based learning or project-based learning
- ☐ Discovering learning's essence through dance
- ☐ Reflecting

References

Benzwei, T. 1987. *A Moving Experience: Dance for Lovers of Children and the Child Within.* Chicago: Zephyr Press.

Carroll, K. 2000. *Science for Every Learner: Brain-Compatible Pathways to Scientific Literacy.* Chicago: Zephyr Press.

Cornell, J. 1998. *Sharing Nature with Children.* Nevada City, CA: Dawn Publications.

Delisle, R. 1997. *How to Use Problem-Based Learning in the Classroom.* Alexandria, VA: Association for Supervision and Curriculum Development (ASCD).

Deming, W. E. 1993. *The New Economics for Industry, Government & Education.* Cambridge, MA: Massachusetts Institute of Technology Center for Advanced Engineering Study.

Dryden, G., and J. Vos. 2001. *The Learning Revolution.* London, England: Network Educational Press.

Esch, C. 1998. "Project-Based and Problem-Based: The Same or Different?": The Challenge 2000 Multimedia Project (San Mateo County Office of Education). http://pblmm.k12.ca.us/PBLGuide/PBL&PBL.htm (accessed June 15, 2005).

Hannaford, C. 1995. *Smart Moves: Why Learning Is Not All in Your Head.* Arlington, Virginia: Great Ocean Publishers.

Jensen, E. 1995. *Brain-Based Learning and Teaching.* Del Mar, CA: Turning Point Publishing.

Jensen, E. 1998. *Teaching with the Brain in Mind.* Alexandria, VA: ASCD.

Kagan, S. 1994. *Cooperative Learning.* San Clemente, CA: Resources for Teachers, Inc.

Kellert, S., and E. Wilson (ed.). 1993. *The Biophilia Hypothesis.* Washington, DC: Island Press/Shearwater Books.

Liem, T. L. 1992. *Invitations to Science Inquiry.* Chino Hills, CA: Science Inquiry Enterprises.

Lyman, F. 2003. *Think-Pair-Share Smart Card.* San Clemente, CA: Kagan Publishing.

Lyman, F. 2005. *ThinkTrix Smart Card.* San Clemente, CA: Kagan Publishing.

Piaget, J. 1962. *Play, Dreams, and Imagination in Children.* NY: Norton.

Sylwester, R. 1998. Art for the Brain's Sake. *Educational Leadership* 56:31–35.

Torp, L., and S. Sage. 2002. *Problems as Possibilities: Problem-Based Learning for K–16 Education.* Alexandria, VA: ASCD.

von Oech, R. 1983. *A Whack on the Side of the Head.* NY: Warner.

4

Field Trips Are for Learning!

"When it's all over, you want them to learn something, you want them to learn how to learn, and you want them to want to learn, to become persistent."

—FRANK LYMAN

Some teachers focus so much on the logistics of a trip—how to get there, keep organized, and take care of all the details—that they forget the most important part: the learning! This book has a whole chapter on logistics (see chapter 5) because handling the details *is* necessary. But planning for student learning deserves just as much time and effort. After all that's the point of the field trip, isn't it?

In chapter 3 we considered two of the foundations for learning on a field trip: caring and curiosity. The many ideas and strategies presented about caring and curiosity are certainly about learning too, and need to be incorporated here. In this chapter, though, as we focus on learning intentions, one word stands out: *alignment*. This chapter presents a systematic way to ensure that the class reaches the goals of the trip. You will learn how to use a graphic organizer, the Domain Matrix, to guarantee that what your students do before, during, and after the trip is in alignment with what matters most. The Domain Matrix addresses the three most important questions for teaching and learning:

1. What do the students need to learn?
2. How will we and *they* know they learned it?
3. How are they going to learn it?

It is best to address these questions in that order. When you ask "What do the students need to learn?" you start with the standards or objectives. Perhaps those standards can come together into an Essential Question or several Essential Questions. Essential Questions are addressed more fully in chapter 3 (see page 111) as a means to spark students' curiosity. Prior assessment helps ascertain whether students already know some of the objectives or whether they have the prerequisite knowledge needed to learn the objectives at hand.

If the first question is "What do students need to learn?" then it is usually wiser to choose a field trip that will best help students achieve those standards or objectives, rather than choosing a field trip and then looking for standards for the trip. See chapter 5 (page 217) for a process for choosing the best field trip to meet your students' needs.

The same criteria, maximizing students' learning, applies in deciding when to have the field trip. Should you have the field trip at the beginning of a unit as a motivating introduction? In the middle to reinforce? Or at the end of the unit to tie all the learning together and celebrate? What about taking the field trip at the beginning and again at the end to help students realize how much they have learned about the subject?

The next question, "How will we and the students know that they learned it?", speaks to what assessment gurus Grant Wiggins and Jay McTighe refer to as "backward planning" (2005). Traditionally teachers start planning activities once the objectives have been determined (or occasionally, even before!). Assessment, in this scenario, becomes an afterthought. Instead, with backward planning, you design assessments that will show that students have truly mastered the objectives and then plan activities that will help students succeed with the assessment. Backward planning really is more logical. Once the objectives are clear, doesn't it make sense to plan how we will know that students truly understand, and then plan activities to help students succeed in that understanding? This doesn't mean what is often referred to as "teaching to the test"—drilling students to memorize information so that they will be able to circle in the right answer on a standardized test. It means teaching to the authentic test—a product or performance that demonstrates mastery, the ability to transfer understanding to new situations. (By the way, students with that level of mastery will be able to circle in the right answer on the standardized test. But they will also be able to do so much more.)

Notice the emphasis on making sure that the students know they have learned. Students are motivated to learn more when they are clear that they used to be at one level of understanding, and now they are at a new, higher level of understanding. Appropriate assessment leads to motivation and persistence.

We will address the third question, "How are they going to learn it?", by offering a variety of learning options before, during, and after the field trip. Options include differentiation using the multiple intelligences, a learning cycle that integrates the arts, and strategies for special skills that may be needed for field trips such as observation, listening, questioning, interviewing, and note taking. This question also refers back to the approaches for making caring and curiosity foundations for the field trip (see chapter 3). The third question addresses traveling time. In addition, it addresses the use of technology for research, production, and communication in field trips, including how to design a virtual field trip. You will find a step-by-step plan to use the Domain Matrix for your own field trip's curriculum near the end of the chapter.

The Domain Matrix—for Alignment and Validity

Some teachers believe they have to sacrifice meaningful and involving learning experiences to meet required standards or objectives. Others may get so involved in making learning exciting that they forget about meeting standards and achieving worthwhile goals; they get lost in the process.

The Domain Matrix, which I first learned about from Sybil Carlson of Educational Testing Service, is a powerful tool to create a balanced learning experience. The Domain Matrix helps ensure alignment of activities and assessments with goals and objectives. The matrix allows teachers to analyze each aspect of the unit or session, to make sure that all objectives are being addressed adequately. The matrix also allows teachers to examine activities—to make sure they are worth doing, and, perhaps, to massage them into addressing more objectives in the same amount of time. The Domain Matrix enables teachers to make learning engaging and, at the same time, stay focused on the objectives.

There are a number of reasons for using a Domain Matrix when planning your field trips. Use the Domain Matrix

- ❍ to stay true to what is most important.
- ❍ for validity—to ensure that you are teaching what you intend to teach and assessing what you taught and nothing else.
- ❍ to check the appropriateness of particular activities and assessments. Do these activities actually teach and assess the listed objectives or standards?
- ❍ to make sure that the summative assessment at the end of the study includes all of the stated objectives or standards and no others. Students are only assessed on what they are taught.
- ❍ to provide formative assessment, to find out what the students already know and don't know at the beginning and whether or not students are grasping the material along the way.
- ❍ to improve a particular activity, by aligning it better to the objectives or changing an activity to address more objectives, to achieve more in the same amount of time.
- ❍ to weave in other objectives, such as cooperation, communication, and leadership development, your own special gift, and the learners' needs, into the same activities that address the required curriculum.
- ❍ to show the powers-that-be that your field trip and creative activities using the multiple intelligences are totally aligned with the required objectives.

The Domain Matrix serves as a valuable tool to align all aspects of your field trip with your goals. The nature of field trips almost guarantees that other learning will also happen because students will soak up information from everything they see and do. But the Domain Matrix will help assure that students learn what is intended. The Domain Matrix also provides a way to justify the trip to the powers-that-be. Principals, parents, and district office administrators will see at a glance that the trip, its assessments, and related activities are all aligned with the standards.

The Domain Matrix is a tool that is well worth the time it takes to learn to use. Let's start with a simple version. Look at the Domain Matrix on page 145:

The Domain Matrix

Activities and Assessments	Objective A	Objective B	Objective C	Objective D
Activity 1	×		×	×
Activity 2	×			×
Activity 3				
Activity 4			×	×
Activity 5	×		×	
Assessment needs to address all objectives and only those objectives		×	×	×

Objectives

Objective A Description

Objective B Description

Objective C Description

Objective D Description

Activities and Assessment

Activity 1 Description

Activity 2 Description

Activity 3 Description

Activity 4 Description

Activity 5 Description

Assessment Description

Notice that the standards for this field trip are represented across the top with capital letters. The activities are listed down the left-hand column, represented by numbers. The summative assessment, the final assessment at the end of the study, is at the bottom.

Let's assess the plan laid out by this Domain Matrix. Is the plan appropriate as it is? If the standards or objectives are suitable, then we are clear about Question 1: "What do students need to learn?" Now let's look at Question 2: "How will we and *they* know they have learned it?" Does the assessment assess the chosen standards? Notice that Objective A was left off the final assessment. The Domain Matrix shows that for the assessment to be valid, meaning that it fully addresses the standards the teacher said he or she will address, Objective A needs to be included in the assessment.

An example of this comes from a teacher I know who had taken her students on a field trip to study monarch butterflies. She planned the final assessment as a Performance Task in which students would make a folding card where one page showed a representation of a caterpillar's egg on a leaf, the next page showed the caterpillar, the next, a chrysalis, and the final, a butterfly. But when the teacher looked back at her Domain Matrix, she found that something was missing. One of the objectives was for students to show how monarch butterflies travel down the continent to winter in Central Mexico. So she added a panel to the folding-card Performance Task where students would show the monarchs' migration. Thanks to the Domain Matrix, her final assessment was in alignment with her objectives.

There have been times where I have chosen a certain number of standards or objectives for a field trip, but when using the Domain Matrix to plan the assessment, I have realized that I had bitten off more than I could chew. The assessment would be too unwieldy. Under those circumstances, I have reduced the number of standards for the Domain Matrix. Students still might be introduced to the standards left off, but they wouldn't be held accountable for them until later. I would plan to teach these standards more fully at another time in another way.

Next let's consider the third question "How are they going to learn it?" The Domain Matrix shows whether all the activities are in alignment. Are there any activities that don't address the standards at all? Note Activity 3. This might be a favorite activity for the teacher and the students but, in its present form, it doesn't help meet any of the stated goals. As it is, the Domain Matrix shows that the activity either needs to be rehauled or sacrificed.

Now look to see if there are any objectives that lack activities. Note Objective B. The Domain Matrix indicates that the teacher needs to adjust the activities to address Objective B. Alternatively, the teacher might decide to teach Objective B at another time. If so, he or she would need to remove Objective B from the assessment.

This version of the Domain Matrix works well for a single lesson. You can make a matrix in five minutes to see if the lesson is in alignment. Every time I have used the Domain Matrix to check on a lesson, I have found ways to tweak the lesson and make it better.

Over the years, though, my colleagues and I have experimented with ways to extend the Domain Matrix and have it accomplish more. The Extended Domain Matrix is useful for a whole unit of study which might include a major field trip or several trips to the same site. See the reproducible on page 148 to find what has been added in the Extended Domain Matrix.

Extended Domain Matrix

Extended Domain Matrix for a Field Trip to _____

Essential Question(s): _____

(1) What do they need to learn?

Standards/Objectives

A. B. C. D. E. F.

Formative and Summative Assessments

Rubric for Summative Task

Gauges

(2) How will we and *they* know they learned it?

(3) What do they need to do to learn it?

Activities / Performance Tasks

Before the Trip
1. Preassessment
2.
3.
4.

During the Trip
5.
6.
7.
8.

After the Trip
9.
10. Summative Assessment(s)

Multiple Intelligences

- Verbal/Linguistic
- Logical/Mathematical
- Visual/Spatial
- Bodily/Kinesthetic
- Musical/Rhythmic
- Interpersonal
- Intrapersonal
- Naturalist

First we will concentrate on the additions, next we will look at an example, and then we will consider each aspect of the Extended Domain Matrix in more detail. On page 151, there is a step-by-step guide to planning a unit or a field trip using your own Extended Domain Matrix.

In regard to the additions in the Extended Domain Matrix, notice that the three questions are present and that there is a place for Essential Questions. To the left there is space to check how well the multiple intelligences are addressed in the activities and assessments. To the right there is a place for formative assessments to gauge students' learning from each task or activity and a place to plan a gauge for the summative or final assessment(s). If the summative assessment is a Performance Task, then a rubric is probably appropriate. See the filled-in Extended Domain Matrix on page 150 for an example.

Extended Domain Matrix for a Field Trip to The Zoo

Essential Question(s): What does it mean to be endangered?

(1) What do they need to learn?

(2) How will we and *they* know they learned it?

(3) What do they need to do to learn it?

Standards/Objectives

A. Understand characteristics of organisms
B. Understand organisms and their environments
C. Be proficient in use of technology
D. Apply knowledge of language to create print texts
E. Develop social skills
F. Develop observation skills
G.
H.

Formative and Summative Assessments / Gauges

1. Count number of correct responses
2. Written checklist
3. Anecdotal records
4. Venn diagram of students' responses
5. Observation checklist
6. Written work and discussion
7. Rubric
8. Peer assessment
9. Rubric used by self and teacher
10. Rubric for Summative Task

Multiple Intelligences

Activities / Performance Tasks	Verbal/Linguistic	Logical/Mathematical	Visual/Spatial	Bodily/Kinesthetic	Musical/Rhythmic	Interpersonal	Intrapersonal	Naturalist	A	B	C	D	E	F	G	H	Formative and Summative Assessments
Before the Trip																	
1. Preassessment. Mind Map knowledge of endangered animals.	4	3	4	2	1	3	4	4	4	4	4	4	4	4			1. Count number of correct responses
2. Research your animal in books and on the Internet; ask experts.	4	4	4	2	2	3	4	4	4	4	4	4	4	3			2. Written checklist
3. Practice observation skills.	3	1	1	2	1	3	2	4	4	4	4	4	4	4			3. Anecdotal records
4. Read children's books and analyze elements; compare with partner.	4	4	4	4	4	4	4	4	3	1	1	1	4	4			4. Venn diagram of students' responses
During the Trip																	
5. Observe animal, read, and interview expert.	4	4	4	4	1	3	3	3	3	3	1	4	4	4			5. Observation checklist
6. Draw/photograph your endangered animal.	1	4	4	2	1	1	4	4	4	4	3	4	4	4			6. Written work and discussion
7. Compare your findings with other students' findings on their animals.	4	4	2	2	1	4	4	4	4	4	3	1	4	4			7. Rubric
8. Sing songs on bus; make a stanza about your animal.	4	4	1	2	4	4	4	4	4	4	1	4	4	4			8. Peer assessment
After the Trip																	
9. Mind Map *endangered*; compare with first Mind Map.	4	4	4	3	1	1	4	4	4	4	1	2	4	3			9. Rubric used by self and teacher
10. Summative Assessment(s). Make a book on your animal for first graders. Read to them.	4	4	4	3	1	4	4	4	4	4	4	4	4	4			10. Rubric for Summative Task

Question 1: "What do the students need to learn?"

The most successful field trips are the ones with clear and appropriate goals. In his research on field trips, author Martin Storksdieck has found that rather than focusing only on narrow test-driven goals, it is wise to include other longer-term goals such as introducing students to their community's resources, increasing curiosity and a motivation to learn, and enhancing class cohesion (2006).

To begin, make a list of standards or outcomes/objectives aligned with the district's standards, as well as other objectives that would be appropriate for a field trip. Field trips lend themselves to interdisciplinary studies. The standards in the Extended Domain Matrix Example on page 150 draw from Standards from the National Science Teachers Association (NSTA), National Council of Teachers of English (NCTE), and the National Educational Technology Standards (NETS). You may decide to address standards that come from more than one discipline. You may add several objectives that are not explicitly in the district standards, based on students' interests and/or your own view of what students need such as building responsibility or self-efficacy. Notice that the teacher in the example added her own objective to develop social skills.

- Decide on an appropriate field trip to help students achieve the standards or objectives. (See chapter 5, page 217.)
- Develop an Essential Question or several that connect the standards. The Essential Question or Essential Questions may reflect other worthy goals, too. (See page 111 in chapter 3 for a description of Essential Questions.) If your school or program does not use state standards but you want the field trip to be in accordance with worthwhile academic goals, you might refer to some of the following Web sites to help you choose objectives.

National Standards and Curricula Resources

Science: National Science Teachers Association, www.nsta.org/standards

Math: National Council of Teachers of Mathematics, www.nctm.org/standards/

English/Language Arts: National Council of Teachers of English, www.ncte.org/about/over/standards

Social Studies: National Council for the Social Studies, www.socialstudies.org/standards/

Music: National Association for Music Education, www.menc.org/
publication/books/standards.htm

Art: National Standards for Art Education, www.artteacherconnec
tion.com/pages/standards.htm

Technology: National Educational Technology, http://cnets.iste.org/

State and Local Standards and Curriculum

Go to your state's Department of Education Web site.

Check with your school district.

Plan diagnostic assessments once the standards or objectives are clearly
stated. What do they already know? The diagnostic assessment can be as simple as an individual, small group, or classroom Mind Map (see page 161–162)
or other graphic organizer where students demonstrate their prior knowledge. The open-endedness of graphic organizers allows you to ascertain not
only which students already know the subject and which need to be taught the
prerequisites, but also underlying misconceptions that may not appear in a
multiple-choice or fill-in-the-blank pre-test.

The diagnostic assessment might also be a written pretest, which is
administered again at the end of the unit. There are many ways to do diagnostic assessment. What the diagnostic assessment provides is a clearer sense of
who already understands the objectives, in which case you can provide learning experiences that build on that understanding and keep them engaged. It
also helps you know who needs additional instruction to learn the current
standards successfully. Sometimes pacing guides are written as if all your students are the same; however, you know this isn't true. The diagnostic assessment gives you documentation to validate your instructional choices. Once
you are clear about what your students need to learn, the next step is to
address Question 2.

Question 2: "How will we and they know they learned it?"

With Question 2 we address three aspects of assessment. One aspect is to
make sure that the final assessment actually measures what we determined
was important from Question 1. Another aspect is to assess continuously
along the way, so that the teacher can keep track of how well students are
learning and adjust the teaching when needed. The third aspect is to recognize
the importance of self-assessment; students need to know when they have
learned. Self-assessment motivates students and gives them skills for life.

Start with backward planning, planning a summative assessment that will address each objective and only the objectives listed. Performance Tasks (see page 158–159) are particularly apt summative assessments because they show that students can transfer their learning to new situations, a criterion for true understanding. Performance Tasks are most motivating when there is a real audience. The audience might be parents who download a podcast—an audio show about the field trip from the Internet. The audience might be students in a classroom halfway around the world who watch your PowerPoint presentations about the field trip. The audience might be a class of younger students in your school who listen with awe to the stories your students tell of their adventures.

Plan gauges for measurement, such as a rubric for the summative assessment at the end and a variety of measures for formative assessment, to assess how well students are getting the idea along the way.

The primary purpose of assessment should be to help people learn. It follows then that formative assessment—assessing throughout the learning process rather than just at the end—is the most important form of assessment. Just as a plane successfully makes its way across a country through constant feedback, "on course, off course, off course, on course," learners can constantly adjust to improve their learning through formative assessment. In the same way, teachers constantly get the information they need to improve their teaching. The word *assess* comes from the Latin *assidere*, which means "to sit beside." Through formative assessment, teachers, peers acting as "critical friends," and the learners themselves (acting as their own assessors) literally or figuratively sit beside the students. Together they consider the students' work in order to help them learn. As educator Arthur Costa has stated, "The purpose of evaluation is for students to learn self-evaluation." Formative assessment is the key to achieving this purpose.

The following are some reasons for using formative assessment throughout the learning process:

- To find out what is needed along the way to assure the student's ultimate success
- To make assessment as accurate as possible by assessing by many different means
- To make the assessment itself a learning tool, not just a tool for grading
- To help teachers improve their own practice
- To teach the value of self-evaluation and personal responsibility for lifelong learning
- To help students feel good about assessment, rather than fear it

Formative assessment strategies can include the following:

- **Observation Checklists.** Matrices with name, date, and activity where a teacher notes the presence or absence of particular behaviors. Record at the time of the activity; interpret later and discuss with students.
- **Written Checklists.** Lists of elements to look for in a student-made product. Teacher, peers, or the student can check off whether the elements are present.
- **Anecdotal Records.** Teacher notes based on observations of students during activities. Record what happens on cards, sticky notes, or record sheets. Keep a file for each student.
- **Notes from Interviews.** A record with notes, based on conversations with each student. To know what a student is thinking, ask. Find out the student's goals, thinking, conclusions, problems, current self-assessments, etc. Record responses.
- **Portfolios.** A systematic, organized way to collect and review growth of knowledge, skills, and attitudes over time. Whether they are writing, subject-specific, electronic, audio, or video, use portfolios to enable students/teachers to reflect on, question, and look for patterns in their own learning process. Often students choose their own work samples and share their thinking about their work. Portfolios serve both as formative assessments and summative assessments.
- **Journals.** Written collections of the students' or teachers' reflections. Use prompts (e.g., "The most valuable thing for me ....", "I felt confused when ....", "An assumption I had been making was ....") or Learning Logs with matrices to be filled in; Mind Map journals (subject specific; free form, etc.)
- **Written Tests or Quizzes.**
- **Tickets Out.** Assessments where students give the teacher their answers to one to three questions on cards as they leave the classroom. The teacher divides the cards into a pile of those who definitely understand and can move on and a second pile of those who don't understand or show only partial understanding. Students whose tickets out are in the second pile need to be retaught.
- **Rubrics.** Scoring tools based on a number of different criteria, delineating what counts in a product or performance, with indicators that articulate gradations of quality. Rubrics make the assessments of products or performances more valid. Rubrics are often matrices with indicators, describing performance levels, for each assessment criterion. Choose criteria based on objectives. Describe indicators, achievement levels for each criterion, by collecting and observing

learners' work over time. Rubrics externalize the assessor's internal, often intuitive way of assessing. With rubrics, learners self-assess their progress and make improvements as they go instead of waiting until the end for a grade. When learners help design the rubrics, their discernment about quality soars. There are Web sites that can help you design rubrics such as Rubistar (www.4teachers.org).

○ **Self-Assessments.** (This type of assessment is often used with a written checklist or rubric to increase objectivity.) Make student self-assessment a priority. Self-assessment, through a rubric, reflective writing, hand signals, or discussion, is key. The highest purpose of assessment is for students to learn self-assessment. Self-assessments help students know that they have learned. That awareness is important to self-efficacy.

○ **Peer Assessments.** These help all learners develop discrimination. Peers can give their assessments on written checklists or rubrics, along with teacher assessment and self-assessment. Students may assess others' work. Here are two ways:

> *Star-Wish-Star.* Write on a sticky note a Star(*), a positive; a Wish, a suggestion to make it better next time; and a Star(*), another positive.

> *"Critical Friends."* A student critiques another's work to help his or her partner prepare a performance or product for its final presentation.

Competence in providing peer evaluation is a useful social skill and is a means to develop discernment about quality work. Even if your district doesn't allow for peer assessment for grades, students may still help each other with formative assessment.

○ **Assessment Quickies.** (see page 156–157). These are instantaneous ways to check each student's assessment of his or her understanding.

○ **Others.** There are many other ways to get formative assessment. Use the formative assessment to assess the effectiveness of your own teaching. How well are students developing the understanding they will need to succeed? What do you need to reteach? In what ways might you change to help students learn more effectively?

Assessment Quickies—Assess Your Whole Group Instantly

Thumbs Up—Thumbs Down

To check for understanding of directions or information learned, suggest that each student make a fist with his or her thumb

 1. up in front of the chest if his or her answer to a question is a definite yes.

 2. down in front of the chest if the answer is no.

 3. horizontal to signify maybe or not sure.

Levels of Understanding

After explaining a set of directions or a new idea or technique, ask students to display their level of understanding.

 Students hold up four fingers and repeat after you "I understand this so well, I can teach it to someone else."

 Students hold up three fingers and repeat "I understand this, but don't ask me to teach it."

 Students hold up two fingers and repeat "I'm a little confused."

 Students hold up one finger and repeat "I haven't got a clue."

About Assessment Quickies

Assessment Quickies provide the teacher and students with immediate feedback from the group. Students who understood the directions or lesson become resources to others who may not have understood the idea the first time. Students like these processes so much that they remind teachers to use them. These processes contribute greatly to safety, clarity, reflection, and self-responsibility. Many teachers in my workshops have reported that these strategies are favorites with their classes.

Assessment Quickies

Why Use Assessment Quickies?

To instantaneously assess the group's

- opinions
- understanding of directions
- understanding of new learning
- understanding of each other

To encourage

- metacognition—students become aware of their own thinking
- self-assessment and peer assessment, rather than relying on the teacher as the only judge
- a sense of personal responsibility for getting the information
- students to use each other as resources

To provide a means for teachers to evaluate their effectiveness in the moment

When to Use the Assessment Quickies

Thumbs Up, Thumbs Down, Thumbs Horizontal. Use this during a meeting or class discussion before a field trip, to check for students' clarity about what to do or what they are learning during a trip, and/or to get the group's opinions or learning after a trip. Keeping fists in front of the chest for privacy reduces the likelihood that a student's vote is influenced by others. Or make the vote public, so that students can see others' responses to their questions or statements. Questions may come from the teacher. Even better, questions may come from the students themselves. In this way, they are assessing others' answers and also learning to listen to other people's point of view.

Levels of Understanding. Use this to find out if the students understand the directions or content given. If most students hold up three or four fingers and there are only a few two's and one's, ask the two's and one's to find a four. The four may be able to explain the information better than you did. If most of the students hold up one or two fingers, you probably weren't very clear and you need to explain it again. This simple tool provides you with immediate feedback on the effectiveness of your communication. This is far better than finding out days later on a test that the students didn't understand. The Levels of Understanding give you and the students an immediate second chance.

I learned the Levels of Understanding while teaching at SuperCamp, a program that helps enhance students' self-esteem while improving their academics. See www.supercamp.com for more information on SuperCamp.

Performance Tasks

An Example of a Performance Task After a Field Trip to a Music Concert

Background. For the last three weeks you have learned about sound, including causes of sound waves, loudness, pitch, and how sound moves from the air through the ear and to the brain. You have also learned about technological design and musical instruments. Last week you attended a concert and heard an orchestra.

Task. Using inexpensive, readily available materials, you will design and make a musical instrument to perform a song. Then you will explain how you made your instrument, how it makes sounds, and an instrument in the orchestra that make sounds in a similar way.

Audience. The parents at parents' night

Purpose. To experience the usefulness of your study of sound as you educate and entertain others

Procedure

1. Brainstorm in groups of three or four a list of musical instruments you could make.
2. Choose materials from school or home from which to make the instrument.
3. Draw a plan for the instrument.
4. Make the instrument and write how you made it.
5. Describe any changes from your original plan and why you made the changes.
6. Share with a critical friend. Help your friend succeed. Let your friend help you.
7. Play the instrument and show how to change the loudness and pitch.
8. Describe how the sound is made and how it gets through air, the ear, and to the brain.
9. Name an instrument in the orchestra you heard last week that makes sounds in a similar way.

Use Backward Planning. Design the Performance Task as soon as you are clear on the objectives. Make sure the Performance Task includes all the objectives. Then plan activities that will meet the objectives and help the student be able to do the Performance Task. It usually takes a number of trials to design an appropriate Performance Task.

Validity is an essential word in assessment. Validity means that you assess what matters. With the performance assessment previously described, the student demonstrates understanding by transferring the learning to a new situation, rather than regurgitating predigested information. Performance tasks, whether used on the job or in a school setting, are valid assessments because they measure what matters.

Why Use Performance Tasks?

- To improve learning (this is the primary purpose)
- To improve teaching practice
- To evaluate methods and programs
- To evaluate the field trip
- To summarize and certify students' achievement
- To report to parents and the public

About Performance Tasks

Assessment involves one of the deepest and most personal issues that arise in the human experience—that of being judged. The judgment is valuable if the assessment helps students find out what they know and to clarify their next steps. The assessment is doubly valuable when the assessment increases learning and understanding at the same time as it assesses. This is the value of performance assessment.

Performance assessments are products or performances that indicate the degree to which the student has mastered the objectives. The objectives assessed in a Performance Task can include academic understanding, social skills, problem-solving proficiency, and whatever else the facilitator and students deem important.

Performance Tasks

How to Use Performance Tasks

To design a Performance Task, use a second person. Speak directly to the learner. Consider the standards or objectives and the Essential Question and complete the statement suggested by assessment guru Grant Wiggins, "The students REALLY have the idea only if they can . . . ."

Give students instructions for the Performance Task such as the following:

- **Background.** Refer to the field trip students have taken and/or the knowledge and skills they have gained that have prepared them for this task.
- **Task.** Have the student design a performance or product that meets all the instructional objectives and is based on a simulation or real-world problem for students to solve.
- **Audience.** Name a real or imaginary audience to experience the product or performance.
- **Purpose.** Show students why this is a worthwhile project in terms of the goals of the course or subject.
- **Procedure.** Outline each step the student must take to complete the performance.
- **Assessment.** Design a rubric that provides the criteria and indicators by which the performance will be assessed. Students can assist in designing the rubric by comparing models of excellence with mediocre examples. Some Web sites that provide ready-made rubrics or help in designing yours are www.rubrics4teachers.com, http://rubistar.4teachers.org/index.php, and www.teachervision.com/lesson-plans/lesson-6364.html.

When to Use Performance Tasks

A Performance Task of this complexity is usually the culmination of a unit or course. Simpler Performance Tasks for formative assessment can be used continuously and can be evaluated with checklists.

For more information, read *Understanding by Design* by Grant Wiggins and Jay McTighe (2005). For more on the Performance Task format read *A Teacher's Guide to Performance-Based Learning and Assessment* by Michael Hibbard and the Teachers of Connecticut's Pomperaug School District 15 (1996).

Examples of Performance Tasks After Field Trips

art show modeled on art gallery

bulletin board display

business letter

cartoon or comic

cause and effect essay

children's book

cinquain poem

classroom blog

clay animation

collage

composing and performing a song

consumer decision making

creation myth

data table or chart

display

drawing or illustration, creative

drawing or illustration, technical

editorial

ethnic food

event chain graphic organizer

experiment, designing and troubleshooting

expository essay

fairy tale

field guide

folktale

friendly letter

geographic game

grant application simulation

graph

graphic design

group work

history book chapter

Idea Web Graphic Organizer

information problem solving

interview

invention

issue controversy

journal, geographic

land-use survey

letter asking for information

letter to the editor

management plan for a group project

math problem solving

Mind Map

models, 3-D or 2-D

movement map

multimedia show

museum replication

musical instrument, make or play

music video

newspaper article

observations

oral report with visuals

pamphlet

peer editing

persuasive writing

photo journal, online

podcast—online radio show

portfolio of field trip

poster

PowerPoint show

reading journal for a novel

research report

science fair display

scrapbook

skit

slide show or photo essay

sound map

story

survey

time line graphic organizer

travel brochure

tribute or eulogy

Venn Diagram

video

virtual field trip for other students

weather map

Web page, perhaps on the school Web site

writing fiction

writing nonfiction

Adapted from a list made by a districtwide team of teachers from Pomerang School District 15 in Connecticut.

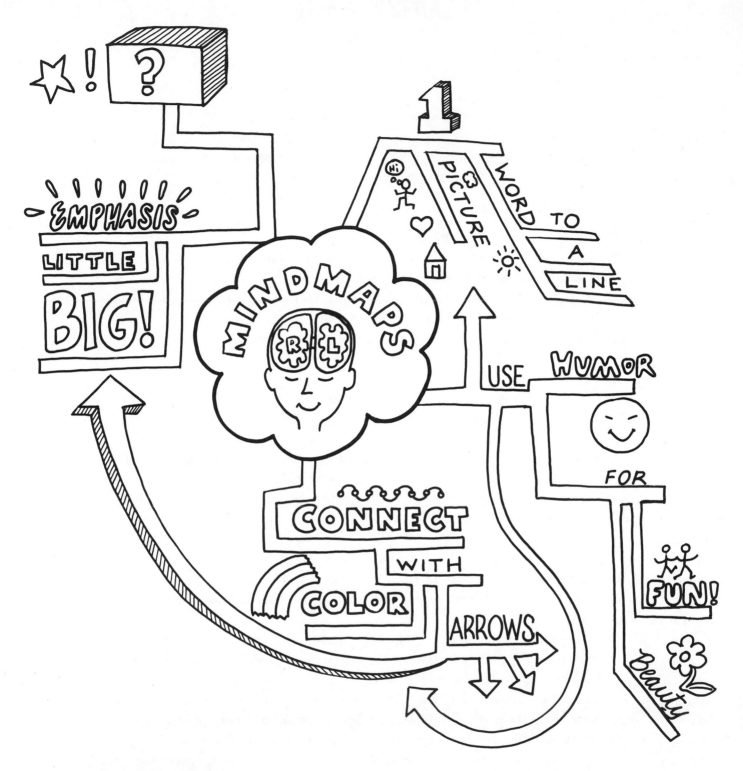

About Mind Mapping

Students all over the world are writing notes line-by-line or, in some languages, column-by-column. But the brain stores information by pattern and association. Mind Mapping was designed by Tony Buzan as an alternative to outlining and as a means of tapping into the enormous potential of the brain. Mind Maps actually look like the tree-like, neurological connections in the brain they reflect. Corporations, schools, and individuals report that Mind Mapping enables them to make huge strides in meeting their goals.

Mind Mapping

Why Use Mind Mapping?

- To think faster and more creatively and organize your thinking
- To get more done in less time
- To improve memory—retention of information
- To generate and record a huge amount of information in a small space
- To reflect the ways brains actually store information—through patterns and association
- To enable a teacher to literally see students' thinking

How to Make a Mind Map

- Use colored pens and highlighters.
- Draw a colorful doodle and write a title for the topic in the center of the page.
- Radiate lines off from the center with the main ideas.
- Use one key word to a line (to get to the essence and to allow for more associations).
- Branch out from the main lines with associations and/or supporting ideas.
- Draw many pictures because "a picture is worth a thousand words."
- Use CAPITAL LETTERS to make it easier to read later.
- Include color and arrows to show connections.
- Use color, highlighters, exclamation points, asterisks, stars, and boxes to show importance.

Use Mind Maps with

- the whole group—on a chalkboard, flip chart, or computer that is projected onto a larger screen.
- teams of two, three, or four. Each person uses a different color to show participation.
- individuals. Students may keep Mind Maps in portfolios, journals, or on their laptop computer using software programs such as Inspiration.

When to Use Mind Maps

- To brainstorm ideas for the field trip
- As a preassessment before the field trip to uncover students' previous knowledge and possible misconceptions
- To take notes during the field trip. Using keywords and doodles, students quickly jot down observations and information from the docent or from written descriptions. Students become active organizers of the new information.
- For reading—students base the Mind Map on their own questions, to read smarter
- For problem solving—Mind Map elements of problems, possible solutions, action plan
- For review—at the end of class or beginning of next class for long-term memory
- For assessment—compare Mind Maps before the field trip and after the field trip: celebrate new learning

For more information, refer to Tony Buzan's *The Mind Map Book: Radiant Thinking* (1993), Nancy Marguelies and Nusa Maals's *Mapping Inner Space: Learning and Teaching Visual Mapping* (2001), or Michael Gelb's *Mind Mapping: How to Liberate Your Natural Genius* (1998).

Software programs, such as Inspiration and Mind Mapper Jr. for kids, enable students to make Mind Maps with color and pictures directly on a computer.

Question 3: "How will the students learn it?"

Plan activities and Performance Tasks that are aligned with the outcomes and objectives and are exactly what is needed for the student to succeed at the summative assessment. For each activity and Performance Task, plan a gauge (described previously) to formally or informally measure students' understanding. While these ideas apply to any learning experience, in the rest of this chapter we will apply Question 3, "How will the students learn it?", to field trips. We will look at many ways to help students learn before, during, and after their field trips.

Appeal to Multiple Intelligences

The multiple intelligences (MI) theory is based on the premise that human beings perceive the world in at least eight different, equally important ways and that schools should foster all those ways of perceiving (Project Zero www.pz.harvard.edu/Research/Research.htm). This theory was first proposed by Dr. Howard Gardner (1993). One reason why students usually enjoy field trips so much is that field trips encourage them to use their multiple intelligences. Activities based on the multiple intelligences can also differentiate instruction by giving students some choice in how to learn the subject.

The Domain Matrix includes a way to gauge how well your plan addresses the multiple intelligences. In the Domain Matrix, check off which intelligences are being addressed by each activity and Performance Task to make sure you reach all kinds of students. Note that every activity involves a variety of intelligences. Use the matrix to ensure that there is some balance in the use of intelligences. Do your best to include all the intelligences at least somewhere in the unit.

The following is a list of each intelligence with some suggestions for using that intelligence before, during, and after the field trip:

Verbal/Linguistic

Some Possibilities Before the Trip

- Discuss the purpose of the trip and how it relates to the current studies.
- Learn vocabulary words that will be used by docents during the tour.
- Practice asking good questions.
- Listen to stories told or read by the teacher that relate to the trip.
- Hear a lecture.
- Research key topics that relate to the trip through the Internet, library, experts, or books provided by the teacher.
- Develop Essential Questions based on your interests and the required standards.

- Focus on certain concepts alone or in small groups.

Some Possibilities During the Trip

- Write observations. Your observations could be based on an Essential Question or on your assigned or chosen focus.
- Keep a field book with data gathered in response to prior questions, new questions, sketches, reflections, etc.
- Write answers to teacher's questions or your own questions.
- Interview experts.
- Take oral histories.
- Lynn Wagner is the educational coordinator of Camp Silos, a Web site that highlights the development of American agriculture (www.campsilos.org or www.silosandsmokestacks.org). (Contact her at info@silosandsmokestacks.org.) She suggests that you choose an object that interests you and write about the following:
  > Expand the title or name of this object into a detailed caption (sentence or paragraph) in your Field Book.
  > Describe the setting in which you might have found this object.

Some Possibilities After the Trip

- Give oral presentations based on Essential Questions or particular focus to your own class, another class, or a group of parents.
- Use storytelling to describe what was learned.
- Take part in a debate.
- Write poems, myths, legends, plays, stories, or nonfiction.
- Write a story about a character in a painting.
- Develop vocabulary lists based on field trip observations.
- Record field trip observations in a classroom journal.
- Write an article on the field trip for the local, school, or class newspaper.
- Write an article critiquing the paintings or sculptures viewed.
- Publish a museum guide book.

Logical/Mathematical

Some Possibilities Before the Trip

- Using ThinkTrix anchors (see pages 122–125 for information about ThinkTrix), you and your teacher develop questions to answer on the trip.

- Help plan logistics:
  - > Help with grant proposals and documentation
  - > Help keep track as money comes in from fund-raising
  - > Plan out the itinerary, in a step-by-step fashion
  - > Make a budget
  - > Make a system to organize materials for the trip and then keep everything organized
- Use math skills to calculate the cost and/or the distance to be traveled (see page 220 for a reproducible sheet).

Some Possibilities During the Trip

- David Dennis is the Southern Field Director of the Algebra Project, a nationwide project to help poor minority children become proficient in mathematics. He offers the following suggestions for making mathematical connections with field trips. Students can calculate
  - > travel time over distance.
  - > gas mileage.
  - > square miles and acreage.
  - > linear distances such as golf course yardage.
  - > sales tax, discounts, volume buying, profit margins, advertising, and labor costs.
  - > menu math and algebraic functions.
  - > linear graphs that graph cars per day/week/month.
  - > volume and ratios at water treatment plants.
  - > estimating, cost accounting, budgets, and square footage.
- According to walking guide Peter Chausse, you can involve students in a variety of math activities on any walk. Here are some of his suggestions:
  - > Bring a tape measure to measure the circumference of trees and other round objects. Have students guess what the circumference of a tree will be (reminding them that the circumference is 3.14 times the diameter), and then start measuring. Their initial guesses may be way off, but their approximation skills will improve with practice.
  - > Find many types of geometric shapes. Have students compile lists of geometric shapes seen in the windows of buildings: squares, triangles, rectangles, octagons, etc.
  - > Look for symmetry on buildings or in parks.
  - > Look for patterns.
- Educational coordinator Lynn Wagner of Waterloo, Iowa, suggests using logic to answer questions such as the following:
  - > How are these two objects different from one another?

> What clues does this artifact provide about ... ?
> In what ways do these two objects relate to one another?
> List the objects in the exhibit in order of usefulness.
> Which object took the most time and effort to produce?
> If you could change one thing in this exhibit, what would it be?
> Pretend you are an archaeologist in the future who is observing this object. What would you be able to conclude about the culture of the past?
> Pretend you are an astronaut on a mission to another planet. Gather data and send a report home as an e-postcard.
> Have time studies (How many seconds is the traffic light red?) or traffic studies (How many cars pass by this spot in one minute?) to see the importance of math in the real world.

- Keep track of the sequence of events.
- Test hypotheses.
- Solve problems that arise in a systematic way.
- Solve a mystery with teacher-provided clues.
- Play 20 Questions on the way home. Someone thinks of a person, place, or thing he or she experienced on the trip. Others have 20 questions to guess. Students must give a logical rationale for their guesses.
- Rank in order the value or significance of different aspects of the trip.
- Collect data.
- Answer ThinkTrix questions (see pages 122–123). Students look for causes or effects, similarities and differences, the essence and/or examples of that essence. Then they make evaluations.
- Follow the Taxonomy for Discovery (see pages 114–115). Write observations, organize findings, look for patterns, and develop hypotheses or theories.

Some Possibilities After the Trip

- Graph the data; interpret the data.
- Complete the Taxonomy for Discovery by developing hypotheses or theories, based on observations during the field trip.
- Do further research to validate or disprove the hypotheses.
- Develop student-generated ThinkTrix questions to review the trip.
- Use student-generated ThinkTrix questions for posttrip tests.
- Make a milepost in the classroom or school hall, suggests Peter Chausse. The milepost is an artwork that looks like the posts seen in M*A*S*H units. The post points to locations in several directions and

tells the reader the distances to those places. Young children might create signs for the post telling how many paces and which direction it is to the gym, office, auditorium, etc., while more advanced students can consult maps and use compasses to record locations and distance of places throughout the local community, the United States, and the world.

Visual/Spatial

Some Possibilities Before the Trip

- Explore the Web site of the destination.
- Do a teacher-monitored Web search about the topic.
- See photographs. Teacher and consultant Sarah Shellow suggests that teachers get postcards or other photographs related to the field trip. Students sit back to back. One student describes the photograph while the other student draws. Then they compare the photographs and drawings and celebrate their communication success.
- See videos of the site or about the topic.
- Develop visual observation skills. Students might describe objects around the room in detail to their partners.
- Brainstorm a list of open-ended questions to focus the trip. Write them in field trip journals.
- Immerse students in the culture first—set up the classroom as a farm or another country.
- Use postcards. Educational consultant Bonnie Tsai points out that the average visitor to an art gallery spends 10 seconds in front of a painting. Imagine if we only gave a piece of music 10 seconds! Art needs time. To sensitize students before going to an art exhibit, Tsai suggests passing out postcards of artwork and inviting students to ask questions such as the following:
  - > "Why did the artist make the sky so high?"
  - > "How did the artist feel?"
  - > "What if the lines were straight?" (Then students draw or paint their own version with straight lines or a lower sky or whatever else the student wondered about.)
- Gail Heidenhain of Atlanta, Georgia, president of the International Alliance for Learning (IAL), has another suggestion for using postcards to give students keys to focus on art. She passes out postcards to each student of paintings with people in them. Then she invites each student to study his or her painting, looking for as many details of line, spacing,

and color as the student can find. Next students exchange postcards with their partners and, without looking, describe as many details about the painting as possible. Finally each student looks at his or her original postcard, imagines becoming a person in the painting, and shares a story of that person's life with a partner. This exercise gives students both an objective view of the painting and an emotional connection with it. When the students visit the art gallery, they can use these tools to help them appreciate the artwork more fully.

Some Possibilities During the Trip

- Use sketch books. Molly Pirrung, a teacher in Silver Spring, Maryland, suggests having students sketch artifacts, structures, scenery, etc. If they cannot complete their sketches, encourage them to label them for future completion as to color, detail, etc. When students draw what they observe on the trip, their perceptual skills are heightened. When they describe what they see before they draw, their drawings become more accurate and detailed.
- Make Mind Maps (see pages 161–162) or other graphic organizers. Students can quickly record important ideas using key words and doodles. This is especially useful if there isn't enough time to write all the information and reflections.
- Look through peepholes in construction paper. Cut different-sized round holes in construction paper. Students view a part of the exhibition through the peepholes. Ask them to describe what they see, what they notice now that they missed before, and how their perspective changes with each new view.
- Wear costumes. Maryland teacher Anne Fretz tells of her students dressing in colonial costumes as they took a tour through the old city of Alexandria, Virginia.
- Complete partial drawings of objects found in the exhibits, based on observations.
- Make hand-drawn postcards and write a summary of the field trip visit. Summarizing is one of the most effective ways to ensure learning.

Some Possibilities After the Trip

- Make videos.
- Make a gallery of photographs with descriptions on the wall at school.
- Make a photo album.

- Make PowerPoint shows, posters, or murals.
- Develop a classroom museum(see page 194) that replicates and extends displays students observed on the field trip. For example, have an art show with a setup for students' artwork, with captions, like the art gallery visited or have a museum exhibit like the museum exhibits visited.
- Set up bulletin boards for the classroom or the school with materials developed or collected during the field trip such as photos, drawings, write-ups, or a time line to show the sequence of events.
- Make a paper, cloth, or digital quilt. Each student makes a square that represents learning from the field trip. If the quilt square is digital, it can even be animated!
- Make video animations about your field trip. Students who live in the San Francisco area can take a field trip to Zeum, where they can create animations, experiment with digital graphics, produce music videos, and explore hands-on exhibits (www.zeum.org/education/fieldtrips/ main.html).
- Make graphic organizers.
- Make books and illustrate them.
- Make dolls.
- Make brochures to sell or market the trip.
- Have a cartoon strip for each field trip. At the end of the school year, make a comic book.
- Draw, paint, or sculpt what was learned.
- Make an architectural drawing.
- Make maps.
- Make a board game or card game.
- Make a school art gallery to display students' paintings, sculptures, and other works (with captions) based on their field trips.
- Make murals, ceramic tiles, or mosaics.

Bodily/Kinesthetic

Some Possibilities Before the Trip

- Act out what you will do and how you will behave to "pave the way" for appropriate behavior on the trip.
- Role play what you expect to see on the trip. For instance, before I took my sixth grade students to see Shakespeare's *Merry Wives of Windsor*, I gave them a summary. Students took turns playing the characters and making up their own dialogue. When they actually saw the play, they were easily able to follow the dialogue and plot.
- Link learning with exercise. Susan Fort suggests finding out the distance

to the field trip site and walking, running, or dancing that distance over days, weeks, or months in advance of the trip.

Learn Through Exercise

Goal: Students exercise while learning about geography.

Example: Students are taking a year-end trip to Florida. Florida is 880 miles from Baltimore. As part of the learning experience to prepare for the trip, the teacher challenges the students to "exercise" their way to Florida.

- Students can determine the route they want to take. This will teach them how to read and use a map.
- Teacher and students should determine how many miles a certain activity warrants. For example:
  > Walking for 20 minutes = 1 mile
  > Biking for . . . .
  > Running for . . . .
  > Playing basketball for . . . .
  > Dancing for . . . .
  > Playing baseball for . . . .
  > Playing games at recess for . . . .
- Each day the students tally up the number of miles they have traveled toward Florida in class, based on the amount of time they have exercised. They should plot the distances traveled on a U. S. map in the classroom.
- Teachers can focus lessons on "stops" along the way. Lessons could include geography, science, history, math, etc. and focus on local food, weird facts, and interesting trivia. Students could be encouraged to share stories if they have actually visited the "stops" along the way.

—Susan Fort, educational consultant, Baltimore, Maryland

Some Possibilities During the Trip

- Use agreed-upon physical gestures for students to know when to be quiet, when to move on, etc.
- Touch, walk, do.
- Take a movement-oriented field trip where students carefully observe the movements of people, animals, machines, clouds—whatever is moving. Students can make a "movement map," noting where the movements were observed.

- Take stretch breaks during the bus ride or between parts of the trip.
- Take part in scavenger hunts where students must find information, objects, or places relevant to the trip's objectives. According to field trip guide Peter Chausse:

Sometimes a well-planned scavenger hunt can be lots of fun. A teacher in Portland came up with a creative idea for her students after we took a tree walk to learn more about tree identification in a local park. After discussing tree leaves, cones, and seeds as we circled a park, she created a series of task cards for four groups. The cards read something like this: Find a Douglas fir cone, a gingko leaf, an acorn for an oak tree, etc. Students had to recall where those trees were. Then they ran to those trees in search of the requested items. Once they returned, they were given another card. Four sets of cards were made (one set for each group) and the cards were arranged so that the teams were not searching for the same items at the same time. This was great fun as it reinforced learning, while providing physical activity and group cooperation.

In organizing a scavenger hunt, be sure the area is safe to run in (find an area free from roads, sharp objects, or slippery terrain), and be sure that students can be seen from a central location. Keep groups together and provide a reasonable amount of time for the activity. I'd recommend 10 to 15 minutes.

- Take a free-play break to allow students to get some exercise and run off excess energy.

Some Possibilities After the Trip

- Play charades where students pantomime some aspect of learning from the trip while others guess to recall sequence of events or what was learned on the trip.
- Design a movement or sequence of movements to explain what was learned.
- Reenact the field trip for other classes.
- Make models of what was learned. Have a corner with a variety of materials such as glue, tape, construction paper, colored spaghetti, buttons, feathers, straws, balloons, packing material, small boxes, etc. The point is not the model itself but how well students can explain what the elements of the model symbolize and how those elements relate to each other.
- Become a living museum. Dress up as a famous person. Use a poster to help describe that person's achievements. Answer questions as the person.

- ❍ Participate in improv theater skits about the field trip.
- ❍ Make three-dimensional figures with clay or Legos.
- ❍ Make clay animation. Build clay figures and then use multimedia tools to make a short animated film. Build storytelling and sequencing skills while depicting a scene from a play, a historical event, a scientific principle, or the field trip itself.
- ❍ Make a time capsule of each trip and open them at the end of the year.

Firsthand Learning About Endangered Animals

My fourth grade students took a field trip to the zoo. The focus was endangered animals of the tropical rainforest. Our guide gave us a hands-on experience of what *endangered* means. He told us a story about a happy marsh where many alligators and other animals lived. He put a sticky note on the wall to represent each alligator. In his story, some people who lived nearby had a great idea for making money. They would use the hides of alligators to make belts, shoes, and purses. The guide removed a sticky note for each item mentioned. Customers liked the alligator products. As demand went up, the alligator population went down. The guide removed the sticky notes until only a few were left. "There comes a time," he said, "when the population gets too low to continue. When that happens, the animal species becomes extinct. Now, what we humans have to do is distinguish between needs and wants. People need shoes and belts. But they don't need to be made out of alligator skin." In a discussion that followed, students applied the point of that story to other endangered animals.

Next, we went out to see the animals. Different groups of students zeroed in on different animals. They carefully drew the animals, which definitely enhanced their observation skills. They collected as much information about their animals as possible when they were at the zoo. They read about their animals and interviewed the zookeepers.

Later, back at school they researched their animals further. For the final project they made a children's book to teach younger children about these endangered animals. For example one book, a "feely book," was called *Lester, The Golden Lion Tamarin*. These students wrote about a little Brazilian monkey they saw at the zoo, who was being taught how to get its own food. The golden lion tamarins are allowed out of their cages and travel freely across the tree canopy. Bananas and other fruits were tied to trees at the zoo for the monkeys to pick. Volunteers monitor the monkeys' behavior and help keep them safe. The zoo has a program to release these monkeys back to repopulate the Brazilian rainforest.

—Kathleen Carroll

Note: The Extended Domain Matrix Example on page 150 is based on this field trip.

Musical/Rhythmic

Some Possibilities Before the Trip

- Listen to music and/or songs that relate to the time or the culture.
- Listen to and learn songs that teach about the topic to be studied.
- Connect the trip with current music, music awards, television programming.
- Listen to songs with messages that remind students to treat one another well.

Some Possibilities During the Trip

- Listen to the music or sing the songs on the way to the site.
- Listen in silence to the sounds of the environment such as ocean sounds, bird calls, the wind through the trees, city sounds, etc.
- Make a recording of sounds on each field trip. Look for similarities and differences in the sounds of different places.
- Listen for and indicate rhythmical patterns.

Some Possibilities After the Trip

- After listening to sounds of a neighborhood, come back, think through your walk, and make pictures of sounds that you heard.
- Make a sound map. On a map of your field trip, add pictures of what made the sounds heard.
- Make a song or rap that summarizes the trip or the aspect of the trip that a particular group focused on.
- Make a musical video.
- Explain how the music and/or words of a song are similar to what was learned on the field trip.
- Give a presentation with appropriate music to accompany it.
- Make an instrument and use it to demonstrate what was learned.
- Create a dance. After making a song or rap that shows the sequence or summarizes the main learning from the trip, make hand motions or steps that reinforce the words of the song. Or make a sequence of movements that symbolize the trip, and then put the movements to music. Or choose music that you think best represents the idea and then improvise a dance in time with that music. For instance, become a school of fish that switches directions with each imagined threat, or improvise a dance that symbolizes New York City, the ocean during a

hurricane, or a forest awakening in the morning. (See Chapter 3, page 134, for a more detailed description of the use of dance.)

- Design a musical performance about the trip.

Interpersonal

Some Possibilities Before the Trip

- Brainstorm and research together.
- Conduct a planning meeting to decide which trip to take and how to pay for it.
- Make Essential Questions. Small groups plan how they will collect information, who will do what before, during, and after the trip, and how they will show they know.

Some Possibilities During the Trip

- Have trip buddies that look out for each other and answer questions together.
- Think-Pair-Share (see page 100) responses to questions, observations, and personal reflections.
- Take turns describing in detail everything observed. Creativity expert Win Wenger assures us that the more students describe what they observe to each other, the more their perceptiveness increases.
- Problem solve in groups.
- Break up the tasks. Some students do agreed-upon research or other tasks. Other students check to see that they have done what they agreed to do. Use the cooperative learning jigsaw strategy: individual or small groups learn some aspect of the topic and then teach others.
- Interview people to find out about career possibilities.
- Take oral histories.
- Take part in a service project, either as the main focus or as a part of any trip. Even if the main focus is something other than service, students might clean up the area, plant a tree (with permission, of course), or participate in some form of service arranged in advance with the site managers.
- At an art gallery, sit on the floor and look at a representational painting of some complexity for 10 minutes. Then go into another room where each student shares what he or she saw. Students become aware of the differences in perception, differences in cultures, and observational biases. They develop stronger connections with other students.

Graduate students at the Yale School of Management experienced this class-building activity recently; elementary school students could get a similar value from it.

- Take part in trust-building activities (see page 104) to build class community.

Some Possibilities After the Trip

- Have a class discussion about what was learned and how it relates to the curriculum.
- Give feedback to one another.
- Make up questions based on the trip to assess each other's knowledge.
- Do an inside/outside circle review of the trip. The class forms two concentric circles. Partners face each other, one in the inside circle and the other on the outside circle. When the music begins, the outside circle moves in a counterclockwise direction. When the music stops, each student is standing before a new partner. Students ask each other debriefing questions. When the music begins again, each student moves to a new partner.
- Have a quiz show. Students can help design the questions. You might include ThinkTrix questions (see pages 122–125) to assure that higher-level thinking is included.
- Do a round robin. Students in small groups write or speak in turn about what they learned.
- Take a trunk show about your field trip to another class.
- Make up games to help prepare the next group.
- Write thank-you notes to chaperones, docents, bus drivers, funders, and anyone who contributed to the trip. Include a summary of what was learned and favorite aspects of the trip.
- Have group projects. Make sure that each student has an individual responsibility toward the completion of the project. Make sure that students have been taught the social skills needed for successful teamwork.
- Use GameIt! with Word, a collection of over 100 games in five different game formats, designed to support curriculum for language arts, science, math, and social science. Available at www.ftcpublishing.com, these games reinforce learning while creating a motivating environment for the K–5 classroom. You can also design your own games using one of the subject-specific game templates for Word, including game styles for Jeopardy, Millionaire, Tic-Tac-Toe, Bingo, and MatchIt! Students can design games, too.

Intrapersonal

Some Possibilities Before the Trip

- Research the subject to be studied and the field trip site.
- Connect the field trip with current events such as local, national, and world competitions, weather extremes, space travel and its costs, broader environmental legislation, and extinction.
- Connect the field trip with personal interests and/or challenges.
- Design your own Essential Questions to explore on the trip (see page 111).
- Make personal goals.

Some Possibilities During the Trip

- Assess your behavior and learning on the field trip.
- Collect information to answer your Essential Questions.
- Write observations and reflections.
- Come up with metaphors and analogies to represent what is observed such as "the capitol building is like a beehive because it is busy and each person has his or her particular job to do" or "the waterfall is like a mountain of diamonds shining bright."
- Imagine becoming the person, animal, plant, building, or artifact being studied. Record your insights.
- Respond to these questions and suggestions designed by Camp Silos educational coordinator Lynn Wagner of Waterloo, Iowa:
  - > Pretend you are an archaeologist in the future who is observing this object. What would you be able to conclude about the culture of the past?
  - > Which object will be of greatest value in a hundred years? Why?
  - > List the objects in the exhibit in order of usefulness or the story they tell.
  - > Pretend you are a character in this exhibit. Tell us as much as you can about your life.
  - > What does this object tell us about the person's attitude toward . . . ?
- Poll the class. After careful observation of an exhibit, students vote on an artifact or artwork that they consider the most valuable part of the exhibit they viewed. Each student then records one sentence in his or her field book, describing why the student felt the object was of key importance.

Some Possibilities After the Trip

- Reflect in journals on what you learned about the topic, about taking a field trip, or about yourself. How will you use this knowledge? How will it make a difference in your life?
- Answer follow-up questions such as: If you could change something about this field trip site or the trip itself, what would it be?
- Did you meet your goals? Why or why not?
- Write or tell how this trip changed you as a person.
- Record your observations on a tape recorder or iPod.
- Compare observations from different field trips.
- Did you gather enough information to answer your Essential Questions? What could you do to answer them more fully?
- What new questions do you have?
- Write poems in relation to the field trip.
- Write one fact your parents probably don't know. Virginia teacher Jennifer Pavol says this solves the "What did you do today?" "Nothing." problem.
- Find ways to continue learning about what interested you. Will you return to the museum or other site with your family? Will you find an expert to mentor you?

Naturalist

Some Possibilities Before the Trip

- Use an Affinity Chart (see page 110) to find out what students already know and want to learn from this trip.
- Have students write about and share a time they experienced a sense of awe and wonder.

Some Possibilities During the Trip

- Observe plants, rocks, and/or the sky. Make a collage of natural items found (if it is permissible to do so at your field trip site). Draw and describe the plants, animals, architecture, or bridges.
- Tend a flower or vegetable garden; plant a tree. Creative teachers integrate gardening with many state standards in science (botany, ecology), social studies (Colonial farms, medicinal herbs, agriculture historically and in cultures around the world), math (measure the plants' growth, weigh the pumpkins), literature (relating the garden to those in books such as the garden in Beatrix Potter books), and health (cook foods from the garden for healthy eating).

○ Use binoculars, telescopes, microscopes, or magnifiers to extend your senses.

○ Press plants or collect rocks. Compare samples from different environments.

○ Interview naturalists about careers in their field.

Some Possibilities After the Trip

○ Use an Affinity chart (see page 97) to classify new learning from the trip.

○ Make a guidebook with photos, drawings, and descriptions of natural and/or human-made objects at the field trip site. For example, my students were divided into groups to study different aspects of the beach, including plants and animals in the tide pools. They drew pictures and used books and articles from the park rangers to identify and give some background information about what they found. Then they made a guidebook on the beach to share with other classes.

Note: Nuran Kansu of www.casacanada.com contributed to the above list.

Breathe Life into Learning Through the Arts

In an elementary school in Missoula, Montana, students planned and built a Lewis and Clark carousel with larger-than-life-sized papier-mâché animals representing those that Lewis and Clark met on their journey. Students' research for this project included taking field trips to study the real animals' habitats and to observe the old-time carousel in Missoula. They read journals from the Lewis and Clark expedition; looked at photos, paintings, hides, and skulls; and studied with an artist-in-residence and a professional carousel carver. The animals students made included a grizzly bear, fox, raccoon, and eagle. The children decided to sell the animals to local businesses after the school's celebration to raise funds to preserve the animals' habitats in their community. During the unit, students addressed science, social studies, and language arts standards. Along with their carousel animals, students created poetry, drama, visual art, and movements to express their learning. The whole school began to see themselves as a community of learners who work together for the common good.

The Carousel Project is just one example of implementing the Framework for Aesthetic Literacy, a program designed to build a bridge between standards-based reform and local school improvement through integrated curriculum, multiple intelligences, and inquiry-based instruction. State language arts specialist Jan Clinard and art specialist Christine Peña wrote a grant to develop the integration of English and the arts, which was funded in 10 model schools in Montana. As a result of workshops and conferences, other Montana schools implemented a variety of these curriculum cycles into their programs.

The aesthetic literacy learning cycle has three aspects: encounter-learn-create. Students "encounter" new learning through field trips and in-school presentations, selected for their authenticity. As Jan Clinard puts it, at some point "students need to experience a real symphony rather than just listening to a recording." When they hear the recording, they will be able to connect in their minds the music played with the actual conductor, musicians, and instruments that made the recording.

An example of an "encounter" is a field trip students at another school near Missoula took to Flathead Indian Reservation to learn about the Salish-Kootenai Native Americans. For this aesthetic literacy cycle, encounters also included in-school presentations by the Dancing Boy Drummers; storytellers and dancers; and experts on the Salish language, ceremonies, and crafts (e.g., star quilts). In an exploration of the Native Americans' history, the students' Essential Question was "How do you learn if there is no school?"

Project director Jan Clinard points out that the "learn" column captures national standards in the arts and English. The standards guide authentic learning experiences that are couched between real-world "encounters" and the students' personal expressions of their learning in the "create" cycle. In the "learning" aspect of the cycle, students perceive and analyze, communicate, connect cultures and content areas, and interact and reflect. These are categories inspired by the National Standards for Arts Education, but modified to include language arts. During the "learning" aspect of the cycle of this Native American study, students found out what the buffalo taught the Native Americans. They studied folktales and looked for underlying themes to recognize the cultural understandings the Native American children gained through the folktales. The Dancing Drummers helped students learn about the traditional dances, drumming, and costumes.

Clinard says that in the "create" aspect of the cycle, students need to do work of quality that is worthy of an adult's appreciation. "Don't stick the child's art on a bulletin board with a thumb tack!" she admonishes. "That demeans the art. Instead frame it and display it in a way that works."

For the "create" aspect of the cycle in the Native American study, boys made ankle cuffs and girls made shawls to wear during the open house performance. Students wrote folktales of their own in Native American pictographs on simulated buffalo hide. Older students from the middle school helped younger students learn Salish words. The students collaborated on a play called *Where the Buffalo Roam*, which they performed at the open house. The older students made props for the play, provided background drumming, managed the lighting, and prompted the very young performers. At the open house, students drummed and performed a round dance, inviting audience participation. The most common comment from parents was "When is this going to happen again?"

The biggest challenge for the teachers at this school was how to assess this kind of learning. Working together they developed meaningful assessment tools, including performance criteria, portfolios, and rubrics. In fact, these teachers became leaders in their district in the realm of authentic assessment based on integrated curriculum.

Page 181 shows an abbreviated example of how teachers at a third school planned an aesthetic literacy program based on language arts, where students had an author visit their classroom.

A Plan for an Aesthetic Literacy Learning Cycle

Focus Questions: Why do authors write what they do? How do they do it?

Encounter

- **Read the author's books.**
- **Listen to a guest journalist describe interviewing techniques.**
- **Have a conversation with a visiting author.**

Learn

- **Perceive and Analyze**

  Summarize the plot of a literary work.

  Make association with the people, places, and problems in literary works.

  Compare books to identify elements and characteristics of the author.

  Make connections between the author's comments and the literature.

- **Communicate**

  Improvise dialogue or gesture to re-create characters, their relationships, and their situations.

  Vary movement, pitch, tempo, and tone to portray different characters.

  Use media, techniques, and processes to communicate ideas, experiences, and stories.

  Demonstrate an understanding of the effects of basic elements of music.

  Design dance movements that successfully communicate an idea, situation, or feeling.

- **Connect Cultures and Other Content Areas**

  Explain how a person's experience influences his or her art.

  Explain how a person's art reflects the time and place in which he or she lives.

  Compare contemporary literary works with works of other eras and with works in other arts.

  Compare the characters and problems in a literary work with media representations of similar characters and problems.

- **Interact and Reflect**

  Respond to artwork and performances by asking questions and giving feedback. Explain personal responses to an artistic expression, citing specific details.

  Experiment with multiple solutions to artistic problems.

  Analyze team process and offer specific suggestions for improving planning, rehearsal, and performances.

  Establish and apply consistent specific criteria for evaluating the effectiveness of encountered and created works.

Create

- **Perceive and Analyze**

  Keep a journal and sketchbook with responses to the author, the author's books, and related activities.

- **Communicate**

  Create Readers' Theater or pantomime interpretations of a literary excerpt.

  Create a painting, drawing, or mural capturing a situation, feeling, idea, or characterization of one of the author's books.

  Write a new chapter or a new ending to one of the author's books.

  Write an article about the author for submission to a children's magazine.

  Compose or adapt a song capturing a situation, feeling, or idea in one of the author's books.

  Choreograph a dance motif, capturing a situation, feeling, or idea in one of the author's books.

- **Interact and Reflect**

  Relive the Reader's Theater, illustrations, new chapter or ending, article, song, and dance.

Infusing the arts into the learning of any curriculum enhances memory, increases thinking ability and enjoyment, and brings about a deeper and more profound understanding by connecting with a child's inner life. The time and effort required will pay off manifold in children's love for learning and the quality of education. The arts breathe life into learning!

Students Need "Hard Fun!"

Monique Jackson's third grade students excitedly put the final touches on their Colonial costumes before presenting their play, "Dreaming of Democracy." Every student had a part. Parents walked through the gymnasium, feasting their eyes on the portfolios filled with their children's original creations from the unit on democracy. Students followed up their field trip to the Capitol and Supreme Court by taking an imaginary "day off from school" bill through the branches of the government and finally for a ruling by the Supreme Court.

The students were having so much fun they didn't notice that at the same time they were mastering the Virginia Standards of Learning (SOLs). The SOLs, which are sometimes taught as isolated, unrelated facts, were unified into an overarching theme exemplified in stories, plays, games, songs, group projects, and other motivating activities. By using accelerative learning principles, Monique designed a whole environment, a backdrop for learning that developed her students' thinking, creativity, and social skills while fitting with the required standards. She was struck by the fact that in as little as five minutes, students were able to create convincing role-plays about the rights and responsibilities of voting. They internalized the learning, took ownership, and were deeply engaged.

The class is a picture of diversity—of race, culture, economic status, and learning styles. With this social studies unit, all students—the visual, auditory, kinesthetic, musical, interpersonal, and print oriented—had their preferences honored. Tests showed that seven months later, every student, including the ESL and academically low performing, retained the learning without review or reteaching. One student said "Oh yes, I remember all about Ben Franklin. Jake played Ben Franklin." As Robert Sylwester points out, retention improves when the emotion is there because emotion drives attention and attention drives learning (1998).

Monique said "Even eight- and nine-year-olds are already turned off to school. And little wonder when they are sitting at their desks all day while teachers try to stuff them with facts to pass the tests. Last year I was considering leaving the profession. Teaching wasn't satisfying. Occasionally I would take out time for fun, then tell my students, 'OK class, it's time to get back to work.' Now I realize that the learning itself should be fun. . . . This unit was wonderful for me. It made school fun again for me and for the students . . . ."

Some people equate the word *fun* with trivial. "Students need to know that learning is work," they say. However, *fun* here means meaningful learning that is so absorbing that students persist through the most challenging obstacles. I read about a child who, when pressed about whether her computer project was fun, responded plaintively, "Yes, but it's *hard* fun (Negroponte 1995)." It is often the hard fun that engages students most deeply in learning.

But how can teachers find the time or inclination for fun in the face of the standards movement? Many teachers, who have their jobs and reputations at stake with the tests, have felt compelled to give up on the approaches that they know work for students and have resorted to "drill and kill."

What Monique found, though, was that while the social studies unit did take longer than a lecture with worksheets, it paid off in the long run because her students became her partners in learning rather than resistant combatants. And, when the time came to prepare students for the state test, she didn't need to reteach the information. Best of all, the students who were usually academically slow retained the learning just as well as the more verbal and logical achievers.

—Kathleen Carroll about Monique Jackson, teacher, Fairfax, Virginia

Develop Skills for Field Trips

Some skills for field trips may or may not be required standards for your grade level, but they will greatly enhance your students' learning. These include observation skills, questioning, interviewing and listening skills, notetaking skills, and the ability to use technological tools such as digital cameras and video equipment.

Observation Skills

Before taking the field trip, students may need to practice using their five senses and develop the vocabulary to describe what they perceive. Young students enjoy putting their hand into a "feely bag" and using as many words as they can manage to describe the shape, size, and texture of objects before they guess what the objects are. If you list the words on chart paper, the game develops students' vocabulary and reading skills.

For the sense of hearing, go outside and have each student close his or her eyes and hold up a finger for each sound the student hears. One hand could be for sounds from nature and the other for sounds from people or human-made objects. Afterward students can guess what made the sounds. Help them find descriptive sound words such as *loud, soft, screeching, swishing, beeping, twittering,* etc. Play sound recordings and invite students to describe the sounds and speculate about the causes of the sounds.

Bring in a variety of spices and other items with interesting odors. Invite students to guess the sources of the smells. Discuss odors that are especially meaningful to the students' lives such as the smell of popcorn at the movie theater, fresh-mown grass on a summer day, or the salt air by the seaside. If the field trip involves eating, it might be helpful for students to try some new taste experiences.

While observation includes all our senses, most people equate observation with the ability to see. An important aspect of observation is the ability to look mindfully to see both the big picture and the details. There are many ways to help students build their visual observation skills. Pairs of students might practice taking turns describing an object and listing the words they use. They might compete with other pairs to see who can come up with the largest number of accurate descriptors.

Sketching helps students become better observers. A good way for students to learn to draw what they actually see, rather than their ideas about what they see, is to copy a picture by drawing it upside down (Edwards 1999). It is surprising how much most people's drawing improves when we look at the actual lines and curves instead of our ideas of what a face, vase, or tree looks like.

Cambridge College professor and creativity expert Dr. Win Wenger of Gaithersburg, Maryland, has the following suggestion:

Some years ago I ran across a technique involving drawing, which, I think, effectively reprograms the brain and mind to work more efficiently and which probably helps improve learning. Take a sketch pad and sketching material up to some object such as a tree. After you've made an initial sketch of the whole tree, write out six to ten different questions such as

- What does the bark look like?
- What do the leaves look like?
- How does the trunk come out of the ground?
- How do its branches run?
- How does this tree shape the space that surrounds it?
- What is the angle of the light and shadow?
- What is the surrounding ground like?

and so on.

Then, with each specific question, make three different sketches, each using a different representation or technique.

Make three studies with each of the six to ten questions. Each study uses a different representation, a different technique.

Then do a fresh sketch of the whole tree.

Wenger has many more ideas for developing observation skills at his Web site, www.winwenger.com.

New York teacher and consultant Sarah Shellow uses drawings about the field trip to prepare students for a field trip. She suggests that teachers get postcards and photographs of artifacts from the field trip site. Students sit back to back. One describes the artifact while the other sketches it. The student who makes the drawing can ask as many questions as he or she wants to make the sketch as accurate as possible. In this way students are improving their observation skills on the very objects that they will study at the art gallery or museum.

Building Observation Skills

On my downtown walking tours in Portland, Oregon, I usually like students to have their hands free for exploration, so I often ask for parent volunteers to record the information that students provide. Generally, I select a volunteer to record responses for the "boys" team and another parent to record the "girls" team responses. The goal is to create the longest list. In downtown Portland I ask students to look for: Transportation Modes Seen, Animals Seen (both real and in the artwork), and Jobs Noticed. As a student sees a bus, for example, he or she will tell the parent volunteer and that parent will record the response. At the end of the day, lists are tabulated.

Generally, students will be able to find 20 or more responses for each category. Transportation Modes commonly found in Portland include walking, busses, bicycles, MAX trains (light rail), roller blades, skateboards, Union Pacific trains, sailboats, barges, escalators, elevators, wheelchairs, strollers, helicopters, airplanes, and mopeds.

I began using magnets with students in downtown Portland as a way to test for the cast-iron facades of historic buildings along the waterfront. Magnets will stick to iron or steel but will not attach to bronze, copper, or aluminum. Beyond the buildings, students like to test to see what other types of objects on a walk may be made of iron or steel. Those items the magnets will often attach to include hydrants, iron fences, lamp posts, railings, and even cars (not recommended, however, especially when the driver is seated inside!).

I also encourage students to engage all five senses on a walk. Apart from what can be seen, we generally stop and sit in a circle at some point, and then close our eyes for a "silent minute." During that time, students are encouraged to listen carefully to all the sounds around them, distinguishing from natural and human-generated noises. I also encourage students to feel the variety of materials used to create sculptures and buildings: bronze, stone, aluminum, stainless steel, terra cotta, copper, etc., and think about adjectives to describe what they are feeling: *cool, smooth, rough, sharp, zig-zag,* etc. In Portland students also have an opportunity to taste water from the drinking fountains on the sidewalks and smell the food from the street vendors.

Often, teachers compile lists of the responses given pertaining to each of the five senses, and that helps stimulate writing activities back in the classroom.

—Peter Chausse, walking-tour guide, Portland, Oregon

Listening, Questioning, and Interviewing Skills

Everybody appreciates someone who listens to him or her carefully, yet good listeners are hard to find, even among adults. One way to help students learn to listen is for them to paraphrase each other when they use the Think-Pair-Share Strategy described on pages 100–103. In classroom discussions, students might get into the habit of paraphrasing the last person who spoke before they give their own points of view.

Here is a variation on a strategy I learned from Win Wenger that has helped to improve listening skills in many classes I have taught:

1. Each student in a pair thinks of two or three stories about interesting or meaningful experiences they have had that they would be willing to share. The experience could be about an exciting vacation or the arrival of a new sibling or pet.
2. Student A tells his or her story while Student B listens carefully and asks questions such as "Tell me more about . . . ." or "How did you feel about . . . ?" to draw Student A out further.
3. Then Student B tells a story and gets the same attention from Student A.
4. The pairs form groups of four and discuss how it feels to be listened to.
5. The groups make a T-chart, listing on one side of the chart what it *looks* like when someone is listening to them carefully. On the other side, they list what it *sounds* like when someone is listening to them carefully.
6. Each group shares their findings with the whole class.
7. They put their charts on the wall.
8. Thereafter, when students engage in paired or group discussions, they look over the chart to remind themselves how to listen well in that activity.

In our culture, we usually feel listened to when someone looks us in the eyes, nods occasionally, and asks pertinent questions. However, there are other cultures where looking at someone in the eyes is considered rude. It is helpful to become familiar with the cultural norms of the children we are working with.

In regard to field trips, how can we help children learn to ask good questions? Jennifer Smith, who was teaching in Baton Rouge, Louisiana, focused on helping her students become effective researchers and interviewers as they took field trips to learn about their community. Here, in her own words, is how she achieved this aim:

> In the classroom students practiced learning how to listen carefully and come up with thoughtful questions. We practiced listening and interviewing skills by listening to books read aloud, watching videos, and hearing students' personal stories.
>
> To prepare for particular trips, students would brainstorm questions to ask the people who worked in that location. Then they would write the questions that interested them most. Once we were on the field trip, they also practiced the skill of listening to speakers and taking notes of questions to ask when the speakers finished their presentation. For example, we went on a tour at the state capitol building. During the guide's presentation, the students wrote questions as they arose and then waited to raise their hands until the appropriate time came. I thought that was pretty good for eight-year-olds. They used active listening, then followed up with questions. They were able to do this because we had practiced those skills a lot in class. With each field trip, it was interesting to watch the kids get in there and ask questions of every employee. That question-asking habit extended into school the next year.

These communication skills are invaluable, not only for field trips, but also in life. These skills help us understand one another. They also help preserve a natural curiosity about the world around us, a foundation for lifelong learning.

Note Taking

In Jennifer Smith's previous example, she tells how students wrote questions during a guide's presentation so that they could remember the questions they wanted to ask at the end. Rather than laboriously writing every word, it is easier and faster if students learn to use keywords and stick figures as in Mind Maps (see page 161). The Mind Map process encourages students not only to remember ideas, but also to organize the ideas as they write them.

Some teachers give students reflection time between exhibits or at other natural breaks during the field trip. This is a time for students to write their reflections in their field trip journals, a quiet time to digest what they learn as they learn it.

Students may also make sketches of interesting aspects and artifacts on the field trip. This is another form of note taking. Clipboards give students a hard surface to write on. Field notebooks are another option. They help students stay organized by keeping their notes and sketches in one place.

Some teachers divide their class into small groups of students, each group with a chaperone. Peter Chausse, field trip expert in Portland, Oregon, likes students to have their hands free on their walks through the city, so he has the chaperones take the notes for their group. Another way is to give each group an iPod with a voice recorder or some other recording system. Students in a group take turns giving their reflections about what they are learning. If the groups focus on a different aspect of the curriculum and/or a different Essential Question, then the whole class will be informed by the recordings of each group.

In order to get the most value from a field trip, students need ways to keep track of their impressions, reflections, and new learning during the trip. This encourages students to assimilate the experience and make it their own.

Technological Tools

Cameras add meaningful ways for everyone to participate in field trips. Digital cameras allow you to review the photographs immediately and share them with parents, the school, and the wider community by posting them on the school Web site or another place online where people can retrieve them. The photographs can also make attention-grabbing bulletin boards for the classroom or school. Video cameras provide some of the ultimate memory enhancers. And what an empowerment it is for the students when they are the ones who make the videos.

Durango, Colorado, media specialist and consultant Bliss Bruen suggests that not only does video familiarity and production help improve media literacy, making videos can build confidence in students who learn differently. According to Bruen:

> Producing videos gives some kinesthetic and visual students experiences of success that have previously eluded them in school. Putting together video presentations draws on a variety of talents. Some students will have a good eye for framing what's important, while others will have the interpersonal skills to be effective, sensitive interviewers. Working with cameras together, a range of students may demonstrate abilities and aptitudes that previously were hidden. Many important characteristics and intelligences do not necessarily correlate with our increasingly standardized measures of academic achievement. Students who struggle to express themselves in writing (or speaking) may, with training, begin to formulate and articulate powerful ideas using video and photographic essays.
>
> If you are going to venture out with kids and video cameras, check in with the audiovisual teacher to get some initial coaching on using the equipment. If there's no AV teacher at your school, try using one of the many user-friendly video production guides online or in books.

Bruen suggests some basics to keep in mind in helping students get usable footage in both picture and sound:

1. **Picture.** Beginners have a tendency to move the camera around too much and stop recording way too soon. Bruen's tip is, as a general rule, "Hold the camera steady and let your subject do the moving. Use a tripod if possible or at least steady the camera on a wall, desk, or tree branch. Too much movement can distract from what could have been a great 30 second piece."
2. **Sound.** Try to use an inexpensive microphone or just make sure you get close to your subjects; there's nothing more disappointing than coming back and finding out that traffic noises or wind muffled or distorted your conversation with the poet laureate, fire chief, wildlife biologist, or a classmate.

Technology extends our eyes, ears, and memories. Photographs, videos, and audio recordings allow all to enjoy their field trips for years to come. Editing and assembling these memories helps students review their learning and find its essence. These remembrances also provide material to prepare future classes for their trips to the same site.

Learning Through Caring and Curiosity

Learning through caring and curiosity are so important that a whole chapter is devoted to them. Those foundational qualities are expressed well in Daniel Goleman's concept of emotional intelligence (EQ). In chapter 3 you will find many strategies to enhance students' sense of caring including service learning (page 89); personal responsibility for one's behavior (page 94); social skills, including cooperative learning (page 104); and stewardship of the environment (page 93).

Curiosity is equally vital. As Dr. Frank Lyman has simply stated, "Why take students on a field trip unless there is something there that they are curious about?" Be sure to design your field trip so that students' curiosity is piqued. Chapter 3 provides strategies to arouse students' curiosity through discovery learning. These include learning through exploration (page 108) and the K-W-H-L-N Chart, a graphic organizer where students keep track of what they know, wonder, how they will find out, what they learned (page 109), and new questions that arise. Chapter 3 also includes Essential Questions (page 111), where the field trip is structured around meaningful questions derived from the students themselves and the Taxonomy for Discovery (page 112). When students make their way through the Taxonomy for Discovery, they (1) experience (do, observe, write); (2) organize (make a chart or other graphic organizer); (3) share (with other students or groups of students); and (4) process (develop theories or hypotheses to test). When they develop their own Essential Questions (page 111), they will be motivated to learn. This natural inclination to follow their curiosity can lead them to mastering the standards through a well-planned field trip. Chapter 3 shows ways to motivate students with "an itch that must be scratched" by making dissonance or cognitive incongruity through discrepant events (page 119) and weird facts (page 120). Chapter 3 also includes discovery techniques that expand students' perceptions, questioning and thinking abilities (e.g., ThinkTrix [pages 122–125] is a questioning method that extends thinking by using seven fundamental types of thinking, Six Thinking Hats [pages 126–129] is a way to delve into a problem or academic subject matter, such as a play, a piece of literature, a historical event, or a scientific discovery from many perspectives). Finally, chapter 3 introduces problem-based learning (PBL) (page 130), which is about using the field trip for students to address real-world problems as they master the standards.

Include caring and curiosity—the foundations of field trips—in the Domain Matrix. Goals, such as the development of social skills, stewardship in the environment, questioning skills, and problem solving, can go right next to your content standards as objectives for your unit. Strategies, such as the Taxonomy for Discovery and PBL, can serve as Performance Tasks for summative assessment. Use discrepant events and weird facts before the field trip or during the trip to make learning motivating and fun. Helping students keep the curiosity they had when they entered school and develop their sense of caring for themselves, others, and the environment is crucial in developing healthy families, a strong workforce, and thoughtful and responsible citizens—lifelong learners who work to improve our community. Now what can they learn in school that is more important?

Inquiry at an Aquarium

In studying fish adaptations, I always start with the children's own experience. I ask the students what they need in order to survive. Then we try to relate their own experiences to what a fish needs. We talk about what it feels like to be in the medium of water because we all have had that experience, if only in the bathtub. We talk about how meeting our survival needs might change if we lived in this different environment.

I spread out a bunch of books about fish and water environments, and our first class is dedicated to free exploration of our topic through reading and looking at pictures. I ask the children if they have any burning questions about what they are noticing and we chart them. Getting questions up on paper as a group also generates discussion among the students and more questions.

The children then make theories about how fish might survive in water. We make some goldfish aquariums so that students can observe fish firsthand over time. During our study of fish, we keep track of the new ideas they are learning on a knowledge time line or continuum. We start with a discussion of time lines: they are used to chart change over time of, in this case, an idea. We make a time line of some experiences all the students have had such as the growth of a plant from a seed. The students write a question and then keep track of what they learn about the answer to the question over time, including the resources they use to find out new information.

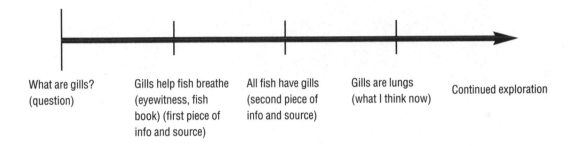

What are gills? (question)

Gills help fish breathe (eyewitness, fish book) (first piece of info and source)

All fish have gills (second piece of info and source)

Gills are lungs (what I think now)

Continued exploration

This way, the students have ownership over their own process of discovery. At this exploratory stage, I do not correct misconceptions. As our study becomes more in-depth, I may point the students to resources to help them revise their thinking and expand their knowledge base.

When we take the field trip to the Aquarium for Wildlife Conservation and students experience the diversity of fish there, many new observations and questions arise. Since the gallery space can be very loud and distracting, and students may have a hard time imagining themselves in the world of their fish, I hand out earplugs for the observation phase of our visit.

Students are in groups of six. Each pair presents their discoveries about their chosen fish at the aquarium to others in their group. They include in their discussion why they chose that fish, the colors, shapes, and patterns; how the fish moves through water; whether they saw their fish breathing, eating, escaping, or chasing other fish; and if they think they saw the fish use its environment to survive.

Follow-up activities have included making a salt water aquarium; a tropical fish pattern quilt where each student contributes one square, based on drawings they made at the aquarium; a 3-D fish, and discovering the essence of "fishness" through dance.

—Sarah Shellow, national consultant for curriculum development
and discovery-based learning, Santa Fe, New Mexico

Travel-Time Learning

Every minute of a field trip can be used productively, including travel time. If students have maps on the bus, they can follow their path to the site and practice their map-reading skills at the same time. They can use compasses to keep track of the direction they are moving in. Or they can observe the street signs, write the directions, and then compare their results with other students and with the official directions. When students have a sense of the directions, they will be more likely to use this resource in the community. Some classes have fun looking for license plates from as many different places as possible. Some compete in finding each letter of the alphabet on signs, billboards, and license plates.

Peter Chausse, a walking-tour guide in Portland, Oregon (www.walkport land.com), advises to provide activities for every part of the trip. From the moment they leave the school, have the students focus on the direction they're traveling, the distances covered, the speed of travel, and the weather conditions. Chausse has students work in groups on the bus, or on public transportation, to note traffic flow, the different modes of transportation they are seeing, local businesses, and other aspects of the environment around them.

Younger students enjoy having pictures of different forms of transportation. They make a mark next to the picture when they observe a bus, bicycle, train, truck, etc.

Transportation on My Trip

Name: _____

Put an "X" next to the picture of each mode of transportation and each type of weather you see.

Transportation

 car _____

 van _____

 truck _____

 police car _____

 fire engine _____

 bicycle _____

 train _____

 airplane _____

Weather

 sunny _____

 rainy _____

 cloudy _____

 snowy _____

Both young students and older students enjoy singing while traveling. Kindergartners and first graders like to sing "Wheels on the Bus" as they ride the bus, making up verses based on what they observe or "Old MacDonald's Farm" in anticipation of their farm trip. Older students might sing songs that relate to the historical period or songs they make up themselves about the subject.

Students can practice singing songs that will be their gift for the guides at the site as they travel there. When my students took a trip on the canal barge, they sang old canal songs. Just for fun they also sang "Proud Mary," a riverboat song. The guides and other passengers were delighted. Songs enhance students' emotional connection to the trip. Singing songs also builds community. Maine teacher Catherine Razi tells of a graduating student's commencement speech recounting his favorite memories. "It was the songs on the bus!" he said.

Consciously plan to make all aspects of the trip, including travel time, as valuable as possible. Your students will be grateful if all parts of the trip are fun and interesting. In addition, the time and energy required in planning the field trip will pay off in many ways as students learn, grow, and connect with one another more fully.

Make Your Own Museum

How can you extend the learning trip to the museum or art gallery? Here are some ideas:

First graders in Muncie, Indiana, assembled hands-on inquiry kits for their school museum exhibit "Mammals in the Schools: Collecting, Classifying, and Preserving." Second graders in Falls Church, Virginia, built their knowledge of science, art, literacy, and "museum making" as they constructed environments, inhabited with native species, from around the world for their school museum. Fourth graders in Potomac, Maryland, demonstrated how the Chesapeake Bay becomes polluted and what people can do to clean it up.

In schools around the country, students are motivated to learn the curriculum by building exhibits. After visiting a museum or art gallery, students brainstorm exactly what they want their audience to learn, which artifacts could facilitate teaching their objectives, how visitors are likely to move through the exhibit, and how to set up and arrange the exhibit to convey their objectives most effectively. They learn not only what to present, but also how to present it. They think and problem solve like museum curators.

The source of this innovative trend is Museum-in-Progress—a program designed by Peg Koetsch, an education consultant who has worked for major museums, including the Smithsonian Institution's National Museum of

Natural History. You can learn more about her work at www.learningin sights.us.

When students tour a museum in the Museums-in-Progress Program, they study both the content of the exhibits and how the exhibit is set up. They interview curators and analyze the exhibit with questions such as "What are the connections between the objects on display?" and "How did this exhibit help me learn?" They watch visitors move through the exhibits and observe, "Do they read the captions?" and "Which parts of the exhibit captured their attention?" They also study placement of the lights and choices of colors to see how these design elements enhance visitors' understanding of the exhibits' themes.

Back at school, students participate in activities to apply their museum-building skills. For example, students might experiment by designing a mini-exhibit in small groups with a few objects, using sticky notes for captions.

Here is an activity example Peg Koetsch uses to guide students through the design and construction of their museum exhibits:

Connecting Artifacts and Concepts

Purpose
To demonstrate how curators make conceptual links among exhibit items

Materials
☐ Assortment of art images on postcards (one for each student)
☐ Assortment of small objects/artifacts (another option)

Planning/Management
☐ Create groups of four to six students each
☐ Assign space for each group to spread out (large tables or floor space)
☐ Each group forms a circle
☐ Distribute the picture postcards
☐ Allow 30 minutes for this activity

How to Play
One player shows a card to the rest of the group, and then puts it down on the table or floor. If the other players see a connection between one of their cards and the initial card, they place their card alongside it. The connections may be visual or conceptual or connect with a color, pattern, the composition, subject, or a personal association. The activity continues as students lay down their postcards to make connections to any other card that has already been shown. After all the cards are down, the children

take turns questioning the connections between any cards, and players explain their conceptual connections.

Discussion Questions
☐ How can a museum exhibit help visitors learn?
☐ What decisions go into creating an exhibit?
☐ How does the placement and order of objects change the learning potential of the exhibit?

Students use the insights gleaned from their museum field trip, interviews with curators and other exhibit designers, and awareness-building activities in the classroom to think through the goals of their exhibit. They bring these together with their research on the subject matter, analysis of the space available, and student-made and other artifacts to build their own exhibits. At their exhibit opening, students act as tour guides to other students, parents, and the community at large. Each time the student tour guides present information on their exhibit to visitors, they reinforce their knowledge of the subject matter and their public speaking skills. At the same time as they learn the curriculum, they learn about aesthetics, the optimal use of space, and how to help others learn.

Learning Through Art

One of the most productive and meaningful ways of enhancing learning is through the use of art and museum visits. Children immediately respond to art because it is directly accessible and multisensory. It communicates to them through their five senses in very meaningful ways. An example of this was a young Chinese boy in an English as a Second Language (ESL) class who, upon seeing Van Gogh's *Starry, Starry Night,* recognized his village in China.

One of the main purposes of using art is to create a climate of "meaningful thinking" in children. To do this, choose a reproduction of a painting such as *My Village* by Marc Chagall.

This picture is particularly appropriate because it represents the complex relationship among humans, animals, and nature. There is a kind of puzzle in it that brings children to a state of creative and meaningful thinking.

Children look at a large reproduction of the painting and freely begin to brainstorm questions beginning with "What if . . . ? How . . . ? Why . . . ?" This is very important because it leads children away from a purely descriptive way to see a picture to really entering into the picture and thinking about it.

Examples of questions are "Why is the man green?" "Why are some of the people upside down?" "What if we could see the entire form of the cow and the man and not just their heads?" "What if the picture was painted with blues and purples instead of reds and greens?" and "How are the cow and man communicating?" The questions go on and on and instead of the teacher lecturing about the picture, the children are discovering it for themselves.

The next step is to ask the children to select one question and draw and paint the picture, putting their question into the painting. So if a child chooses "Why are some of the people upside down?" the answer would come through painting the picture with all the people right side up. Children would share with one another what they have discovered about the painting. A child might discover that the upside-down people made the painting turn in a circle like the world. If the people are right side up, the movement would disappear.

The final step would be an exhibition of the children's paintings with the questions and answers posted beside each one. Other classes and parents would be invited to the exhibition and children would guide them through it, explaining their pictures.

If a museum nearby has some of Marc Chagall's paintings, this would be a wonderful opening to take them on a museum visit.

—Bonnie Tsai, educational consultant, Brooklyn, New York

Integrate Technology with Field Trips

Teachers who use technology most successfully never treat it as an end in itself, but as a means of communication and a vehicle for students to develop higher levels of thinking and creativity. Portland, Oregon, Principal Tim Lauer doesn't have his students living in a virtual world in front of computers all day. His students go outside and walk to a farm a mile away. They dig down into the rich soil. They plant the seeds and pull the weeds. Then they use technology to make maps of the garden's location and share their photos and reflections. Technology is the means; communication about real-world learning is the end.

Technology engages many of the multiple intelligences at the same time. Students exercise their verbal/linguistic intelligence with iPods and voice recorders to interview others or to state their observations; they use logical/mathematical intelligence with calculators to plan budgets or distances. They draw on their visual/spatial intelligences with Web sites and by recording the trip with video and digital cameras. They can use these technologies to incorporate music and songs into their reports. Most of these technologies involve the bodily/kinesthetic intelligence as students move and do, interpersonal intelligence as they work together and learn from one another, intrapersonal intelligence as they answer their own questions in ways that motivate them most, and naturalistic intelligence as they learn the skills needed to survive and thrive in the 21st century. Technology is a powerful way to make the world the classroom.

Following are some ways that technologies can enhance your field trips. Use technologies as tools for the following:

- **Research.** Use search engines, specific Web sites, and online encyclopedias. Students ask questions, search on approved sites, and use criteria to discern the quality of the information found. A search of the field trip's Web site can show students what to expect and help them generate more questions to delve into when they reach the site.

- **Students' production.** Students combine any or all of five types of media: (a) images—use digital cameras, drawing or painting software, or scanners, being careful to observe copyrights; (b) text—summarize the information learned; (c) sounds—incorporate music and sound effects; (d) motion—use screen transitions, video clips, animations; (e) interactivity—such as hyperlinks. Use authoring programs, such as iMovie and MediaBlend, to make combining the media natural. These products can serve as authentic assessments of student learning and treasured keepsakes of the school experience.

- **Public exchange of ideas.** This includes parents' reviews of their children's online portfolios, real-time chats with experts or adventurers in faraway places, and students on opposite sides of the world sharing perspectives (Brunner and Tally 1999; Simkins et al. 2002; Burke 2002).

Innovative Technology Tools

The technologies that can serve as tools for research, student production, and public exchange of ideas as described are evolving at faster and faster rates. Here are a few innovative technological tools that teachers are using to make the world their classroom:

- **Classroom Blogs.** The term *blog* is short for *Web log*. Web logs are journals or newsletters that are frequently updated and reflect the personality of the bloggers. Usually the teacher decides what gets posted. People may respond from anywhere in the world. Again for the students' safety, the teacher can control which responses students read. Blogs certainly give students a voice and motivation to develop their writing skills! Students share about their field trips and people from all over the world learn from them. In some cases the blog is only available to parents and the school community. The blog enables parents to keep up with their children's activities in and out of school and enhances their children's ability to express themselves. See www.blogger.com or www.typepad.com.

- **Vlogs.** "Vlogs" take the blog a step further. A *Vlog* is a video Web log, or a blog with video. According to Dionne Searcey of the *Wall Street Journal* (2005), all that is needed to make a Vlog is a digital camera that can take moving images and a high-speed Internet connection. The directory for iTunes includes Vlogs in its podcast directory as video podcasts (see the podcast description that follows). Vlogs include video and text. Viewers are able to respond to the Vlog. If you want, you can edit your video with Movie Maker or iMovie. A free tutorial for Vlogging with a step-by-step guide to setting up a videoblog using free tools and services is available at http://freevlog.org.

- **Podcasts.** Digital recordings of audio shows are made available on the Internet for downloading to a computer or personal audio player such as an iPod or other MP3 player. You can subscribe free to a choice of thousands of unique audio programs produced by public radio stations, museums, subject-area experts, educators, and creative individuals. You can download these for playback on your computer or on a portable music player. Depending on your learning objectives, podcasts from experts can serve as preparations or follow-ups to your field trip. The Web site www.learnoutloud.com/Podcast-Directory is one place with podcasts for learning about a variety of subjects. Students can also make their own podcasts with reports, songs, poems, reviews, or other reflections on their field trips using a computer, access to the Internet, and a microphone. The advantage over the old-style taped presentations is that since the shows are digitized, they are easily edited. Music can be added with free software such as open source Audacity (http://audacity.sourceforge.net/). Some students design podcasts that sound like old-time radio shows. Parents or anyone can download the podcast onto an MP3 player or onto a computer that has the technology to play it. Podcasting allows students to share their own unique voices with the world. Podcasts are also authentic demonstrations of student learning. KidCast, available from www.ftcpublishing.com, is another software program students can use to get started. KidCast has directions to help you learn how to find and listen to podcasts on the Internet and organize your own podcast shows. Another option is to use the program CastBlaster (www.castblaster.com), which creates podcasts for you. If you are interested in looking into podcasts further, go to http://recap.ltd.uk/podcasting, a British podcast directory for educators, or the Education

Podcast Network (www.epnweb.org). These Web sites have podcasts made by educators to share. They also provide avenues for you to share your own or your students' podcasts with schools internationally.

- **Wikis.** A *wiki* is a Web site, or software to make a Web site, which allows users to add and edit content collectively. (*Wiki wiki* means "rapidly" in Hawaiian.) Students can edit each other's work and add digital photos, commentary, or links to related articles or information. At principal Tim Lauer's elementary school in Portland, Oregon, all the teachers have wiki Web sites. These wikis are open only to students in the teacher's class. Wikis can be shared more publicly if a teacher wishes. Imagine a wiki report on a class field trip where students contribute their photographs, poems, reflections, and reflections on one another's reflections.

- **The Green Machine.** This is a $100 laptop that could greatly expand the number of children we can connect with on the Internet. The MIT Media Lab has launched a research initiative to design, manufacture, and distribute laptops that are sufficiently inexpensive to provide every child in the world access to knowledge and modern forms of education. To achieve this goal, a nonprofit association, One Laptop per Child (OLPC), has been created. These laptops are not for sale but will be distributed through governments in the developing world. The initiative was first announced by Nicholas Negroponte, lab chairman and cofounder at the World Economic Forum at Davos, Switzerland, in January 2005. Go to http://laptop.media.mit.edu to find out more.

- **Flickr.** This is a photo-sharing Web site (http://flickr.com) that may change the Internet. While the photo sharing can be public or private, 80 percent of the photos are public. One way that Flickr is special is its policy of tagging. You can put a "tag" with a few keywords that let others who are interested in your subject find your photos and comment on them. So if you are interested in wildflowers, Russian Easter eggs, or skateboard champions, your pictures may attract others with the same interests. Communities form around common interests. People may find your photo years after you take it because it may be pulled up in someone's search.

Portland, Oregon, elementary school principal Tim Lauer's students place photos and reflections about their field trips on Flickr. These students enjoy the excitement of sharing their learning with a huge audience. At the same time, they are learning to use forms of technology that are the wave of the future. In the next few years, new

Internet-based sharing of files—from photos to video and audio recordings—will be even more ubiquitous than they are today. Flickr and other Web sites are generating the most unlikely and creative new communities of people with similar passionate interests. The social networking aspects of the Internet are tantalizing. These technologies may serve as the new literacy for the next generation of adults.

- **Mapping.** Mapping is taking on new meaning in this age of information. Google Earth (http://earth.google.com) is a free, downloadable virtual globe program that helps students understand their place in the world. Students can use Google Earth to see an aerial view of their own home, school, field trip destination, or pen pal's location. Then they can broaden the view to the city, state, country, continent, and position on the globe.

Another example of mapping is the horned toad project sponsored by Washington State's division of NatureMapping, a nationwide movement to encourage ordinary citizens to collect data on the plants and animals in their area, working with scientists to help preserve our biodiversity. Each student partners with a local farmer, who keeps track of horned toads' behavior on his or her farm. The students record and analyze data and find trends over time—activities that are usually considered way beyond the level of fourth graders (www.edutopia.org/magazine/ed1article.php?id= Art_1251&issue =apr_05#).

According to archaeologist Dr. Jim Judge, in a project planned for southwest Colorado, students will work with archaeologists to map fields that centuries ago were used by indigenous people to grow corn, beans, and squash. During the course of a year, the class will gather and integrate information on climate, soil, and water, both from today and from A.D. 1200 when the population of the area was possibly quite similar. Their Essential Question is "Can our region feed itself?" Today farmers living on the same land depend on distant suppliers for their food while using the same fields to grow alfalfa, a cash crop that must be shipped to buyers hundreds of miles away.

Greenmap.org is a worldwide network of students and adults who are mapping the ecological and cultural aspects of their communities. Green Mappers from around the world learn from each other and use agreed-upon icons to describe everything from areas for watching birds, bugs, or frogs to sites for pollution sources.

Green Mapping Through Field Trips

Children all over the world are making maps of what is "green" in their communities, deciding what to map and taking field trips to collect information and gain knowledge as they map their communities. This process is called *Green Mapping*, designed and developed by Green Map System (www.greenmap.org).

In rural Robeson County, North Carolina, students expanded green mapping to not only include environmental and ecological assets in their community, but also historical, cultural, civic, and recreational assets and resources. According to Mac Legerton, executive director of the Center for Community Action and developer of the project, students take field trips to talk to elders, family members, community leaders, and other keepers of knowledge and wisdom to learn about their communities. They collect the information and draw their own map of their community, starting with a very large map made from rolled paper or poster board taped together. They collect and compile information on each site. They transfer their drawings and site descriptions to smaller paper and eventually print and distribute their maps. The Robeson County Green Map Project is the only rural project in the world that was selected for the first international Green Atlas (www.greenatlas.org), which provides portraits of communities based on locally led projects around the world.

Community mapping is a way for students of all ages to acquire competency skills and civic knowledge. Green Maps are also community service projects that preserve and promote the diverse natural and cultural assets in our communities. They can be used as classroom curricula and continuously expanded and updated. Because of the Web-based, international Green Map program and introduction of more sophisticated mapping instruments, students can also acquire significant technological skills through the project. Students can communicate with other children around the world who are engaged in similar projects as well.

Schoolyard Habitat Mapping uses the same procedures right outside the school door. At Fairgrove School in Robeson County, North Carolina, students identified the various habitats on their school property and developed a habitat map. They spent hours in each habitat and documented the distinct plant and animal life that lived in each habitat. According to Mac Legerton, executive director of the Center for Community Action and developer of the project, the habitat mapping experience provides a way for students to learn firsthand about habitats and the unique beings that live in each habitat in their school community. Students also plan and develop projects to improve the quality and diversity of animal and plant life in each habitat. Teachers develop curricula enhancement materials and projects that can be used and improved year after year.

For more information, see the National Wildlife Federation's Schoolyard Habitat Program (www.nwf.org/backyardwildlifehabitat/programoverview.cfm), the Roger Tory

Peterson Institute (www.rtpi.org), and the Rural School and Community Trust's place-based education emphasis (www.ruraledu.org).

—Mac Legerton, executive director of the Center for
Community Action, Lumberton, North Carolina

All of these real-world projects involve students in mapping. Some projects are low-tech, such as a group of students and teachers in North Carolina who are making hand-drawn maps with photographs and narratives about every neighborhood in their county. Some projects involve Global Positioning System (GPS) units, handheld devices that send and receive information from satellites orbiting overhead, to mark precisely where the user is standing by providing longitude and latitude coordinates.

○ **Geotagging.** This takes mapping beyond the neighborhood and around the world. Geotagging automatically gives the latitude and longitude of the place where a photo is taken and provides a map for students to locate the site of the photograph. For instance, a photograph on Flickr, the photo-sharing site described previously, can be geotagged to show where the photo was taken. Students can also Geotag to find out where Web sites are located. Geotagging helps students learn to read maps and understand where places are in relation to each other. The world becomes the classroom.

Mapping and Sharing Field Trips on the Internet

At Meriwether Lewis Elementary School in Portland, Oregon, fourth and fifth grade students are involved in a learning-garden science curriculum that incorporates five field trips per year to JEAN's Urban Forest Farm. The farm is an outdoor laboratory designed to provide students with an understanding of farm, forest, and watershed ecology. The farm is located just over a mile from the school, and students visit the farm to learn about agriculture and sustainable food production. In preparation for the trips, students have utilized Web-based tools such as Google Maps (http://maps.google.com), which offers access to street maps and satellite images for the whole world as well as a route planner. Using this tool, students are able to plan their walks to the farm and are able to see aerial views of the farm and surrounding areas.

Students are documenting their field experience with digital photography and by writing about the experience in their garden journals. Some of the images and journal entries are making their way onto the Web, providing access to this work to a larger audience. At Lewis they are using online tools such as Flickr (http://flickr.com) to post images, along with written documentation about the farm field trip experience.

Using the Firefox Web browser and a Firefox extension (www.firefox.com) the students are able to Geotag their Flickr images. Geotagging, sometimes referred to as Geocoding, is the process of adding geographical identification metadata to various media images. The use of this extension to the Firefox browser makes it very simple to find and add the geo-coordinates to an image.

With the help of another Web tool, Flyr (http://flyr.whatfettle.com), students can pull up their collection of field trip photos overlaid on a Google map with markers that indicate the specific location where the picture was taken, along with the writing associated with that image. By utilizing tags that describe a specific group of images in a few words, students and teachers can call up a Google Map with markers showing photo locations on an interface. This gives students a visual geographic reference and record of their field trip experience. Students use tagging to utilize this tool to create photo-maps for any number of trips.

Combining the easy Web publishing of tools such as Flickr, and the extendibility of Web tools such as Firefox, opens up a world of publishing and documentation possibilities that help teachers and students extend and build on their field trip experiences and share the experiences with many others.

—Tim Lauer, principal, Portland, Oregon

Safety with the Internet

In response to safety concerns, many schools or school divisions have established guidelines for the appropriate use of computer networks, including both the Internet and Intranets (networks within and between classrooms in a school or district). Such a list of guidelines is called an Acceptable Use Policy or AUP. An AUP is a written agreement in the form of guidelines, signed by students, their parents, and their teachers, which outlines the terms of Internet and Intranet use, including rules for online behavior.

In some schools, teachers have parents sign permission slips whenever students take an online field trip. In other schools, parents sign one permission form for the whole school year.

Online Virtual Field Trips

Online virtual field trips were first described in chapter 2 (see pages 78–81 for examples). In this section we will discuss some practicalities for using these field trips with students. Students can design their own online virtual field trips as Performance Tasks after a field trip. The audience may be friends and family and other classes in their school. The student-made virtual field trips may be designed to exchange information with another nearby school or one on the other side of the world.

Here we will discuss teacher-planned trips where students go online to learn from others. Walter McKenzie, an education consultant and technology director for the Northborough-Southborough, Massachusetts Public School District, will be our guide. He has written and taught courses on virtual field trips for Connected University and has published several books and articles on instructional technology. He is the Webmaster of Surfaquarium (http://surfaquarium.com), which includes his Virtual Field Trips page found at http://surfaquarium.com/IT/vftguide.htm.

In planning an online virtual field trip, Walter McKenzie suggests that teachers prepare the following:

- **Task:** a short four- or five-sentence paragraph introducing the purpose of your online virtual field trip. It should name the topic or destination and generate student interest by asking the questions you want your students to answer as they visit each site on the trip. (The task will be especially motivating if you set it up as a problem, a mystery, or a scavenger hunt.)

- **Resources:** an alphabetical, annotated list of the Web sites students will use on their trip. Each entry should include the Web site title, the URL address, and a one-sentence description of the site.

- **Itinerary:** an outline of the sites the students will tour in the order you want them to be visited. For each stop, describe what the students can look forward to seeing and doing on the site.

- **Souvenirs:** a list of the artifacts you would like students to collect from each site. Remember to be descriptive and indicate the quantity of each souvenir you would like collected.

- **Project:** a step-by-step set of instructions for completing the Performance Task at the conclusion of the virtual field trip.

- **Performance Tasks:** activities the student must complete at each Web site, as well as the culminating task at the completion of the virtual field trip. (This includes a URL, the souvenir the student will find, and what he or she will do with that souvenir once it is identified).

Here is an example:

Objectives: Students will visit www.history.org/Almanack/places/places.cfm, view examples of architecture in Colonial Williamsburg, identify three buildings that show good examples of symmetry in their design, and sketch an example of symmetry viewed in each building in their online virtual field trip notebooks.

Walter McKenzie has made a list of dos and don'ts to help you make your online virtual field trip as successful as possible.

Virtual Field Trip Dos

1. Select a trip which has a clear connection to the standards you are studying in class.
2. Collect signed parental permission slips to take your class online.
3. Be responsible as the chaperone while your class is online.
4. Plan ahead for your trip.
5. State a measurable objective for your culminating activity.
6. List your online virtual field trip in your lesson plans.
7. Place a time limit on the trip.
8. Be the tour guide; help students pace themselves.
9. Consider using a projector and touring as a whole class.
10. Consider pairs or small groups if students work on their own.
11. View all monitor screens from one vantage point.
12. Use the story folder to see where a browser has been.
13. Extend the experience to word processing, desktop publishing, and multimedia presentations.
14. Follow through on a plan of assessment for completed student work.
15. Have at least one follow-up lesson after the trip.

Virtual Field Trip Don'ts:

1. Don't allow students to wander online on their own.
2. Don't present the site without knowing it in detail.
3. Don't go on a trip without preparation ahead of time.
4. Don't use online virtual field trips as an unstructured use of free time.
5. Don't complete an online virtual field trip without follow-up.

Technology will never replace getting students outside to learn about the world firsthand. Used properly, however, technology serves as an invaluable tool to extend students' learning and give students a voice in sharing their perspectives on the world they will inherit.

Technology-Based Projects

In my country, New Zealand, nearly all young primary-school students can take their experience of a field trip and turn it, in under a day, into a complete multimedia story: with videotape, animations, cartoon characters, or whatever is required. But only in very rare instances would any one student do all that work. The talented wordsmiths would translate the field trip experience into a video script. Kinesthetic and tactile learners might fashion the historical characters, animals, buildings, or artifacts into Play Dough to use with the class Clay Animation Kit. The musically talented would use electronic software to create music as the background theme. Some of the visual learners might photograph the models using digital cameras or video and use videos shot during the field trip to add to the script. The IT experts among the students would start to turn all this material into digital images, again using templates such as Apple iMovie or Microsoft Movie Maker. And while they were doing this, their teacher might be sitting in a corner with two foreign-born students, assisting the students as they write their own stories about the trip to help them catch up with English. And by the end of the day, the entire team would have produced a Disney-style movie, learned to develop their own talents, gained a whole new range of skills, and worked together combining their talents with others. Now imagine their reaction when they go off to high school or college and get confronted with a boring lecture!

—Gordon Dryden, coauthor of *The Learning Revolution*

The Extended Domain Matrix: Step-by-Step

Now that we have examined all the aspects of the Extended Domain Matrix (see page 148) and considered the three questions from many perspectives, you are invited to try out the Domain Matrix in planning your own field trip.

1. What do they need to learn? List the standards and/or objectives you plan to address. Depending on your goals, you may use more or fewer spaces than listed.

    A. _____

    B. _____

    C. _____

    D. _____

    E. _____

    F. _____

    Plan a preassessment to find out if some students have already mastered the standards, in which case you will need to plan ways to take them further, or if some students need to be taught some prerequisites.

    Preassessment_____

List the Essential Question or questions that make the standards meaningful to students _____

_____

2. How will we and *they* know they have learned it? Use backward planning. Plan one or more summative or final assessments that will show whether students have mastered all the standards or objectives. If the final assessment is a Performance Task, plan a rubric or checklist to assess the Performance Task.

   The summative assessment is _____

   _____.

   It will be measured by _____

   _____.

3. How are they going to learn it? Decide which field trip destination will best achieve the learning goals and is most doable. Choose pretrip, during trip, and posttrip activities that are specifically designed to help students succeed at the summative or final assessment.

   Before the Trip

   1. _____

   2. _____

   3. _____

   4. _____

   During the Trip

   5. _____

   6. _____

   7. _____

   8. _____

   After the Trip

   9. _____

   10. _____

Assess your plan. Are the activities aligned with the learning goals? To the right of each activity, mark (either on a scale of 1 to 4, with 4 being the highest or with an x) which standards will be addressed. Modify the activities if some standards have not yet been addressed adequately.

Does the plan address the multiple intelligences well? To the left of each activity, mark which intelligences the activity will address. A goal might be to include every intelligence somewhere in the unit to meet the preferences of as many students as possible.

When you have determined which activities are best to help students succeed at the final assessment and show that they have met the goals of the unit, plan formative assessments for each activity to determine whether students are learning or if some parts of the unit need to be retaught. Formative assessments may be as simple as thumbs up, "I got it" or thumbs down, "I didn't get it." Or the formative assessments may be as complex as little Performance Tasks with rubrics. To the far right of the Domain Matrix under gauges, there is a line to plan a gauge for students' learning for each activity:

Before the Trip

1. _____

2. _____

3. _____

4. _____

During the Trip

5. _____

6. _____

7. _____

8. _____

After the Trip

9. _____

10. _____

Once you have completed your Extended Domain Matrix for your field trip, you will be assured that the plans for the trip are in alignment with the trip's learning goals. Share this with administrators and parents to let them know that the trip is well planned and worth taking.

In summary, take the time to be crystal clear about why you are taking this field trip, how you and the students will know that they achieved the goals, and how students will learn before, during, and after the trip. Include ways for students to exercise their caring and curiosity. Through these efforts you will make the field trip a trip to remember!

Checklist: Field Trips Are for Learning!

Look at the list below and check off the ideas or activities that you would like to incorporate into your field trip:

☐ Domain Matrix to align a lesson
☐ Extended Domain Matrix to align a unit

Question 1: "What do they need to learn?"

☐ Standards and objectives
☐ Essential Questions
☐ Diagnostic assessment

Question 2: "How will we and they know they have learned it?"

☐ Backward planning
☐ Helping students know they know
☐ Summative assessments—at the end
☐ Performance Tasks
☐ Rubrics
☐ Formative assessments—along the way
   ☐ Observation checklists
   ☐ Written checklists
   ☐ Anecdotal records
   ☐ Interviews
   ☐ Written quizzes
   ☐ Ticket out
☐ Self-assessment
☐ Peer assessment (Star-Wish-Star, Critical friends, Trip buddies)
☐ Mind Maps and other graphic organizers

Question 3: "How are they going to learn it?"

☐ Multiple intelligences—before-during-after
   ☐ Verbal/Linguistic
   ☐ Logical/Mathematical
   ☐ Visual/Spatial
   ☐ Bodily/Kinesthetic
   ☐ Musical/Rhythmic

- ☐ Interpersonal
- ☐ Intrapersonal
- ☐ Naturalistic

Breathe Life into Learning Through the Arts

- ☐ Develop special skills
- ☐ Observation skills
  - ☐ Listening, questioning, interviewing
  - ☐ Note taking
- ☐ Have a caring focus
- ☐ Use curiosity-enhancing strategies
- ☐ Include travel-time activities
- ☐ Use technological tools
  - ☐ For research
  - ☐ For production
  - ☐ For communication
  - ☐ Classroom blogs
  - ☐ Podcasts
  - ☐ Wikis
  - ☐ Geotagging
- ☐ Virtual field trips
  - ☐ Planning
  - ☐ Dos and don'ts
- ☐ Step-by-Step Domain Matrix

References

Brunner, C., and W. Tally. 1999. *The New Media Literacy Handbook, an Educator's Guide to Bringing New Media into the Classroom.* New York: Doubleday.

Burke, J. 2002. The Internet Reader. *Educational Leadership* 60:3.

Buzan, T. 1993. *The Mind Map Book: Radiant Thinking.* London, England: BBC.

Carroll, K. 2000. *Science for Every Learner: Brain-Compatible Pathways to Scientific Literacy.* Chicago: Zephyr Press.

Hibbard, M., et al. 1996. *Performance-Based Learning and Assessment.* Alexandria, VA: Association for Supervision and Curriculum Development (ASCD).

Edwards, B. 1999. *The New Drawing on the Right Side of the Brain.* NY: Jeremy Page Tarcher/Putnam.

Gardner, H. 1993. *Frames of Mind* (10th ed.). NY: Basic Books.

Gelb, M. 1998. *Mind Mapping: How to Liberate Your Natural Genius.* Audioprogram. Niles, IL: Nightingale-Conant.

Marguelies, N., and N. Maal. 2001. *Mapping Inner Space: Learning and Teaching Visual Mapping.* Chicago: Zephyr Press.

Negroponte, N. 1995. *Being Digital.* NY: Alfred Knopf.

Searcey, D. 2005. "Vlogger (noun): Blogger with Video Camera." *Wall Street Journal,* December 16, 2005, B1.

Simkins, M., K. Cole, F. Tavalin, and B. Means. 2002. *Increasing Student Learning Through Multimedia Projects.* Alexandria, VA: ASCD.

Storksdieck, M. 2006. *Field Trips in Environmental Education.* Berlin, Germany: Berliner Wissenschafts-Verlag.

Sylwester, R. 1998. Art for the Brain's Sake. *Educational Leadership* 56:31–35.

Wiggins, G., and J. McTighe. 2005. *Understanding by Design* (2nd ed.). Alexandria, VA: ASCD.

5

Handling Logistics

A Field Trip Essential

"Success is in the details."

—KATHLEEN CARROLL

The world-famous architect Ludwig Mies van der Rohe is quoted as saying "God is in the details." We might use his perspective with this truth about field trips: "Success is in the details." Careful logistical planning is essential for a field trip to be successful. You can have the best idea for a great and enjoyable learning experience that is perfectly aligned with your standards. But the trip will only succeed if the children are allowed to take the trip; the bus finds its way to the site; the students see, hear, and do what they came for; and all return home safely. This chapter focuses on logistical matters that are the sine qua non for safe, effective, and enjoyable field trips. I invite you to look for ways to include students wherever possible in planning and handling the logistics. Helping to handle the details required of field trips gives students real-world opportunities to build skills in mathematics, language arts, computer literacy, communication, and conflict resolution, to name just a few.

Susan Fort, educational consultant and a former Master's degree student of mine in the National Institute for Teaching Excellence (NITE) program at Cambridge College, is an expert on logistics for field trips and has contributed greatly to this chapter.

In this chapter I will

- suggest structured ways to keep track of data on field trips from year to year.
- consider several strategies for determining which field trip to choose, based on criteria such as educational benefits, costs, time and effort required, ease of travel, and probable enjoyment levels.
- review options for financing the trip, including fund-raising possibilities.
- look at getting permissions from the district level, school or other organizations, parents, and the site managers and arranging transportation.
- plan for special needs.
- consider pretrip preparations, setting goals based on standards and students' needs and interests and getting students ready for the trip.
- make plans for posttrip evaluations of student learning and of the trip itself.
- consider how to recruit chaperones and prepare them for the field trip and how to stay in communication with chaperones, other drivers, parents, and school officials.
- examine ways to keep students safe, focused, and happy throughout their trip so that they can enjoy maximum educational benefits.

● think about a timetable and checklists for things to do and items to bring.

Using all the suggestions in this chapter with every field trip would be overwhelming. Keep in mind that the field trip you are planning will benefit from only certain aspects of this chapter; the next field trip may involve other aspects. Think of this chapter as a smorgasbord from which you can pick and choose what is relevant to you at any particular time.

Choosing the Right Field Trip

How do you know which field trips will best fit your group's needs? How can you maximize the value of the trips you choose? Successful field trips require thoughtful analysis.

Collect Data

In some schools, teachers take the same field trips every year because "That's what we have always done." There are advantages in returning to the tried and true, perhaps refining and improving on the trip each year. As field trip research expert Martin Storksdieck put it in a conversation recently, "It may not be until the third trip that you get it right!"

Anne Fretz, a Rockville, Maryland, teacher and the field trip coordinator for her grade level for 30 years, has found certain trips that are optimal for her curriculum. She keeps a field trip journal from year to year with notes on each field trip and folders with information on each trip site to help remember information such as the following:

● How and when to schedule the trip
● Who the contact person was
● How long it took to get to the site
● How long the visit took
● Which guides were most helpful and worked best with children
● Which activities were most and least successful (including pretrip, on-site, and posttrip activities)

Every September Anne contacts all the sites for her field trip plans throughout the school year. She contacts them early to maximize the likelihood that she will get the best times of year for her trips. She refers to her field trip journal with information she has collected from past years to help optimize her field trip plans for the new school year.

Planning Field Trips for the School Year

We take 10 to 12 field trips per school year because there are so many rich things to see and do on the topics we study. I make a list in September of places to call, noting the dates we visited the place last year and how that worked. Some places want you to schedule online instead of calling. Some have you download a form and then fax it. I keep folders on each trip with that kind of information. I also keep notes on what we did and how the trip went on previous years, such as who the contact person was, activities that worked or that we should do differently next time, guides that were particularly helpful or who didn't relate well to children, how long it took us to get there, and how long the program was. It's a field trip journal—this journal helps me improve future trips.

Parents sign up for field trips on back-to-school night. From there on I leave organizing the chaperones to the room parents. They do it by e-mail most of the time. A day or two before the field trip, the room parent lets me know who is coming. There are some trips where you need more parents than others. Sometimes there are parents who follow the school bus or work near the site and meet us there.

I send a letter for every field trip. I always give outside times for our return—the latest time I expect that we would return so that parents or others at school won't be inconvenienced or concerned. I give this letter to my supervisor, all the tutors, the special teachers, and the lunchroom people—whoever may be affected. I send the letter out at least a week in advance.

Even on half-day field trips, we always have a snack before the students go into the site. We bring extra saltines for those who didn't bring a snack from home. We just don't want them complaining of being hungry at 11:00 A.M. Some buses don't let you eat on the bus. In that case we just eat outside before we go into the site. We also bring along tissues, a huge trash bag, and a bell to get the students' attention.

When we go back to school, we take the kids outside for unstructured free play. They need some time to unwind after a field trip.

Field trips take a lot of planning, but they are well worth the effort.

—Anne Fretz, teacher, Rockville, Maryland

While a field trip journal can help you improve on a trip to the same site the next year, it may also help you improve on the next trip you take to a new site. Just ask yourself "What can we learn from our last trip to make our next trip better?" Consider using the Six Thinking Hats process described in chapter 3 (see pages 126–129) to address many perspectives. It is helpful to include the ideas of other teachers, students, chaperones, and others. You may be surprised at how helpful the perspectives of even young children can be. Add your findings and thoughts to your field trip journal.

> *Excerpt from Anne Fretz's Field Trip Journal*
> ## Potomac Overlook Park
>
> Beautiful spot—took about 45 minutes to get there. Cindy was the naturalist (very good). Her indoor slide show was a full hour—interesting but too long! Then she divided us into two groups. I stayed inside to view nature center, other group went outside for 15 minutes for the nature walk.
>
> If they don't have two naturalists to split the walk, maybe Terry and I should go on separate days. Ask Brenda about bus expenses for this.

Field Trip Criteria

Sometimes the person coordinating the trips is new to the job and doesn't have years of experience to fall back on. Sometimes the coordinator would like to try some new sites to visit. Again, think about including students in the decision-making process. When considering new field trips, it is helpful to think through what might be most beneficial and weigh the criteria for various possibilities. In this case, you will need to choose criteria that best fit your situation. The following are some examples:

Educational Benefit

For most field trips the first criterion is the educational benefit: "How will this field trip help students to learn?" You may want to start with your standards. If you don't already have a list of your state or district standards, they are only a Google search away at your state's Department of Education Web site. If you are in a school or program that is not required to use state or district standards, national standards might serve as helpful guides for you. Look in chapter 4 (see pages 151–152) for some Web sites that list national standards for different subject areas.

Developing Caring and Curiosity

You might also consider the field trip's potential for developing caring and curiosity, including the development of emotional intelligence (EQ) as discussed in chapter 3. The EQ potential benefits include self-awareness, self-control, self-motivation, altruism, empathy, and social skills. While any field trip could be structured to address these EQ traits, certain field trips, such as those involving service projects and that lend themselves to discovery learning, may be particularly appropriate.

Cost

Suppose you found five field trips that could satisfy your educational objectives. You would need to use other criteria to narrow down your choices. For most of us, cost is a major factor. Susan Fort designed a table for cost analysis that you can copy and use with each of the field trips you are considering.

Costs Worksheet

Location _____

Item	Amount	Donation Possible? (Y/N) Amount?	From Whom?
Pre-Trip			
speaker/video/other			
Food			
lunch			
snack			
water			
other			
Transportation			
bus			
Entrance Fees			
other			
other			
other			
TOTALS			

Time and Effort Required

For most of us, time and money are the big issues that place boundaries on what we do with our lives. If you happen to work in a school or program where money isn't an issue, time probably will be.

The criterion of time can be considered in several ways. One way is the amount of time the field trip will take students away from their regular studies. Another is the amount of time and effort that planning for and executing the field trip will take you. Different field trips might require very different amounts of planning and time away from school. The question is "Do the benefits of that more distant or labor-intensive trip justify the extra time and effort required?"

Ease of Travel

This criterion relates to the cost, the time, and the enjoyment of the field trip. Long trips on buses can be exhausting. But if the drive is beautiful or the destination fabulous, it can be worth it. What if the trip were on a train or boat though? In that case, the travel itself might be the best part of the trip (unless a student suffers from motion sickness, which is something you would wish to know in advance).

Timing

Is this a time when you can expect huge crowds at your chosen destination? Or is it a time when the weather is likely to be inhospitable? What will you do if it rains? The contact person is likely to be able to help you with information on timing.

Enjoyment Levels

"Emblazon these words in your mind: learning is more effective when it is fun!" This quote from educational author Peter Kline validates the criterion when planning your trip. If two possible field trips were equal in every other way, wouldn't you want to pick the most enjoyable one?

Occasionally, motivating activities have been taught at the expense of designated outcomes—a tendency known as "process-creep" (Hibbard 1996). However, fun here means meaningful learning that is so absorbing students persist through the most challenging obstacles. Brain research indicates that all students will retain the learning longer if there is a positive emotional component to the learning experience (Caine et al. 2005). Chapter 3 (see page 108) presents many strategies for arousing and maintaining students' curiosity and interest during field trips.

Most field trips can be made enjoyable if, in the planning, we include enjoyment as a goal. Feedback from the other teachers, parents, and the students can provide useful information on how to make the field trip as enjoyable, challenging, and engaging as possible. This is also the best way to achieve academic goals.

Decision-Making Tools

In making decisions about field trips or other issues for that matter, getting others' viewpoints can be very helpful. One way to get feedback from students, parents, and other teachers when deciding on which trip is best is to use the Six Thinking Hats Strategy (see pages 126–129). The Six Thinking Hats strategy provides for parallel thinking, as hats originator Edward de Bono calls it. Everyone considers the facts about each possible trip (White Hat), the feelings (Red Hat), the positives (Yellow Hat), the cautions (Black Hat), the possibilities (Green Hat), and the overview (Blue Hat) when deciding on which field trip to take. Six Thinking Hats is also a useful tool for reflecting on and evaluating the trip at its conclusion.

Another way to get feedback is a decision-making tool designed by creativity expert Dr. Donald Treffinger called the ALU: "A" is for advantages, where you list all the positive aspects of the trip; "L" is for limitations, where you list the disadvantages of this particular trip; and "U" is for the unique potential, where you list interesting connections and hidden possibilities that may not have occurred to you before. "Unique potential" helps one to break out of the dichotomy of good and bad, with aspects that are neither positive nor negative but are intriguing. Sometimes an idea may have more minuses than plusses, but the "unique potential" list is so fascinating that we decide to do it anyway. The Six Thinking Hats and ALU can be rich sources of data if you ask students, other teachers, and parents their perspectives on each trip. Students feel particularly empowered when they find that their voice counts (www.homestead.com/peoplelearn/decisionmaking.html).

A third way to compare possible field trips is to use the table on page 223 to analyze and rate the relative educational benefits, costs, time required, ease of travel, and probable enjoyment levels to compare each field trip you are considering.

Which Field Trip to Choose?

Rate each field trip on each criterion you consider relevant:

	Location	Educational Benefits	Cost	Time Required	Ease of Travel	Timing	Enjoyment Level
Field Trip 1							
Field Trip 2							
Field Trip 3							
Field Trip 4							
Field Trip 5							

Most Cost Effective _____ Ideal Time _____ Best Travel _____ Most Enjoyable _____

Which trip will you choose? _____

_____

_____

_____

Paying for the Field Trip

If parents can pay for the trip, the only money issues are in planning how to inform parents, collect the money, and keep your paperwork straight. In some schools with wide disparities in parental income, some parents are willing to pay a little more so that all students in a class can attend the trip. Use your contacts; a strategic phone call or e-mail might cut the cost of your trip. Some schools have the resources so that it isn't necessary to collect money from the parents directly. Often though, in this time of cutbacks in school funding, financing field trips isn't that easy. There are many opportunities for students to learn mathematics and a variety of other real-world skills when they get to help with the fund-raising and with keeping track of the funds needed and the funds that are raised.

Grants

Grants can be one source of funding. Grant funders may be very sympathetic to a request for funding for a worthwhile field trip, especially if the students will learn about topics that are dear to their hearts. When the school is in a poverty-stricken area or the fund-raising is to include disadvantaged students, funders may be doubly inspired to help you.

When I was teaching in a poor, urban school and wanted to use the school grounds to help students learn about plants and ecology, garden clubs were delighted to fund us with trees, flowers, and soil for our projects. At times we also worked out agreements with trip organizers. Our students got trips on the Chesapeake Bay. In return, we promised to make a film they could use that showed what our students had learned.

There are foundations and Web sites that were established especially to help fund students' field trips. DonorsChoose (www.donorschoose.org) is a Web site that connects people who want to contribute with classrooms in need of financial support. Initiated by Charles Best, a teacher in New York City, DonorsChoose has raised millions for schools in states around the country. Individuals have funded projects requested by more than 6,000 public school teachers for classroom materials and field trips.

Teachers must submit an essay describing their need and how the materials or trip requested would contribute to student learning. Volunteers screen and validate each request before it is posted online.

As a charity, DonorsChoose has some advantages over many others; the gift is personal. Donors know exactly where their money is going, how the money is spent, and who benefits. Teachers send photos and thank-you letters from students. (DonorsChoose sends teachers disposable cameras and guidelines for writing class thank-you notes.)

Children's expressions of appreciation are very meaningful to the people who receive them. For example a fifth grader in the Bronx wrote "No one has ever done anything that nice for me before. I want to do something for you. Just tell me what you need and I'll take care of it." A fourth grader in North Carolina wrote "My children's children's children will treasure this book" (Bower 2005).

DonorsChoose also teaches children about philanthropy. A group of first graders in Brooklyn held a bake sale and used the proceeds to fund "Big Floor Puzzles" for a classroom in North Carolina. When DonorsChoose gets big grants, with directions from the funder, student grant makers read through the proposals and choose which proposals will best help their peers. Students meet with the funder and give a rationale for their choices.

You may want to make www.donorschoose.org one of your first stops in raising money to pay for your field trip and supplies.

Local example of funders include the Field Trip Foundation (www.field tripgroup.org), a volunteer-based, nonprofit organization dedicated to providing environmental educational field trips to low-income San Francisco Bay–area school children. The Field Trip Foundation partners with local public elementary schools in low-income areas to connect their students with educational outdoor resources in the Bay Area. On the East coast, the Chesapeake Bay Trust, www.chesapeakebaytrust.org/fieldtrip.html, also assists in funding field trips. Most grants are for one-half of field trip costs including: program fee, transportation, and substitute costs. Students who participate in trips funded by the Chesapeake Bay Trust gain awareness with the field trip and then apply their knowledge by participating in a project that benefits their local watershed and the Bay. Projects might include planting trees or native grasses near streams; making a Schoolyard Habitat: a "No Mow Zone," a native grass and wildflower meadow with habitat structures; or storm-drain stenciling "Don't Dump! Chesapeake Bay Drainage." When applying for grants, it can be wise to include a student service project in line with the purpose of the foundation.

Once you are funded, be careful to keep track of what you do and how you spend the money. Keep the funders informed. Send them photos. If they are local, invite them to see what you are doing.

Fund-Raising Projects

A great deal of learning can take place when students themselves raise some of the money for the trip. Students learn practical skills such as cooking, cleaning, or making handicrafts. At the same time, they develop entrepreneurial skills, including marketing and keeping track of money raised. Fund-raising is a natural and motivating way for students to learn real-world math skills. At the same time, students' energy investment makes the field trip more valuable to them and gives them a sense of ownership.

In lieu of the usual selling candy or gift wrap, there are many creative ways to raise funds for field trips.

Auctions

Auctions, where parents and/or local businesses donate anything from someone's homemade jam to dinner for two at the neighborhood restaurant to a weekend trip to a beach house, can bring in a lot of money. But the auction needs to be well publicized, and placing bids needs to be easy and convenient. One way to make the auction accessible is to place the items for auction and ways to bid on the school Web site. Another way is to combine the auction with some other school function such as a school play, PTA meeting, or other school gathering.

Service to the School and Neighboring Community

There are many ways to raise money by serving the school community. Students might help in ways such as the following:

- Make pizzas or soup and sandwiches to be served at the school lunch, after school, or at school sports events
- Rake leaves
- Walk dogs
- Wash cars
- Collect family recipes for a classroom, school, or community cookbook
- Make a book of student, parent, and staff poems and sell them
- Make little handmade gifts, postcards, or holiday cards to sell
- Help make a large item, such as a doll house or quilt, to raffle

Earth-Friendly Fund-Raisers

Everything we do with students teaches values. It is helpful to think about what values we are promoting with our fund-raisers. Earth-friendly fund-raisers accomplish at least three worthwhile goals. They help improve the environment and they teach students a sense of responsibility toward the environment. At the same time, they raise money for your field trips!

The following are a few ideas from the Funding Factory, the largest free recycling fund-raising program in the United States and Canada. The Funding Factory helps schools and nonprofit organizations, such as libraries or sports teams, unlock the power to fund-raising success. The Funding Factory suggests clean-up projects that help the environment and serve as big money makers for your group.

- You could agree to remove a certain number of pounds of trash or clean a certain distance along a park path or local stream. Sponsors pledge an agreed-upon amount of money by weight of trash or distance cleaned. If students are very young, they might take part in a project like this with their parents. Be sure to have rubber gloves for each child. Sometimes the Park Service or other overseers of the land will provide your group with gloves and trash bags. For fund-raising, you would need to write a one-page letter describing the project and suggesting an amount to pledge, say 1 cent to 10 cents per pound of garbage, with a $20 cap. If 20 students each had 5 sponsors who pledge $20, you will raise $2,000 for your trip.

- The Funding Factory offers free technology, sports and recreation equipment, playground systems, and cash in exchange for empty inkjet and laser printer cartridges and used cell phones. Empty printer cartridges and used cell phones can be refurbished and resold. Therefore the core product still holds value even after the ink is consumed or a wireless customer has changed plans or upgraded phones. More than 300 million cartridges are thrown away each year, while 30 million cell phones are discarded. Collecting these items is a service to the environment and a way to earn needed funding for your school. The Funding Factory describes a way to raise funds and reduce the landfill all year long:

> Collection boxes are supplied at no cost and prepaid shipping labels are already attached to boxes. Your group's name, address, and account number are included on labels. Your group places the collection boxes at local businesses and other convenient locations such as retailers that sell new printer cartridges. Many times a person buying a new cartridge brings in the old one to ensure a perfect match. Every time a box is full, you call UPS and arrange for the box to be picked up. Then you replace the box and start the process again. Your group can collect cash or earn technology prizes for your recycling effort, demonstrating once again that "doing the right thing" pays handsomely.

For more information, go to www.fundraiserhelp.com/earth-friendly-fundraisers.htm or www.fundingfactory.com.

Crunch Time (www.crunchtime.org) is another company that is dedicated to using fund-raisers to help the environment. Crunch Time offers environmentally friendly products to sell, such as energy conserving lights, water conserving gadgets for the sink or shower, and fast-growing trees.

Crunch Time also offers Newman's Own pure organic chocolate bars for sale. Actor Paul Newman is famous for his salad dressings and spaghetti sauces. These chocolate bars are of the same high quality his other brands are known for. The chocolate in the bars is grown in environmentally friendly ways by indigenous people in the rain forest. Educational curricula available related to the fund-raiser are available. The class or school makes a minimum of 52 percent profit on the chocolate bars. Thirty-five percent of the money that goes to the company is used to buy and preserve acres of rain forest.

In addition, Crunch Time fund-raisers are set up for people to go to the Crunch Time Web site to order in your school's name. That feature spares students from selling from door to door, which could be dangerous. It also spares the teacher from the mounds of paperwork that sometime accompany fund-raising.

Pledges—Fund-Raisers for Learning
While the fund-raising products at Crunch Time include educational curricula, there are other fund-raising options that are directly related to classroom goals. The following are a few curriculum-based ideas:

- People contribute an agreed-upon amount of money for each word a child spells correctly, each book a child reads, or each math problem the child solves
- Sponsors participate in or back students in a game show, based on the theme of the field trip
- Students help put on an international potluck, choosing food, music, and decorations that reflect the culture(s) the students are studying; guests pay to attend
- Students participate in an intergenerational talent show; guests pay to attend
- Students participate in a bike race or walk-a-thon

Spelling Challenge for Fund-Raising and Learning

Because of budget cuts, all our district-sponsored field trips have been canceled. We have tried selling cookie dough and candles as fund-raisers, but we haven't made much money and participation has been low. What has worked is a fund-raiser we developed that brings in $5,000 to $8,000 a year, doesn't cost a lot, and where everything we earn is ours. Best of all, this fund-raiser helps our children learn while they raise money. It's called the Spelling Challenge. On a special Friday morning in the spring, our students take a spelling test of from 20 to 50 words, depending on the grade level. Friends and relatives pledge money for each word the student spells correctly. Here are the details of how it works:

- ● The Spelling List
  - > Our teachers design two lists of spelling words, one easy and one hard, for their grade level, based on their curriculum.
  - > Since we have weekly spelling tests all year, students have studied many of the words already.
  - > Kindergartners see a picture and have to write the first letter of that word.
  - > First and second graders have 20 words. Third graders have 30. Older grades have 50 words.
  - > Teachers change the list slightly from year to year, based on changes in what they study.
- ● Accommodating Special Needs
  - > We have a high ESL population, so some of the words are easier.
  - > Some special education students get involved. (A fourth grade student may get a second grade list.)
  - > Some children choose to learn both lists. A second grader chose to be tested on the fifth grade list and only got a few wrong from the 50.
- ● The Pledges
  - > Two weeks before the test, we send out letters about the fund-raiser in an envelope with space for 10 names on the front.
  - > People might pledge a quarter per word or a penny per word. There is space to just give a donation, if preferred.
- ● The Day of the Test
  - > The test takes place on a Friday morning in the spring.
  - > The whole school takes the test at the same time.
  - > Parent volunteers grade the test and add up what each person who pledged should pay.
- ● Collecting the Pledges
  - > Volunteers staple what each person owes, along with a copy of the test, onto each child's envelope.
  - > The children take the envelope home and tell friends and family how much to pay.
- ● Celebration
  - > If students fill out all 10 names on the sheet or get 100 percent on the spelling test, they get a pizza party.
  - > The top two classes, the one with the most 100 percent scores on the test and the one that raises the most money, get a special breakfast served by the principal and assistant principal, who dress as waiters or waitresses.

> In the past, the students decorated the principal as an ice cream sundae, covered with ice cream, whipped cream, and sprinkles. The principal had to be hosed down before getting in the car to go home. Students loved this reward, but the new principal preferred giving the breakfast.

In a school of 500 children, 75 percent participate in the fund-raiser. Everyone takes the test though. We have considered using the same format with math instead of spelling.

The Spelling Challenge fund-raiser has allowed our children to continue to take field trips even though the money is no longer available from the school system. For instance, 100 kindergartners were able to take trips to the butterfly garden, the Science Center, and the zoo this year. The Spelling Challenge fund-raiser has made this possible.

—Tracy Lengeling, PTA president, Des Moines, Iowa

Keep Organized When Fund-Raising

Fund-raising requires you to be organized and address many details at the same time. Here are some suggestions:

- **Make a time line for the fund-raiser.** Plan in advance what needs to be done, who will do it, and how long it will take.
- **Listen to feedback.** Be open to the suggestions of people you know who have done fund-raisers before and to the suggestions of helpers who are working directly with some aspect of the fund-raiser.
- **Consider sales tax.** Be careful to comply with all federal, state, and local tax regulations, even if your school or organization is tax exempt. For more information see www.fundraisetaxlaw.org.
- **Keep records.** Take the time to keep careful records. Make copies of all tabulations, order sheets, and money collected.

Make Fund-Raising Fun

Fund-raising is most successful when it is fun. As part of your plan, arrange ways to bring fun into each aspect of the fund-raising. Fun will make your fund-raiser more profitable and enjoyable for everyone. The following are a few suggestions:

- **Show appreciation** to everyone all the way through.
- **Have fun incentives.** Perhaps if a certain amount of money is raised, the teacher has to do something silly such as dress in a funny way, sing a

song, or be the recipient of water balloons.

- **Take pictures or film the fund-raising.** The pictures or video make everyone feel important. They can also serve as incentives or models for next year's volunteers.
- **Make the actual sales fun.** If you have a bake sale, you could bring more fun—and profit—into the sale if you make the sale a cakewalk. People can purchase tickets to play. Fifteen participants walk around 15 numbered chairs while the music plays. When the music stops, everyone sits in a chair and a number is drawn from a jar. Whoever's chair matches the number gets the pleasure of choosing one of the donated cakes.
- **Give heartfelt thanks** in words and deeds.
- **Celebrate at the end.** Have a party to acknowledge the workers. Show the pictures or video at that time.

Note: adapted from http://fundraiserhelp.com.

Permissions

If you are in a school where the permission slips are standard and your field trip is typical, then all you need to do is get your administrator's approval and send out the school permission slips with a letter providing more complete information to the students' parents. If your trip is far away, to an unusual place, or uses unusual modes of transportation, you may also need your district's permission. The National Council of Teachers of Mathematics (NCTM) suggests that permissions and/or the accompanying letters offer opportunities for authentic student writing.

The following is an example of a simple parent permission form.

I give my permission for my child to go on this day, _____,

to _____. The transportation will be by _____.

Or

I give my permission for my child to go on this day, _____, on foot in the neighborhood to look at birds.

Longer trips need other important pieces of information such as medical conditions, medications, and emergency phone numbers. Loudoun County, Virginia, teacher Jennifer Pavol says to keep this information with you on the field trip, then shred the information after the trip to preserve privacy for your students and their families. Maryland teacher Anne Fretz reminds us to leave duplicates of the emergency information in the office back at school. Information should include the itinerary, destination, departure and return times, a list of all children and adults participating, permission slips, and cell phone numbers.

Special Needs

There are a number of considerations when children in the class have medical issues. If a child has asthma, it may be necessary to bring a bronchodilator to help the child breathe in case of an emergency. If a child is allergic to bee stings or has an extreme allergic reaction to certain foods, bring along an injection of epinephrine and someone who knows how to administer it. (Remember that strong fragrances such as perfumes attract bees.) Some children are on medications for Attention Deficit Disorder (ADD) or Attention Deficit Hyperactivity Disorder (ADHD). While many of those medications only need to be given once or twice a day and can be given at home, a child may need a dose during the field trip. Diabetes is another condition that needs to be noted.

Different districts address children's medical needs on field trips in different ways. Some districts require a doctor's order for students to receive medications. Some require parents to fill out a special permission form for medications. Some schools ask that the parents accompany their child on the field trip to administer medicine, if it is needed. Some districts require that parents sign a special permission for medications to be given to their children. (Some districts require permission even to apply sunscreen to a child.)

What can you do that will not isolate a child who needs medication? One major action you can take is to communicate with the parents well in advance of the field trip. This will allow the parents to take necessary steps with the child. One such step could be to adjust the medication the child is on.

There may be other special needs to consider. For instance, is there a child who needs wheelchair access? If so, the trip may require a special-needs bus and special provisions at the field trip site. A special-needs child may need an adult buddy on the trip.

Information and Requests to Parents

Parents need more information than a permission slip provides. A letter should accompany the parent permission form that provides information on the following:

- Educational purpose of the trip
- Date and location

- Trip itinerary
- Supervision plans
- Provisions for students with special needs
- Cost of the trip, if any
- Money needed, if any
- Kind of clothing needed
- Lunch and/or snack needs
- Whether to bring a water bottle
- Whether or not electronic games and music are permitted
- Whether or not the student should bring reading material for the trip
- Whether or not the student may bring a camera

On the day before the field trip, students may write an "I need" letter to remind parents to have their child dressed appropriately with a lunch and whatever else is needed, including a good night's sleep and a substantial breakfast.

The teachers I have talked with were not in favor of electronic games and music on field trips because it can isolate students and detract from the focus. One way to deal with the issue is to make the travel part of the learning experience, so that there is no time for the electronic games and electronic music.

Anne Fretz suggests that you bring a box of saltines or other snacks for students who don't bring snacks from home. Allow students to enjoy their snack before going into the field trip site. Peter Chausse, a walking tour field trip guide in Portland, Oregon, has similar advice. He recommends that students eat lunch early on field trips because, for some reason, field trips make kids hungry. Think through ahead of time how to keep the lunches cold and safe, where and how students will wash their hands, what will be needed for cleanup (e.g., garbage bags, wipes), what to do with the garbage, and who will be on the cleanup crew.

Many teachers are opposed to allowing students to buy souvenirs in gift shops. One reason is that they don't like the commercial aspects, where the trip becomes about buying rather than learning. Another reason is that some children may be given large amounts of money while other children might have none; this can result in unnecessarily painful situations for children.

One solution is to raise enough money for the field trip so that there is some left over to buy a few remembrances for the classroom. Another is to include enough money from the field trip fund-raising to provide each child with a small amount for a souvenir. I appreciate the desire not to make the trip too commercial. One of my few memories of a field trip in elementary school, however, was clutching my quarter tightly in my fist as I poured over the prints at the National Gallery of Art, trying to choose the one to take home. Somehow, buying that print, something that I could take home from the gallery and keep, was tremendously important to me. Some teachers have students use the pictures, brochures, and other memorabilia from the gift shop as a jumping off place for writing and illustrating their experiences of the field trip.

What if a parent doesn't want her child to take the field trip? Miriam Kronish, former principal in Needham, Massachusetts, points out that parents have a right to say no to a trip. If parents don't want their child to take the trip, then find a teacher who will look after the child. The child will need to have work to do in his or her own curriculum.

Site Manager's Permission

In addition to parents and school officials, permission may also be needed from the managers of the field trip site. Agree on a date, time, the number and grade level of students and adults attending, the goals of the trip, special needs of your group, and how the site manager can contact you. You may also want to agree on an alternate date if the weather fails to cooperate. Keep a file of various site managers in your field trip journal with their phone numbers and e-mails for future trips.

Often, the site mangers will have useful materials to help you plan and follow up on your trip. They may also be able to tell you the best time of year and time of day to take the trip, as well as costs, restrictions, and suggestions. When you contact the site managers, this is also a good time to inform guides of particular goals that you might have for the trip in line with your curriculum and any particular needs of your group of children.

Visit the Site in Advance

Make visiting the site in advance a priority, if possible. There are so many ways this can enhance the field trip. The advance visit may enable you to

- collect pictures, postcards, and brochures.
- send for or collect materials the site has prepared for school visits. Determine whether these fully address your needs or if you need to adapt materials to fit your needs.
- explore the exhibition(s) you plan to visit to get ideas for pre–field trip activities.
- take photographs or videos.
- plan clues for mysteries for students to solve on the trip.
- design scavenger hunts or booklets. Should they be the same for all or will you differentiate?
- make a tour that fits more ideally with your standards and objectives.

- look for ways you hadn't thought of to connect the trip to your standards and objectives.
- plan for safety. This is especially important for walking tours.
- find restroom facilities and spaces for lunch and/or snacks.
- meet the site facility managers and tour guides and plan for your group's unique needs.

Arrange Transportation

Plan for transportation as soon as you know where you are going. If you plan to use school buses, you need to find out well in advance whether the buses are available. Anne Fretz told me that years ago they used to pile children into parents' cars for trips, but they never do that anymore. Not only would most schools find this inadmissible, but the parents' car insurance probably doesn't cover using the car in this way. Parents can take their own children and their children's friends in their car informally, but they probably shouldn't transport children in their cars on official school trips.

When arranging for transportation, it is important to make sure the driver knows how to get you where you are going. I have had several disappointing trips where the bus driver got lost. Anne Fretz suggests that you get the directions in advance online from www.mapquest.com or http://maps.yahoo.com. Sit up front, close to the bus driver, to say when to turn right or left. It would be smart to have a cell phone contact who knows the way if in spite of your best efforts, the bus still gets lost.

If you plan to take students on a longer trip, perhaps to a faraway city where they will stay for several nights, you may want to consider working through an agency. Tim Rider, president of Adventure Student Travel in Kirksville, Missouri (www.adventurestudenttravel.com), suggests that the pitfalls of planning without help can include the need for liability insurance and potential difficulties in planning for the bus, hotel, and food. He recognizes that advantages include the fact that you can totally customize the trip to your needs. Sometimes you can save money, too.

Taking children on a field trip is a responsibility. Responsibility implies liability. It is very sad that some teachers or schools are afraid to take field trips because of concerns about liability. As Miriam Kronish says, "When people are afraid to do field trips, the children are the losers. While all students benefit from field trips, students who learn through hands-on activities and coaching are starved for field trips." We just need to do everything we can to make the trip safe. Kronish suggests that one way is to go to the site in advance, look around for what could go wrong, and then make sure make sure it goes right.

Prepare Students for the Field Trip

Part of the planning needs to go to preparing students for the experience. Chapter 4 (see page 141) goes into some detail about planning for learning in relation to field trips. First identify the academic standards and other goals (e.g., communicating, problem solving, teamwork, or finding connections). Then identify the field trip site. Next have a brainstorming session or a pretest to find out what the students already know, what they want to know, and what their expectations are about the field trip. One kind of pretest could be a Mind Map (see pages 161–162). Students might make Mind Maps before and then again after the trip, so that they can see how much they have learned. Use all the information you can gather from students ahead of time to form measurable class learning goals for the trip. It may be appropriate for students to have individual goals, too.

In finding out students' knowledge, interests, and expectations, you may want to use the Taxonomy for Discovery in chapter 2. Either alone, in pairs, or in small groups, do the following:

1. **Experience.** Students take part in pretrip preparations, looking at the Web site, books, articles, and/or brochures, or they do research on some aspect of the field trip. Students write their observations.
2. **Organize.** Students organize their observations in some way by searching for similarities and patterns.
3. **Share.** Students share their organizations with other individuals, pairs, or groups.
4. **Process.** Students share their learning with the whole class. Out of this process, along with the required standards, students and teacher design learning goals for the field trip.

Use the Taxonomy for Discovery again or some other process for students to give their input about expected behavior for the trip (see page 112 in chapter 3). If students help make the code of behavior, they are more likely to remember to abide by the code.

The following is a list of possible ways to prepare students for a field trip. Are you going to

- ○ have a speaker to prepare the students?
  - > Will that cost money?
  - > Will you prepare the speaker with the knowledge level of the students and the goals and details of the field trip?
- ○ order a kit from the field trip site with hands-on materials? How much in advance to you need to order it?

- show the students photographs of the site and/or provide materials for students to study?
- take students to the Web site of the field trip or to other sites? Have you reviewed the sites yourself?
- collect books and/or magazines about the site?
- plan Essential Questions? (See chapter 3, page 111.)
- plan for a service aspect to the trip?
- plan for ways to make the travel time productive? (See chapter 4, page 192.)
- have students do research for the trip to increase their knowledge base and focus?
- visit the site in advance to maximize the academic benefit and the likelihood that all will go smoothly?
- plan how to manage if the weather is different from what you had hoped?
- eat on the field trip? Who will provide the food? How will you clean up after yourselves? Do you need trash bags?
- give students an itinerary of the trip so they won't be wondering when lunch is?
- plan for students to evaluate themselves with questions such as the following?
  - Did you meet the class learning goals?
  - Were you able to answer your own questions?
  - Did your behavior match the agreed-upon standards of conduct?

Plan to Evaluate the Trip

Plan ways to evaluate the field trip and share your findings with other teachers, administrators, and the site managers. Value student input; they may tell you about observations and experiences that you missed. You may also want to collect data from the chaperones, site managers, guest speakers, guides, and other parents. The evaluation questions might be as simple as these:

1. What worked?
2. What problems arose?
3. How could we improve next time?

The evaluation might also include questions such as these:

- What were the greatest educational benefits of this field trip?
- Did students achieve the objectives? How do you know?

- Were students properly prepared for the trip? What worked best in preparing the students? How might you prepare them better next time?
- What was most memorable?
- Were there enough chaperones and were they well prepared?
- What were the most productive activities or aspects of the trip?
- What were the least productive activities or aspects? How might these aspects be improved next time?
- Did we use our time well? How might we use it better next trip?
- Did we leave the site cleaner than we found it?
- Did we provide adequately for everyone's safety?

Some teachers design a trip booklet with goals, expectations, and activities before, during, and after the trip. Ways for students to show they know could include written and/or illustrated reports, bulletin boards, PowerPoint shows, time lines, role plays, videos, and journal entries. All of this requires advance planning.

Supplies Checklist

Susan Fort put together a list of supplies that you may need for your field trip. The suggested supplies for students is from Molly A. Pirrung of Silver Spring, Maryland. Students may be able to help check the lists to make sure you have everything you need. See which of the following are relevant to your needs. Add whatever is missing.

General Supplies

- ☐ itinerary for each adult
- ☐ nametags
- ☐ cash and change
- ☐ credit card
- ☐ licenses or permits (if applicable)
- ☐ cell phones
- ☐ phone numbers cheat sheet with everyone's number
- ☐ maps and directions
- ☐ guidebooks/field trip location materials
- ☐ camera
- ☐ film
- ☐ camcorder
- ☐ tape recorder for docents remarks (with permission)
- ☐ items for assessment

Food Supplies

- ☐ cooler
- ☐ ice/freezer packs
- ☐ hygiene gloves
- ☐ drinks/water
- ☐ cups
- ☐ snacks
- ☐ plates/utensils
- ☐ napkins
- ☐ garbage bags
- ☐ other _____

Possible Student Supplies

- ☐ clipboard, cardboard, or hard notebook for note taking, sketching
- ☐ journals
- ☐ art materials for sketching: crayons, markers, pastels
- ☐ newsprint for rubbings on gravestones, building signs
- ☐ resealable, plastic bags for collections, labeled with student or group names

First Aid Supplies

- ☐ bandages
- ☐ gauze
- ☐ scissors and tape
- ☐ tweezers
- ☐ needle
- ☐ safety pins
- ☐ tissues
- ☐ aspirin/pain medication
- ☐ antibacterial ointment
- ☐ anti-itch cream
- ☐ sunscreen
- ☐ insect repellent
- ☐ snake bite kit
- ☐ bee sting supplies
- ☐ other _____

Be sure to include time to check over the supplies on the day of the trip.

Plans for Student Safety

The first priority of a field trip is to keep students safe. Work with your students to become your partners-in-safety. We will address several issues about student safety on field trips, including bus safety, student identification, group formation, keeping contact with groups, and restroom plans. If students understand the reasons for these safety procedures and even help in identifying and planning for the procedures, they are more likely to serve as partners in keeping everyone safe.

Anne Fretz's class practices the following rules the day before the trip:

- Stay in your seat; there is no standing up
- Sit face forward with your back on the seat
- Use indoor voices
- Make sure the bus driver doesn't get distracted; safety is most important

Science educator Silvia Shugrue explains how she prepared students to have certain "patterns of behavior" on the bus. Students agreed ahead of time that the first ones on the bus went to sit in the back. Those in the back of the bus would be the first ones out. Students were in partners. If one partner sat by the window on the way to the destination, the other partner would sit by the window on the way back to school. Students sometimes practiced bus patterns of behavior ahead of time. These patterns of behavior helped prevent problems on the bus before they arose.

Virginia teacher Jennifer Pavol tells how students have biannual training on what to do if an emergency occurs on the bus. Students practice using emergency safety exits and even learn how to use the CB radio to contact the dispatcher in case the driver becomes incapacitated.

Students on a walking trip also need to be reminded of safety rules and regulations. Rules include stopping at the curb; looking left, then right, then left again when crossing the street; crossing on a light that has just turned green; and staying on the sidewalk, rather than stepping onto the street.

Where the teacher stands in the line matters. If the teacher leads the way, he or she will not be in a good position to watch over the students. Baton Rouge, Louisiana, teacher Jennifer Smith notes "When I took my kids on trips, I always appointed a trusty line leader, told them where to go, had all others follow that person, then I stood near the middle or rear of the line so I could keep my eye on every child."

Name tags are a tradition for field trips. They are very helpful when a site guide or docent wishes to be able to address a child by name. But there are some safety concerns. One fear is that a stranger with ill intent might engage the trust of a child by calling out the child's name. Some schools have the child's name and school on wristbands instead of on their chests for this reason. If you do decide to have nametags of any type, an assembly line could make the production quick and effortless.

Field trip coordinator Tim Rider suggests each child wear the same brightly colored T-shirts (bright green, orange, or yellow) to make the children on the trip easy to identify. The teacher may wear a special color of shirt so that she or he is easy to spot, too. Rider also suggests that, whenever possible, the teacher and each chaperone carry a cell phone so that they can be in touch at a moment's notice. Cell phones can do so much to make field trips safer and easier. Another tip he gives is that if the trip is overnight and students will stay in a hotel, make sure the hotel has an indoor corridor and security guards, rather than doors that open to the outside.

We will talk about chaperones in greater depth below (see page 243). Here we will consider chaperones in terms of safety. Depending on the age of the students and the nature of the field trip, the number of chaperones may be as few as 10 to 1 if, say, the students are going straight to a theatrical production and then straight back to school; 5 to 1 where students need to be monitored more closely such as a trip to a state park or on a walking tour of their city, or 3 to 1 if students are very young. Give the chaperones the names of each child in their group. Some teachers like to have each group composed of all boys or all girls to make restroom visits easier. You may want to give each group an Essential Question or a particular aspect of the trip as a focus.

Anne Fretz points out that some parents may work near the field trip site and choose to meet the group at the site, rather than riding on the bus. Other parents may need to drive their car behind the bus because they have somewhere to go after the trip. In both cases be sure to exchange cell phone numbers in advance.

It is important to plan how to keep track of students throughout the field trip. One way to keep track of all students is to have chaperones keep track of their group, and then check with the chaperones. Another way is to take role call periodically. Portland, Oregon, field trip guide Peter Chausse suggests the following:

> Teachers can provide every student with a personal number, and then spend some time practicing a roll call of numbers. Let's say each child has a number and the teacher has the name of each student and his or her number on a clipboard. Rather than calling roll, or trying to count heads, the teacher says "Let's go!" Whoever is number 1 shouts out "1," followed by "2," "3," etc. If the line stops prior to "4," the teacher (and usually most of the kids) will know that Number 4 (let's say Tommy) is either not listening or not present. I've seen this work well in most cases. It probably works best if you have practiced it at school frequently, and if nobody decides to be a wise guy and shout out some-

one else's number. Doing that could lead to problems. Another idea is to assign everyone a partner. In counting heads, you can count by two's, and if someone is missing, you will know because one student won't have a partner.

Teachers experienced with field trips have something to say about restrooms! They say that it is wise to check out the availability, number of stalls, and cleanliness of bathrooms in advance. Make sure that students in each group have a restroom buddy available. You may want to bring each group a small packet of flushable, alcohol-based baby wipes to clean toilet seats and small packs of antiseptic soap to wash hands. It is essential to ensure that restrooms are available, safe, and as clean as possible.

Keeping Safe on Our Field Trips

Whenever we take field trips, there are so many aspects of the trip to handle. Once we were late coming home from a trip because there had been a storm. I used my cell phone to contact the parents. If a parent didn't speak English, I had the child speak to his or her parent. We told the parents we would be arriving late. Some of the parents had younger children to take care of and they didn't need to sit in a car for hours waiting for us.

Medical information and cell phone numbers are on the permission slips and I carry them with me during the trip. I shred the information afterward so that the information is not passed around. I sometimes give chaperones my cell phone number, especially any who volunteer to follow the bus. On occasion I have suggested an alternative route to the bus driver to a destination to lessen our driving time.

I encourage parents who have a child with medication needs or a behavior problem to chaperone and place their own child in their group. As the teacher, it is best if I don't have a group so that I can keep my focus on leading the field trip. If the child's parent isn't available, I put these children in my group.

I have taught in a school where students had name tags; in another, name tags were not allowed for safety reasons. (Someone with ill intent might say "Hi Suzie, I know your mom.")

I wear a staff shirt to identify myself and carry a bag with first aid and medications. The first aid pack is prepared by the school nurse. When we return to school, we give it back.

I assign kids to groups and give chaperones a list of who is in their group. I try to give my chaperones either all girls or all boys. If that isn't possible, I make sure that there are pairs of boys or girls so that each has a bathroom buddy.

When we go to Monticello (the home of Thomas Jefferson) or Mount Vernon (the home of George Washington), we get on the Web site in advance. We give chaperones information such as the time for each tour.

In advance of the trip, we show the students photos and discuss the trip. I ask students "What do you want to see?" We want to allow students to have a bit of say.

I mention to some chaperones, "Please, don't smoke. You will have some children besides your own." When students get back from a trip that ends after school has let out, I ask students to come to tell me when they are leaving so that I know they have been picked up.

We have bus safety practice two times a year. Students learn to walk in front of the bus, not behind it. Students are reminded to sit forward and stay on their bottoms. They learn where the emergency doors and windows are and about the hatches in the roof if the bus ever fell on its side. They also learn how to use the CB radio on the bus that goes to the dispatcher and how to say where they are in case the bus breaks down. Students practice going out the emergency door back seats first.

We put a lot of focus on keeping everybody safe on our field trips.

—Jennifer Pavol, teacher, Loudoun County, Virginia

Chaperones

Two major concerns in regard to chaperones are finding them and making sure they do a good job with your students. In regard to the second concern, students can help chaperones do a good job if the students are very clear about what to do on the field trip and the importance of staying close by and in communication with the chaperone, serving as the chaperone's partners-in-safety.

One way to solicit parents as chaperones is to send a letter along with the parent permission slip. Another is to include the request in the classroom newsletter. If all else fails, phone calls usually work. Even better—delegate the job of organizing chaperones to the room parent.

Make sure to have a written request that includes the time frame, responsibilities, and items to bring such as a blanket, picnic basket, camera, or cell phone. Include appreciation in advance. If they are thanked in advance and if students wrote personal thank-you notes the last time they chaperoned, parents are likely to do so again.

When you prepare chaperones for your trip, the goal is to have a balance between structure (As Ted Rider puts it, "Students want defined expectations.") and freedom (As Miriam Kronish says "If they go to a museum and don't have a good experience, then children might hate museums for the rest of their lives. 'Don't touch, be quiet, move in line like a prison!'"). The following are some suggestions for chaperones to help students have a fruitful and enjoyable learning experience while keeping safe and being respectful at the same time.

Guidelines for Chaperones

- Know the meeting time for all groups to get back to the group leader.
- Know the schedule, any tour times, and which exhibits or aspects of the trip your group needs to experience.
- If possible, have a cell phone to stay in communication. Know the cell phone number of the group leader. Give the group leader the number of your cell phone. If you can't use cell phones, be clear about meeting back at the agreed-upon time.
- Get to know the group of students you are chaperoning. Be familiar with each student's name and interests so that you can assist each one in getting the most from the trip.
- Know the goals of the field trip and if students have particular assignments. If there is a scavenger hunt, be familiar with what the students will be looking for.
- Support each student's curiosity and sense of wonder.
- Encourage questions. You don't have to know the answers. Help students find answers with the others in their group.
- Ask questions such as
  > "What are you noticing about . . . ? How does it look, feel, smell?"
  > "What do you think is happening?"
  > "Why do you think that happened?"
  > "How does this work?"
  > "What would happen if . . . ?
  > "Can you figure out how to . . . ?"
  > "How many . . . ? How much . . . ? How long . . . ? How often . . . ?"
- If students are assigned to work with any electronic equipment, such as tape recorders, camcorders, or digital cameras, do your best to make sure you can help them know how to use the equipment.
- Keep the group together in one exhibit area. Count heads before you move to the next area.
- Know the ground rules. Make sure that students are respectful to each other and to other visitors. If appropriate to the trip, help students remember to keep indoor voices.
- Send students to the bathroom in pairs.
- Please don't smoke.
- Don't socialize with other chaperones. Please keep your focus on the students. (Find another time to get together with other parents.)

- Find child care for other siblings so that you can focus all your attention on the children in your group.
- Have fun. Students will be more involved when they see that the adults are interested and having fun.

Sharing the Work

Susan Fort has compiled a list of duties that you can use to share the work required of a field trip with other teachers, parents, volunteers, and students:

1. **Emergency Contact Person.** Gives parents his or her phone number for the day of the trip; has phone numbers of parents in case of an emergency. Exchanges cell phone numbers in advance with parents who need to meet at the site, rather than ride the bus.
2. **Chaperones.** Are directly responsible for groups of children. Chaperone/student ratio may range from 1 to 3, to 1 to 12, depending on the students' age and the nature of the field trip.
3. **Name Tag Coordinator.** Hands out name tags at the beginning of the trip.
4. **Medication Coordinator.** Collects and keeps track of all medication. There should be one medication coordinator for each bus.
5. **Group Leader.** Acts as the liaison with the on-site field trip contact person.
6. **Lunch/Snack Coordinator.** Coordinates distribution of food during the day.
7. **On-Site Cleanup Coordinator.** Makes sure the group does not leave chaos in its wake throughout the day.
8. **Bus Cleanup Coordinator.** Makes sure the bus stays clean throughout the day and is left in order at the end of the day.
9. **First Aid Coordinator.** Keeps track of the first aid kit.
10. **Coordinator of Tipping.** Organizes the group to tip the bus driver or others (when appropriate).
11. **Evaluation Coordinator.** Helps create, distribute, collect, and summarize the evaluations of the trip.
12. **Thank-You Note Coordinator.** Makes sure thank-you notes are written; may write them himself or herself or organize students to write them.
13. **Permissions Coordinator.** Applies for administrative approval from building principal, district administrator (if necessary), and parents.

Walking-Tour Logistics

In planning a walking tour, pre-walk all areas you intend to visit with kids. Check to make sure that students will be walking on sidewalks, will have safe crosswalks, and will not be walking too close to freeways or other hazardous areas for pedestrians.

Consider how weather conditions might change the walk (muddy, slippery). Is the walk handicap accessible, and if not, what alternatives are there for those with special needs? Consider places you can escape from extremely wet, hot, or windy weather. Encourage your students to dress in layers and wear comfortable walking shoes. Hats, raingear, or sunscreen can help make the day more enjoyable.

Keep in mind that you will be sharing space with others. Check ahead to make sure you won't be going somewhere where large unexpected crowds may be gathering. Time your pre-walk and then consider the pace of the students. In most cases, things will take much longer than expected, so I've found that it is better to plan to do less on the walk rather than to overplan. Arrange to have extra time to avoid having to run to catch buses or trains. When you are rushing, safety is sometimes compromised.

In pre-walking or pre-driving the route, you can prepare the students for what they might see, and you can focus their learning on what will soon be coming. If you have extra time on the walk with students, use it to review what you've seen, with questions and discussion. Encourage kids to reflect on their experience or play a trivia game that challenges them to recall what they have learned thus far on the trip. Give students opportunities to get involved in hands-on activities.

Eat early and often. I've found that kids tend to be hungry by 10:30 A.M. or earlier, so frequent snack and lunch stops are encouraged. I'd recommend lunch earlier in the day than normal. For some reason, kids tend to be famished on field trips and may have difficulty focusing on learning until they have had something to eat. Provide hands-on activities before lunch and some kind of recreational activity after lunch or in the afternoon.

Plan for restroom stops and be sure the restrooms will be open. Also, try to find clean places for restroom breaks where there are multiple stalls, rather than single toilets that can really slow things down. Know about emergency restrooms away from the standard stops.

Responsible chaperones are essential. If each parent is responsible for particular kids, then the teacher just checks in with the parents. If all parents are there, and they each have all of his or her kids, then things should go well. I like a minimum of 5:1 student-to-adult ratio, but 3:1 works even better. If the teacher doesn't have to take a group, that can free him or her to handle any situation that might arise. Also, if parents can carry cell phones, along with the teacher, communication is only a phone call away. The teacher can carry a list of cell phone numbers of all chaperones.

Before and during the trip, involve people in the community whenever possible. Welcome their expertise, but brief them about your goals and time restraints. Be sure they can talk to kids in a language they will understand, and try to keep things moving. Encourage guest speakers or community helpers to include hands-on activities, rather than a just a lecture approach to learning.

It is fun to take pictures or videotape to reinforce the learning after the trip. Walking trips like these reinforce the idea that learning can happen anywhere and at any time.

—Peter Chausse, walking-tour guide, Portland, Oregon

The Day of the Trip and Afterward

When the big day for the field trip arrives, have a list to make sure that all the details are handled. Check to make sure that all the supplies are in place, medications are collected, name tags are distributed, chaperones are present, and all students are accounted for. Take notes on how the trip goes in your field trip journal. Remember to pass out the evaluations to students, teachers, and chaperones at the completion of the trip. Collect the feedback and share it with the administrators and other teachers who might want to take a field trip to that site. Use student feedback and student products to gauge how well the students met the trip's goals. There are so many ways that you can use the field trip experience when you return to the classroom to enrich students' personal connection to their learning. You could weave the experience of the trip into the curriculum for the rest of the school year. The authentic encounter gives students a real-world basis for understanding their subject matter.

Remember to write thank-you notes (see page 106). Giving appreciation means a lot to people. If the children write them, the notes can serve as one more assessment piece for the trip. If there isn't time for the children to write them, then write them yourself. Congratulate yourself and others for the gift you have given your students in providing them with a trip to remember!

In summary, a successful field trip requires advance planning with the intention of maximizing students' learning and enjoyment, while focusing on safety. This means anticipating what might go wrong and planning ways to have it go right. When possible, share the workload. Encourage others (other teachers, parents, students) to take ownership and help make the trip a success.

Task	Who	When	Date
☐ Take notes in journal			
☐ Distribute evaluations			
☐ After trip			
☐ Send thank-you notes			
☐ Evaluate the field trip			
☐ Share evaluation results with administration and other teachers			

References

Bower, A. "It's Raining Pencils." *Time*, March 7, 2005, 69.

Caine, et al. 2005. *12 Brain/Mind Learning Principles in Action: The Fieldbook for Making Connections, Teaching, and the Human Brain.* Thousand Oaks, CA: Corwin Publishing.

Hibbard, M. et al. 1996. *Performance-Based Learning and Assessment.* Alexandria, VA: Association for Supervision and Curriculum Development.

Kline, P. 1988. *The Everyday Genius.* Arlington, VA: Great Ocean Publishers Binding.

Negroponte, N. 1995. *Being Digital.* NY: Vintage Press.

Acknowledgments

So many voices have contributed to the writing of this book that it is hard to know where to begin. An educational consultant and former master's degree student of mine, Susan Fort, brainstormed the format and contributed greatly to the contents, especially the chapter on logistics. Portland, Oregon, walking-tour guide Peter Chausse contributed too many ideas to this book to count! Frank Lyman of the University of Maryland provided a unique perspective and powerful strategies for teaching thinking skills. Sarah Shellow, national consultant for curriculum development and discovery-based learning, gave step-by-step ways to make field trips true experiences of inquiry. She also showed me how using dance to integrate learning can enhance children's knowledge of math, language arts, social studies, and art.

Educational Consultant Mardy Burgess of Annapolis, Maryland, contributed many ideas for chapter 2 and edited scores of pages. Jo Ann Lohl Spears, the director and pre-K teacher at the University of Houston, also graciously shared her many ideas about where to go and what to do on field trips. In fact, her suggestions served as the basis for chapter 2.

Jennifer Smith, who taught in Baton Rouge, Louisiana, shared unique ways to teach young children how to think, question, and imagine. Durango, Colorado, media specialist and consultant Bliss Bruen wrote brilliantly about ways to incorporate Essential Questions and technology in field trips. Portland, Oregon, principal Tim Lauer gave practical examples of the cutting-edge integration of technology with field trips currently taking place at his school. Gordon Stokes, coauthor of *The Learning Revolution*, coined the phrase "the world as the classroom" and showed me the thrilling possibilities of using real-world field trips to produce high-tech products. So did Mac Legerton, executive director of the Center for Community Action in Lumberton, North Carolina, whose green mapping project is tying in with mapping projects around the world.

Montana State University Language Arts Specialist, Jan Clinard, shared her whole Aesthetic Literacy Program, where many schools integrated field trips with the arts in mastering standards. And Peg Koetsch's Museums-in-Progress takes field trip follow-up to the highest levels. Retired principal Miriam Kronish of Needham, Massachusetts, shared inspirational stories of field trips to study birds, bugs, clouds, and more. Baltimore, Maryland, teacher Victoria Mansuri gave beautiful descriptions of her students' expressions of personal responsibility. Previous conversations with *The Learning*

Revolution coauthor, Jeannette Vos, contributed to the focus on caring as a foundation for field trips. Chevy Chase, Maryland, teacher Anne Fretz donated hours of her time sharing her 20+ years of experience as the field trip coordinator for her grade level. Prince William County teacher Jennifer Pavol shared useful tips on field trip safety and how to design a Webquest. Walter McKenzie, an education consultant and technology director for the Northborough-Southborough, Massachusetts, Public School District, provided a number of tips for successful online virtual field trips, and teacher Rosella Wallace of Anchor Point, Alaska, showed how to take a low-tech virtual field trip of the mind.

Tim Rider, president of Adventure Student Travel in Kirksville, Missouri, gave logistical support and childhood memories of field trips. Science educator Silvia Shugrue shared helpful ways to use the schoolyard and prepare children for longer field trips. Margaret Jackson showed how to take urban children to Africa on a shoestring and share a science project on two continents. Dave Dennis, director of the Algebra Project in North Carolina, taught us about the "mathematization" of field trips, and Mac Legerton and Jim Judge showed how to extend learning through mapping. Author Peter Kline's field trip memories also showed the lasting value of field trips. Regional Training Center Director, Diana Ramsey, showed me how to connect field trips with current events. Thanks to Mathew Wheeler, director of a nonprofit organization to increase field trips for DC students, and to DC principal Ray Bledsoe, and Rockville, Maryland, teacher Ellen Bauman for describing how needed field trips are. Thanks to assessment experts Neil Davidson, Dale Miller, Chris Christensen, and Sybil Carlson, and to Michael Hibbard, Grant Wiggins, Jay McTighe, and the teachers of the Pomeraug School District in Connecticut for contributions to the assessment portion. Thanks to Ron Fairchild, Summer Program Director at Johns Hopkins University, for providing many useful ideas and a summer program perspective. Thanks to Martin Storksdieck and Lynn Tran, both of whom wrote doctoral dissertations on field trips that summarized research showing the benefits of field trips. The writings of Spencer Kagan, Geoffrey and Renate Caine, and Randy White also helped to show the value of field trips. Portsmouth, Virginia, teacher Aveda Majette and Portland, Oregon, home-schooling parent Teri Brown both showed the value of parental involvement in field trips.

Thanks go to grandnephew Isaac Schaal, a student in Brookings, North Dakota, who did a fine job of remembering his field trip studying the prairie.

Thanks to my editor, Jerome Pohlen, for his patient support in bringing this book to fruition.

Finally my eternal gratitude goes to my husband, Steve Carroll, whose culinary and computer skills made this book possible.

Index